T0293630

Belt and Road Initiative
Interregional Cooperation
Between Asia and Europe

Series on China's Belt and Road Initiative

Print ISSN: 2591-7730
Online ISSN: 2591-7749

Series Editors: ZHENG Yongnian *(National University of Singapore, Singapore)*
Kerry BROWN *(King's College London, UK)*
WANG Yiwei *(Renmin University of China, China)*
LIU Weidong *(Chinese Academy of Sciences, China)*

This book series showcases the most up-to-date and significant research on China's Belt and Road Initiative (BRI) by leading scholars from inside and outside China. It presents a panoramic view on the BRI, from the perspectives of China's domestic policy, China's foreign investment, international relations, cultural cooperation and historical inheritance. As the first English book series on the BRI, this series offers a valuable English-language resource for researchers, policymakers, professionals and students to better understand the challenges and opportunities brought by the BRI.

Published:

For the complete list of volumes in this series, please visit
www.worldscientific.com/series/scbri

Series on China's Belt and Road Initiative – Vol. 12

Belt and Road Initiative
Interregional Cooperation
Between Asia and Europe

RONG Xinchun

Chinese Academy of Social Sciences, China

Translated by

XIA Xia

World Scientific

NEW JERSEY · LONDON · SINGAPORE · BEIJING · SHANGHAI · HONG KONG · TAIPEI · CHENNAI · TOKYO

Published by

World Scientific Publishing Co. Pte. Ltd.

5 Toh Tuck Link, Singapore 596224

USA office: 27 Warren Street, Suite 401-402, Hackensack, NJ 07601

UK office: 57 Shelton Street, Covent Garden, London WC2H 9HE

Library of Congress Cataloging-in-Publication Data
Names: Rong, Xinchun, author. | Xia, Xia, 1976–   translator.
Title: Belt and Road Initiative : interregional cooperation between Asia and Europe /
    Rong Xinchun ; translated by Xia Xia
Other titles: Yi dai yi lu. English
Description: New Jersey : World Scientific, [2019] | Series: Series on China's Belt and
    Road Initiative, 2591-7730 ; Vol. 9 | Originally published in Chinese as Yi dai yi lu :
    bao rong . kai fang de ya ou ming yun gong tong ti in 2015. |
    Includes bibliographical references. | In English, translated from the original Chinese.
Identifiers: LCCN 2019025051 | ISBN 9789811206313 (hardcover)
Subjects: LCSH: Yi dai yi lu (Initiative : China) | International economic relations. | International
    cooperation. | Silk Road--History. | China--Foreign economic relations. | China--Economic
    policy--2000– | China--Economic conditions--2000– | China--Foreign economic
    relations--Asia. | Asia--Foreign economic relations--China. | China--Foreign economic
    relations--Europe. | Europe--Foreign economic relations--China. | China--Foreign economic
    relations--Eurasia. | Eurasia--Foreign economic relations--China.
Classification: LCC HF1604 .R6713 2019 | DDC 382/.30951--dc23
LC record available at https://lccn.loc.gov/2019025051

British Library Cataloguing-in-Publication Data
A catalogue record for this book is available from the British Library.

Sponsored by B&R Book Program

一带一路：包容、开放的亚欧命运共同体
Originally published in Chinese by China Social Sciences Press.
Copyright © China Social Sciences Press, 2016
Belt and Road Initiative: Interregional Cooperation Between Asia and Europe

For any available supplementary material, please visit
https://www.worldscientific.com/worldscibooks/10.1142/11443#t=suppl

Contents

Preface

In September 2013, President Xi Jinping initiated the strategic concept of building a new Silk Road Economic Belt during his visit to Kazakhstan. At the Conference on Interaction and Confidence-Building Measures in Asia (CICA) in May 2014, President Xi further proposed to accelerate the construction of the Silk Road Economic Belt and the 21st-Century Maritime Silk Road. At the Summit of Asia-Pacific Economic Cooperation (APEC) held in November 2014, President Xi expounded the Belt and Road Initiative, whereon China proposed to set up the Silk Road Fund. The Belt and Road Initiative has become a critically important developmental measure during global economic growth.

On March 28, 2015, the Chinese government officially launched the *Vision and Proposed Actions Outlined on Jointly Building the Silk Road Economic Belt and the 21st-Century Maritime Silk Road*, signaling that the concept of the Belt and Road Initiative proposed by China had officially kicked off and was ready for implementation. The countries along the Belt and Road have their own resource advantages and their economies are mutually complementary. Therefore, there is a high potential and room for cooperation. These countries should promote policy coordination, facility connectivity, unimpeded trade, financial integration, and people-to-people bonds as their five major goals, and the major way to realize these goals is to coordinate among the goals and communicate policies to each other. It is a process of cooperation among multiple parties.

By March 31, 2015, the eve of the deadline for registering membership in the Asian Infrastructure Investment Bank (AIIB), which is dedicated to infrastructure investment and construction in Asia and to promote the construction of regional connectivity and economic integration, 57 European and Asian countries had applied to be original members of intention of the bank. An open and inclusive multilateral developmental institution had made its official debut on the world financial stage, expanding its scope from Asia to Europe, Latin America, Africa, and Oceania. A series of events for the signing ceremony of the *Articles of the Agreement of the Asian Infrastructure Investment Bank* were held in Beijing on June 29, 2015, when the finance ministers, or their authorized representatives, from the 57 original members of intention were present at the signing ceremony. The AIIB was officially founded on December 25, 2015. The founding of the AIIB had the right timing, place, and cooperators; it matched with the construction of the Silk Road Economic Belt and the 21st-Century Maritime Silk Road. Its birth is a result that will benefit all the participants, and it will contribute to the integration and development of the Asia-Pacific economy together with other multilateral developmental institutions.

These two events in 2015 have provided new ideas and the China-type "positive energy" for the recovery of the world's economy, which had been in the shade of the financial crisis of 2008 and had been suffering weak recovery since then. A regional developmental strategy, led by European and Asian countries and covering other regions, is taking shape.

The concept of the Belt and Road Initiative has foreseen bright prospects in the countries along the route since it was proposed by China. Statistics show that the total value of exports between China and the countries along the Belt and Road was nearly RMB 3 trillion in the first half of 2015, accounting for 1/4 of the total value of

China's foreign trade in the same period. Of that, the performance of China's exports to the countries along the Belt and Road was better than that of all the exports in the same period, which is a basic fact.[1]

According to the statistics published by the Ministry of Commerce, Chinese enterprises made direct investments in 48 countries along the Belt and Road from January to July 2015, with a total amount of investments of USD 8.59 billion, an increase of 29.5% over the same period of the previous year, accounting for 13.5% of China's non-financing foreign direct investments. The investments mainly went to Singapore, Indonesia, Laos, Russia, and Kazakhstan. The number of engineering projects undertaken by Chinese enterprises in 60 countries along the Belt and Road reached 1,786, producing contracts valuing USD 49.44 billion, thus accounting for 44.9% of the value of newly signed contracts of the projects undertaken by Chinese enterprises in foreign countries, with an increase of 39.6% over the same period of the previous year. Under these newly signed contracts, 176 projects valuing over USD 50 million contributed to a total contractual price of USD 42.09 billion. In the first seven months, the contractual price for service outsourcing established between Chinese enterprises and the countries along the Belt and Road totaled USD 8.23 billion, of which USD 5.94 billion was implemented, with an increase of 22.6% and 12.9% over the same period of the previous year, respectively. These contracts mainly involve information and technology services, engineering design outsourcing, and industrial design outsourcing. In July 2015, the countries along the Belt and Road invested to establish 217 enterprises in China, with an increase of 19.9% over the same period of the previous year; the actual investment to China valued USD 0.76 billion, with a decrease of 1.3% over the same period of the previous year. In terms of the industries that received investments, there were bigger increases of investment in the wholesale and retail industry and in leases and commercial services,

---

[1]The Export Value between China and the Countries along the Belt and Road Nears RMB 3 Trillion for the First Half of 2015. (July 13, 2015). Retrieved from State Council of the People's Republic of China website: http://www.gov.cn/2015-07/13/content_2895851.htm.

with increases of 428.7% and 500.3% over the same period of the previous year, respectively. In terms of the areas that received investments, the investments were bigger in Shanghai, Beijing, and Guangdong.[2]

On October 16, 2015, China Enterprise Combo, led and organized by the China Railway Corporation, officially signed a contract with Indonesia SOE Combo, led and organized by PT Kereta Api (PT KAI) Indonesia, thus establishing a China–Indonesia joint venture. The JV, whose contractual price is valued at around USD 5 billion, will take care of the construction and operation of the Djakarta–Bandung high-speed railway project in Indonesia, marking a historical breakthrough in China's "going global" in the area of railways.

The high-speed railway stretching from Djakarta to Bandung, the fourth largest city of the country, with a total length of 150 km, has the highest design speed of 300 km/h. This high-speed railway was approved for a franchised operation by the Ministry of Transportation of Indonesia in March 2016, thus marking an important legal guarantee for the overall kickoff construction of the Djakarta–Bandung high-speed railway project. Upon its completion, the time for traveling from Djakarta to Bandung will be reduced from 3 hours at present to less than 40 minutes. The project head from the China Railway Corporation pointed out that the Djakarta–Bandung high-speed railway, employing the cooperation model in which the Chinese and Indonesian enterprises jointly invested in the construction and management of the railway, is the first overseas order that involves almost all the aspects of the project, from technical standards, prospect design, engineering construction and machine building, to materials supply, operations and management and talent training; it is also the first overseas railway project carried out through cooperation bridged by both governments and practiced by the business to business (B2B) between the mutual countries. It is a success and a

---

[2] Chinese Enterprises Invested USD 8.59 Billion in 48 Countries along the Belt and Road from January to July. (September 7, 2015). Retrieved from State Council of the People's Republic of China website: http://www.gov.cn/2015-07/13/content_2895851.htm.

significant element of innovation of the overseas model of China's railway, and has produced a significant demonstrative effect in utilizing overseas and domestic markets and resources in a strategic way; moreover, it has advanced the branding of "China's high-speed railway," enabling it to go global more efficiently.[3]

During the period from October 19–23, 2015, President Xi Jinping paid a fruitful visit to the United Kingdom, acclaiming the visit as one in a "golden age." On October 21, China's nuclear industry accomplished a historic feat in the United Kingdom. The Chinese nuclear power enterprises led by the China General Nuclear Power Group (CGN) signed an agreement with Electricite De France to invest 6 billion pounds in the project of the Hinkley Point Nuclear Power Plant in the United Kingdom, with the Chinese party holding 33% of the shares. The Hinkley Point Nuclear Power Plant will become the first nuclear power plant in the last 30 years in the United Kingdom. This is the first time for a Chinese nuclear power enterprise to participate in the construction of a nuclear power plant in a developed country in the West. In the future, Chinese nuclear power enterprises will be expected to obtain a lion's share of the construction and operation of new nuclear power station projects in the United Kingdom by applying the "Hualong technology" developed by Chinese enterprises. On the same day, in London, the Central Bank of China succeeded in publishing the one-year draft of the Central Bank, with the final nominal interest rate of 3.1% and an oversubscription of over five times. Previously, the central banks of the two countries had also signed an agreement on a bilateral standard currency swap and enlarged the scale of the swap to RMB 350 billion from the original RMB 200 billion. The period of validity was three years and could be extended. In the Chinese president's visit, great achievements were made in investment and cooperation between China and the United Kingdom in the areas of the economy, trade, and culture, and the two parties reached around 150 cooperative agreements involving approximately 40 billion pounds, which was beyond expectations.

---

[3] China Won the Djakarta-Bandung High-Speed Railway Project. (October 17, 2015). *Xinhuanet*. Retrieved from http://www.xinhuanet.com/world/2015-10/17/c_128325993.htm.

The British government also announced that it would provide a new two-year visa with multiple entries to Chinese tourists starting from January of the following year, and the visa expenses would be the same as those for the present six-month visa. Before, Chinese tourists could only apply for the six-month visa for traveling to the United Kingdom, which cost 85 pounds, while a two-year visa with multiple entries cost 324 pounds. The spokesperson for the Prime Minister's Office of the United Kingdom said that the change aimed to attract more Chinese tourists to the United Kingdom. In the past five years, the number of Chinese tourists received by the United Kingdom has more than doubled. In 2014, the number reached 185,000, contributing 0.5 billion pounds to the British economy. In the eyes of the British people, however, this "cake" is supposed to grow much bigger as compared to the benefits reaped by France, a big account for European tourism.[4]

In 2015, Chinese enterprises made direct investments in 49 countries involved in the Belt and Road Initiative; the investment amount totaled USD 14.82 billion, an increase of 18.2% over the same period of the previous year, accounting for 12.6% of the total amount of Chinese investments. The investments mainly flowed to Singapore, Kazakhstan, Laos, Indonesia, Russia, and Thailand. Chinese enterprises signed another 3,987 contracts for projects outsourcing with 60 countries along the Belt and Road; the value of the new contracts was USD 92.64 billion, accounting for 44.1% of the total contract value for China's engineering outsourcing for the same period, and an increase of 7.4% over the same period of the previous year. This generated a turnover of USD 69.26 billion, accounting for 45% of the total for the same period of the previous year, with an increase of 7.6% over the same period of the previous year.[5] Statistics from the

---

[4] China and the UK Reached about 150 Agreements, Valuing about 40 Billion Pounds. (October 22, 2015). *Qilu Wanbao*. Retrieved from http://www.qlwb.com.cn/2015/1022/479752.shtml.

[5] Liu Ran and Zhou Suya. (January 20, 2016). Ministry of Commerce: Chinese Enterprises Increased 18.2% More in the Countries along the Belt and Road in 2015. *People's Daily Online*. Retrieved from http://finance.people.com.cn/n1/2016/0120/c1004-28070428.html.

Ministry of Commerce show that the advancement of the Belt and Road Initiative has nurtured new opportunities for foreign investments in China. In 2015, the investments made in China by the countries and regions along the Belt and Road increased by 25.3% over the same period of the previous year. As an important area covered by the Maritime Silk Road, the investments made by the ASEAN community in China increased by 22.1% over the same period of the previous year.[6]

One may associate the present with the peace, development, and prosperity brought by the ancient Silk Road to the Asian–European Continent that took shape out of the need for trade in the Middle Ages a thousand years ago, despite all kinds of mysteries and legends. The modern Silk Road Economic Belt will also become a bond for peace, harmony, and cooperation, and a road to friendship for economic exchanges and cultural integration among countries.

All times have their own changes that are often unpredictable, but what remains unchanged is the Chinese nation's inclusiveness, her concept of harmonious development, and the way she has been dealing with others, that is win–win cooperation. How to activate the conception of connecting Asia and Europe, namely, "China westward and Europe eastward" integration, which has been held by the people in Eurasia for thousands of years, is not only the strategic choice made by China and Europe to realize win–win cooperation, but it is also the realistic demand for China and Europe to realize multilateral benefits in their relations with Central Asia, the Gulf and the Middle East region, Russia, Iran, and Turkey.

---

[6] Countries along the Belt and Road Invested 25% More in China in 2015. (April 12, 2016). *China News Service.* Retrieved from http://www.chinanews.com/cj/2016/04-12/7830688.shtml.

About the Author

Rong Xinchun is an Associate Professor at the Department of China's Contemporary Economic History, Institute of Economics, Chinese Academy of Social Sciences. His research interest mainly include macroscopical economy, transportation and communication industry and more. He has also authored and co-authored monographs of more than one million words. Around ten of his academic papers have been published in key journals, such as *Chinese Economic History Studies* and *A Study of Contemporary Chinese History*.

About the Translator

Xia Xia, PhD., is an acquisition editor at International Cooperation and Publishing Centre, China Social Sciences Press. She is also a translator who has participated in many translation and proofreading book projects, such as *The Handbook of Belt and Road* and *China-ASEAN Relations* (Vol.2).

Historical Origin and Realistic Challenges

According to a piece of enlightened Western reading material in English, *Stories of the Silk Route*, a child asked the author Sanjiva Wijesina: "What is the Silk Route? Is it really paved with silk?"[1] This suggests that the image of a silk country had been deeply rooted among the Western people, and China's light and magnificent silk articles were known by the outside world and delivered to Europe long ago.

1. The Silk Road in History

Silk was the most famous, most valuable traditional product transported and sold at the longest distance and the greatest scale in ancient China's foreign trade. China first introduced silk to India and Western countries in the Spring and Autumn Period and the Warring

---

[1] Sanjiva Wijesina. (1991). *Stories of the Silk Route*. Sri Lanka: Colombo, quoted from Liu Yingsheng. (2014). *The Silk Road*, Nanjing, China: Jiangsu People's Publishing House, p. 315.

States Period in the 4th century B.C. The Western people were unaware of China until the introduction of silk, and they hailed China as Seres, which in Greek means a silk country. After visiting China for seven times during the period 1868–1872, the German geologist Ferdinand von Richthofen was the first to put forward the name "Seidenstrassen" (the Silk Road) in the book *China* (Volume III) published in 1877. Therefore, in a word, the Silk Road was an artery for ancient China's exchange of goods with the outside world. However, in history, ancient China exchanged goods with the outside world through maritime roads as well as land roads. In his book *Documents sur les Tou-Kiue (Turcs) Occidentaux*, the French Sinologist Édouard Chavannes discussed both land and maritime silk roads. The Maritime Silk Road was the maritime transportation artery for trade and cultural exchanges between ancient China and foreign countries and was the oldest known seaway. It was mainly divided into two seaways: one starting from the East China Sea and the other from the South China Sea. As early as the Qin Dynasty (221 B.C.–207 B.C.) and the Han Dynasty (202 B.C.–A.D. 220), exchanges were relatively frequent in regions such as Southeast Asia and South Asia. During the Tang Dynasty (A.D. 618–A.D. 907), fleets that mainly shipped silk departed from Quanzhou and Guangzhou, sailing through the South China Sea, the Indian Ocean, the Persian Gulf, and Europe. During the Ming Dynasty (A.D. 1368–A.D. 1644), Zheng He's fleet arrived at some area in southeastern Africa (Zheng He was a famous Chinese navigator of the Ming Dynasty). Therefore, the seaway connecting the East and the West was commonly called "the Maritime Silk Road." The exported goods gradually shifted to porcelain during the Song Dynasty and Yuan Dynasty (A.D. 960–A.D. 1368); thus, it was known as the Maritime Porcelain Road. It was also known as the Maritime Spice Road due to the introduction of spices. In the Yuan Dynasty (A.D. 1271–A.D. 1368), the Italian Marco Polo traveled to China along the Land Silk Road and returned to Italy via the Maritime Silk Road. In his monograph *An Exploration of the Maritime Silk Road* published in 1967, the Japanese scholar Takatoshi Misugi pointed out that the Maritime Silk Road emerged as early as the Qin Dynasty and the Han Dynasty of China, and flourished extraordinarily during the Tang Dynasty and the Song Dynasty, and the Maritime Silk Road featured two seaways from the East China Sea and the South China Sea.[2] As indicated, as early as the time when Zhang Qian, an envoy and an outstanding diplomatist, was sent to the Western regions for friendly exchanges during the Western Han Dynasty (206 B.C. to A.D. 24), Chinese silk became famous abroad, while the road in which Zhang Qian traversed was hailed as the Silk Road.

1.1 *Overview of the Silk Road*

The cultural contact between China and the outside world was attributable to the opening of the Land Silk Road and the Maritime Silk Road during the Han Dynasty and the Tang Dynasty. Both silk roads enabled China to break through geographical barriers to some extent so that Sino-foreign cultural exchanges could be carried out. The Silk Road was preliminarily opened before Zhang Qian was sent to the western regions during the Qin Dynasty and the Han Dynasty, and it became highly prosperous during the Han Dynasty and the Tang Dynasty, and lasted till the middle of the Ming Dynasty. Until the time when westerners built extensive connections through the seaway spanning the Atlantic Ocean, the Indian Ocean, and the Pacific Ocean, this large channel connecting both the eastern and western ends of Eurasia, being 10,000 km long from east to west and 3,000 km wide from north to south, was regarded as the oldest land artery at an unprecedented scale for human economic and cultural exchanges in nearly 2,000 years from the 3rd century B.C. to the 16th century A.D.[3]

As evidenced by the ancient Chinese book called *The Biography of King Mu* — which recorded the western expedition of King Mu of the Zhou Dynasty, there is a vast open country to the north of the state of Queen Mother of the West, with feathers seen for about

---

[2] Lin Yueqin. (2015). The Conception of the Belt and Road: Challenges and Countermeasures. *Journal of Hunan Finance and Economics University*, Issue 154, Vol. 31, pp. 5–17.
[3] Feng Tianyu. (2014). Three Major Motive Forces for Carving Out the Silk Road. *Hubei Social Sciences*, Issue 9, pp. 107–112.

900 km, and many exquisite Chinese silk articles and pongees embroidered with the phoenix pattern were unearthed at the Pazyryk Cemetery in the Soviet Union; thus, a trade route may have existed between China and the West very early in the history, and Chinese silk fabrics were delivered to Central Asia, and even to Europe, along this trade route. In the 5th century B.C., Chinese silk was the clothing fabric sought after by Greece's upper class, as evidenced by the delicate and transparent silk relics on portraits which were sculpted and made of colored porcelain in Greece, while at that time, people believed that only a remote eastern country called Seres was able to make this delicate and transparent clothing fabric.[4] The archaeological discoveries in Egypt, Baden-Württemberg, Germany, and Greece in recent years have also indicated that westward introduction of Chinese silk fabrics began as early as even before the Shang Dynasty and Zhou Dynasty (1600 B.C.–256 B.C.). Chinese silk and silk technique, ironware and cast-iron techniques, the well-digging technique, and the papermaking technology were introduced to the West along the Silk Road during the palmy days of the Silk Road. Meanwhile, local specialties, music, dance, and religious art were also gradually introduced to the East from European countries.

From 138 B.C. to 119 B.C., Zhang Qian was sent twice by Emperor Wu (156 B.C.–87 B.C.) of the Western Han Dynasty to the western regions for the purpose of expanding the Silk Road. During the Western Han Dynasty, the Silk Road started from Chang'an (Luoyang in the Eastern Han Dynasty [A.D. 25–A.D. 220]) and extended to Dunhuang via the Hexi Corridor. It was divided into northern and southern roads from Dunhuang: the southern road started from Dunhuang and passed through Loulan, Yutian (currently Khotan), Shache, and then crossed Congling (currently Pamirs) to Da Yue Zhi (currently Afghanistan), Parthia (currently Iran), and in the west reached Ndiochia (the name of an ancient West Asian country, currently an area between the Tigris and the Euphrates inside Iraq) and Cippus (the Roman Empire); the northern road started from Dunhuang and passed through Jiaohe, Qiuci, Shule

---

[4] Jin Qiu. (2002). *The History of Musical and Dance Cultural Exchanges on the Ancient Silk Road*. Shanghai, China: Shanghai Music Publishing House, p. 2.

(currently Kashgar), crossed Congling to Da Yuan (currently the Fergana Valley in Central Asia), and to the west, it reached Cippus via Parthia. The commonly known Silk Road refers to the westerly extended Land Silk Road, namely the land way that was opened by Zhang Qian in the Western Han Dynasty and Ban Chao (a famous militarist and diplomatist in the Eastern Han Dynasty) when they went to the western regions as envoys; the Land Silk Road started from Chang'an (currently Xi'an) and Luoyang and went to Central Asia and Western Asia via Gansu and Xinjiang, and connected the Mediterranean countries. This trade route was dominated by silk articles trade; thus, it was called the Silk Road.

In a broad sense, the Silk Road includes the Southern Land Silk Road and the Maritime Silk Road in addition to the Northwestern Land Silk Road. The Southern Land Silk Road (also called the Shu-Hindu Road) refers to the trade route in ancient China starting from Chengdu, Sichuan to reach Myanmar and Thailand via Guizhou and Yunnan, finally reaching India, with a total length of about 2,000 km; it was one of the oldest international routes from China. The Maritime Silk Road refers to the seaway for transportation, trade, and cultural exchanges between ancient China and foreign countries; it prospered during the Song Dynasty and the Yuan Dynasty.[5]

In his book *China: The Results of My Travels and the Studies Based Thereon* published in 1877, Ferdinand von Richthofen officially named the trade route from China to Europe "The Silk Road," which referred to the transportation route mainly used for the trade of silk and silk articles between China's Central Plains and the Amu Darya-Syr Darya river basin in Central Asia and India during the Western Han Dynasty and the Eastern Han Dynasty (202 B.C. to A.D. 220). In 1910, in his book *The Ancient Silk Road between China and Syria*, the German historian A. Herrmann extended the western end of the Silk Road to the Eastern Coast of the Mediterranean Sea and Asia Minor. The monograph *The Silk Road* written by a German geographer gave detailed descriptions of the trade route between

---

[5] Huang Weiping. (2015). New Development of the New Silk Road Economic Belt and the China-EU Economic and Trade Pattern. *China Business and Market*, Issue 1, pp. 84–90.

China and the West in history. The name "Silk Road" was generally used by the people at home and abroad; its definition covers more extensive contents and regions, and it roughly meant the transportation route across the Asian Continent during ancient times that started from the Central Shaanxi Plain in the Yellow River Basin, spanned the Hexi Corridor, the Tarim Basin, Congling (currently Pamirs), Mesopotamia in Central Asia, the Persian Plateau on the south side of the Caspian Sea, and Mesopotamia in Western Asia to the Eastern Coast of the Mediterranean Sea and various areas of Rome. For about 1,000 years since the 2nd century B.C., a number of Chinese goods such as silk were introduced to the West by means of this road, which tallied with the name "Silk Road."

Since the second half of the 20th century, the connotations of the Silk Road had been further expanded; in a broad sense, the Silk Road refers to the whole transportation route connecting the East and the West in ancient times, including the Land Silk Road and the Maritime Silk Road.

The Land Silk Road was further divided into the Northern Silk Road and the Southern Silk Road.

The Northern Silk Road roughly refers to the transportation route starting from Luoyang and Chang'an and unfolding westerly in a fan-shaped way during the Han Dynasty and the Tang Dynasty; it was divided into eastern, central, and western sections. The eastern section started from Luoyang and Chang'an reaching Yumen Pass and Yangguan via the Hexi Corridor; the central section included the southern road (along the northern foot of the Kunlun Mountains, the southern edge of the Taklimakan desert), central road (along the southern foot of Tianshan Mountains, the northern edge of the Taklimakan desert), and the northern road (across the Junggar Basin at the northern foot of the Tianshan Mountains); the western section was the route spanning Congling (Pamirs) and moving westerly reaching Europe, and it was divided into the southern road (through Afghanistan and the Iranian Plateau to Baghdad, Damascus, Beirut, and nearly to the Mediterranean Sea to the east and various areas of Rome via navigation), the central road (namely the northern road during the Han Dynasty, extending westerly along Amu Darya to meet up with the southern road at Teheran), and new northern roads (one road extended westerly along the Syr Darya to meet up with the central road at Merv, while another road extending along the prairie in what is currently northern Kazakhstan, via the route from the north of the Caspian Sea to the Asia Minor Peninsula and various areas of the Roman land).

The Southwestern Silk Road was a trade route that started from Chengdu, Yibin in Sichuan, crossed the Minjiang River (and its tributary the Dadu River), the Jinsha River (and its tributary the Ya-lung River), the Lancang River, the Nujiang River, and The Hengduan Mountains (including Gaoligong Mountain), and reached Myanmar and India via Tengchong. Yunnan was at its crossroads and connected China's Central Plains and Southeastern Asia and Southern Asia.[6]

The Maritime Silk Road took shape during the period of Emperor Wu of the Han Dynasty. An ancient book, *The History of the Han Dynasty-Geographical Section*, recorded maritime trade in which envoys sent by Emperor Wu of the Han Dynasty and the enlisted merchants engaged. After the middle of the Tang Dynasty, with the development of the shipbuilding industry and seamanship, maritime transportation prospered as it never had before. The original Silk Road declined in importance and retreated from the leading position in east–west transportation due to the "An Lushan Rebellion," the development of textile technology in Western Asia, a climate with frequent severe sandstorms, restrictions of means of transportation, pillaging of Silk Road trade by many nomadic people, and the southward shift of China's economic powerhouse. After the Song Dynasty, with the further development of Southern China, the above southward shift was accelerated, and seaways from Guangzhou, Quanzhou, and Hangzhou increasingly prospered and extended from Southeastern Asia to the Arabian Sea, and even to the eastern coast of Africa.

Some scholars discussed the cultural connotation of the Silk Road; they believed that "This road is regarded as the Oasis Road relative to the Eurasian Steppe Road and the Maritime Silk Road. This road spans a vast desert dotted with numerous natural oases, giving rise to

---

[6] Feng Tianyu. (2014). Three Major Motive Forces for Carving Out the Silk Road. *Hubei Social Sciences*, Issue 9, pp. 107–112.

many oasis countries and providing rest areas for travelers and droves. Oases serve as the junction points of the transportation network, and countless points form a transportation route across Eurasia so that an artery for economic and cultural exchanges between the East and the West takes shape. Therefore, this road has been called the 'Oasis Road'. The silk trade is the artery of commercial exchanges on the Oasis Road, hence the commonly-known Silk Road is the Oasis Road."[7]

1.2 *The Silk Road Promoted Trade and Cultural Exchanges between China and the West*

The ancient Silk Road was generally divided into the Northern Silk Road, the Southern Silk Road, the Maritime Silk Road, and the Steppe Silk Road; the Northern Silk Road and the Maritime Silk Road were the most important roads. The Northern Silk Road prospered mainly during the Western Han Dynasty and the Tang Dynasty; it was opened after Zhang Qian was sent again to the western regions as an envoy in 119 B.C., and it was also called as the Desert Oasis Silk Road, the embodied Land Silk Road, or sometimes the whole Silk Road. The Silk Road flourished for the first time during the Western Han Dynasty. At the time of the Eastern Han Dynasty, the control over the western regions was abandoned due to internal troubles; thus, the Silk Road no longer prospered. In the subsequent Three Kingdoms (A.D. 220–A.D. 265) and during the Northern and Southern Dynasties (A.D. 420–A.D. 589), the Silk Road was inter-rupted by frequent wars. The Silk Road started to become smooth again during the Sui Dynasty (A.D. 581–A.D. 618). The Tang Dynasty controlled the western regions once again, and the Silk Road prospered for the second time. However, after An Lushan Rebellion in the middle of the Tang Dynasty, the Central Plains Dynasty gave up the operation of the western regions and shifted its attention to the maritime road; as a consequence, the Silk Road declined again, and

---

[7] Shi Yuntao. (2007). *Changes in the Silk Road from the 3rd Century to the 6th Century*. Beijing, China: Culture and Art Publishing House, p. 61.

the land road gradually changed from a main road to a supplement to the maritime road; the land road and the maritime road were replaceable to some extent. During the Northern Song Dynasty (A.D. 960–A.D. 1127), the Hexi Corridor was occupied by the Western Xia Regime (A.D. 1038–A.D. 1227). The Southern Song Dynasty (A.D. 1127–A.D. 1279) lost control of the whole northwestern region, and it was impossible to restore the Silk Road to its previous status. During the Yuan Dynasty, the Silk Road became the transportation route within the empire; it was less blocked during the Yuan Dynasty than other dynasties, but it mainly served the people with religious faith and the mission of cultural exchanges; thus, it was no longer a Silk Road that was mainly dedicated to merchants, and it failed to prosper again. Great changes in the mode of transportation occurred; with the development of sea transportation and convenient air transportation, the land road was no longer attractive.

The Maritime Silk Road mainly prospered during the period from the middle of the Tang Dynasty to the Song Dynasty and the Yuan Dynasty. The road refers to the seaway from Southeastern China to the Pacific Ocean or to the Indian Ocean, Southern Asia, Western Asia, and Africa via the South China Sea. It may become more important again sooner than the land road. The maritime road was the supplement to the land road before the Tang Dynasty; however, after the middle of the Tang Dynasty, the land road was blocked; furthermore, the economic powerhouse moved toward the south. The compass was invented, and progress was made in seamanship; thus, the Maritime Silk Road started to thrive, surpassed, and gradually replaced the land road. The Northern Song Dynasty and the Southern Song Dynasty adopted a more open policy and gave great importance to commerce and overseas trade, thus guaranteeing continued prosperity for the Maritime Silk Road. In the Yuan Dynasty, the Maritime Silk Road became smoother. After the Song Dynasty and the Yuan Dynasty, porcelain and tea were mainly exported while spices were imported; thus, it was also called the Porcelain Road, the Tea Road, and the Spice Road. Maritime trade was banned at the beginning of the Ming Dynasty. Although Zheng He traveled to the West via a seaway seven times in nearly 30 years, and his expedition was a magnificent feat in the history of worldwide navigation, marine navigation was stopped soon after Emperor Yongle (A.D. 1360–A.D. 1424) of the Ming Dynasty died because there was only official diplomacy without private participation, manpower and financial resources were wasted, and a heavy economic burden was imposed on the government. The situation of the Qing Dynasty's (A.D. 1636–A.D. 1912) closure of the country was even more serious. Emperor Kangxi (A.D. 1654–A.D. 1722) of the Qing Dynasty lifted the ban on maritime trade but did not permit trade with the West. Emperor Qianlong (A.D. 1736–A.D. 1796) of the Qing Dynasty fully secluded China from the outside world; he later only permitted Guangzhou to trade with foreign countries, and no. 13 Trading Company monopolized trade, so the Maritime Silk Road declined in use.

In the 14th and 15th centuries, the Chinese Silk Road was on the wane while worldwide navigation routes sprang up. At the turn of the Yuan and Ming Dynasties in the 14th and 15th centuries, Chinese Land and Maritime Silk Roads declined, but Europe opened new worldwide navigation routes. In 1453, the Eastern Roman Empire collapsed, and the Ottoman Empire rose and controlled the east–west trade route, namely the silk road, extorted excessive taxes and levies from merchants, and increased the prices of goods by 8–10 times in switch trade; thus, some European trading cities declined. Europe's upper class took Asia's articles of luxury as the necessities of life and purchased these articles of luxury at high prices, leading to a trade deficit for Western Europe and massive outflow of gold. The nobilities, merchants, and bourgeoisie in Western European countries were eager to bypass Western Asia and open new navigation routes to India and China. Therefore, Christopher Columbus and other people were sent to embark on oceangoing voyages; they discovered the New World and opened global navigation routes to expand international trade and form the world market. As the industrial revolution occurred in the West, the world trade center and economic powerhouse shifted from the East to the West, and China was replaced by Western Europe as a world economic power. As mentioned by the French scholar Aly Mazaheri, the birth and development of modern technology and industry are among the main factors that contributed to the abandonment of the ancient Silk Road; as a consequence, industrial products replaced the traditional products from China. As indicated, the shift of the trade route resulted not only from political and military factors but also from economic and technological development.[8]

1.3 *Decline and Continuity of the Silk Road*

Since modern times, especially since the second half of the 19th century, China has been invaded by great powers, and so the ancient Silk Road has become a relic of history. After 1895 when the Sino-Japanese War broke out, the Qing Regime hoped to build railways for overcoming China's transportation dilemma. Joseph Charignon, who once worked for the Qing Regime, put forward a grand plan for building 21 trunk railways to form China's railway network, including the plans for building two large international routes from north to south and from east to west. The east–west international route started from China's coastal ports to connect Gansu, Shanxi, and Henan Provinces through railways and then foreign railways. In 1918, in his book *The International Development of China*, Sun Yat-sen mentioned about this plan to build a vast railway network in China and presented three major railway systems: the east–northwest, the east–southwest, and the central railway systems, including the Urumchi–Yili Railway connecting railways in European and Asian countries.

During the second half of the 19th century, Tsarist Russia built the trunk railway connecting the Pacific Ocean and the Atlantic Ocean via Siberia in Eurasia. This railway started from Vladivostok in Eastern Russia and extended through Siberia to Moscow, and then European countries and finally ended at the Port of Rotterdam, in the Netherlands. It was hailed as the first Eurasian Continental Bridge.

In 1956, China and the Soviet Union signed an agreement on extending the Lanzhou–Xinjiang Railway to Aketogay in the Soviet Union. However, the western section of the Lanzhou–Xinjiang Railway was not connected to the Turkestan–Siberian Railway in the

---

[8] Yang Zhengwei, Zhou Baogen. (2014, April 14). New Policy for the Silk Road Belt: Various Silk Road Plans Heavily Overlap. *Caijing*.

Soviet Union until September 1990 after the threat from the Soviet Union disappeared. Since then, the steel artery from China to Europe via Central Asia, reputed as the Modern Silk Road, has become the new competitor for large container vessels between China and Europe. In 1994, Chinese Premier Li Peng visited four Central Asian countries and proposed to jointly build the modern Silk Road to expand economic and cultural exchanges between Asia and Europe.

During the period of the Soviet Union, the famous Baikal Amur Trunk Railway was built. After the collapse of the Soviet Union, Central Asian countries gained independence. In the 1990s, the second Eurasian Continental Bridge was built. It spans both Europe and Asia, starts from Lianyungang, China on the east and goes to the Alataw Pass, a border city in China, via the Northern Xinjiang Railway on the west, enters Kazakhstan, and extends to the Port of Rotterdam, in the Netherlands after passing through Russia, Belarus, Poland, and Germany. With a total length of about 10,800 km, it connects the Pacific Ocean and the Atlantic Ocean. Leading to China and more than 40 countries and some regions in Central Asia, Western Asia, Eastern Europe, and Western Europe, the route is the longest continental bridge in the world. As it connects China and Europe through Central Asia, it actually means the renaissance of the ancient Silk Road.[9]

The United Nations envisioned the building of a pan-Asian railway network as early as the 1960s, but China was amid the turmoil of the Cultural Revolution and Vietnam was plagued by civil war in that period. In 1988, UNESCO announced the launch of the 10-year program *Integral Study of the Silk Roads: Roads of Dialogue.* Afterward, the United Nations carried out a number of activities focusing on the Silk Road. The United Nations Development Programme launched the Silk Road Initiative in 2008.

In the early 1990s, Europe called for building a new Silk Road belt connecting Europe to Central Asia through the European–Caucasus–Asia trade corridor. In the late 1990s, the United States joined this effort and formulated the Silk Road Initiative Act of 1990,

---

[9] Li Yongquan. (2015). *The Silk Road Economic Belt: National Conditions.* Beijing, China: Social Sciences Academic Press.

which, however, was not adopted by the Senate. Afterward, the US presented the Silk Road Initiative Act of 2006, which was also not adopted. In 2005, Frederick Starr, a US expert on Central Asian issues, envisioned a new Silk Road — a network of transportation and economic development with Afghanistan as the hub and connecting countries in Central Asia and Western Asia to India, even Southeast Asia. This is considered one of the most important sources of US Silk Road diplomacy. In July 2011, the US Secretary of State, Hillary Clinton put forward an official version of a new Silk Road plan in India; subsequently, the US Government put it on the international agenda. The new US Silk Road Initiative is designed to further con-solidate the Northern Distribution Network covering nine Soviet states, protect US interests in Afghanistan and Central Asia after the withdrawal of troops from Afghanistan in 2014, and to encourage the integration of Central Asian countries and the South Asia Region to incorporate Central Asia into the new economic, political, and safety framework, in order to push aside China, Russia, and Iran. In 2011, Iran initiated the plan for connecting Iran's railway line to China's railway line through Afghanistan, Tajikistan, and Kyrgyzstan.[10] In 2012, the President of Kazakhstan announced the implementation of a new Silk Road belt program and stressed that Kazakhstan should become the largest transit center in Central Asia and the unique bridge between Europe and Asia. On February 19, 2015, Alexis Tsipras, Prime Minister of Greece, vowed to support and participate in the Maritime Silk Road, the China–EU land–sea express construc-tion plan proposed by China. In his article "Engaging in the Construction of the New Silk Road" published in the French news-paper *Les Echos* on February 27, 2015, Dominique de Villepin, former Prime Minister of France, emphasized the idea that Europe should take advantage of this Silk Road, draw up a development roadmap on the basis of the new Silk Road initiative, and connect it to the investment plan with a total amount of EUR 300 billion put forward

---

[10] Li Jianmin. (2013). Innovative Mode of Regional Cooperation under the Spirit of the Silk Road — Strategic Conception, International Comparison and Concrete Approach to Implementation. *Academic Frontiers*, Issue 23, pp. 20–25.

by Jean-Claude Juncker, the President of the European Commission. Moreover, local European governments, chambers of commerce, enterprises, universities, and think tanks should also take part in it.[11]

2. The Belt and Road Initiative Proposed by China: From Conception to Reality

The Silk Road, ancient or contemporary, presents itself as open and inclusive, rather than exclusive and limited. Although the great significance of rejuvenating the Silk Road has been noticed for long both at home and abroad and several new suggestions and programs for the rejuvenation have been proposed, there has been no significant progress on it, and a huge gap still exists among the exchanges and connectivity in transportation, commerce and trade, investment, finance, and talent communication, impeding the cooperation among relevant countries and their development.

On September 7, 2013, Chinese President Xi Jinping, during his visit to Central Asia, delivered a speech at Nazarbayev University in Kazakhstan proposing to innovate the mode of cooperation and jointly build the Silk Road Economic Belt. The proposal of this initiative evoked strong positive responses both in China and abroad. On October 3, 2013, President Xi Jinping pointed out in a speech he made to the Parliament of Indonesia during his state visit to the country that "China will strengthen maritime cooperation with ASEAN countries ... to develop a maritime partnership in a joint effort to build the 21st-Century Maritime Silk Road." Since then, the Belt and Road Initiative has been gaining extensive attention from the international community and active responses from relevant countries and regions.

On November 12, 2013, it was pointed out in the *Decision of the CCCPC on Some Major Issues Concerning Comprehensively Intensifying the Reform* adopted at the Third Plenary Session of the 18th Central Committee of the CPC that "we should speed up opening up border areas by permitting special approaches and policies in personnel

---

[11] Lin Yueqin. (2015). The Conception of the Belt and Road: Challenges and Countermeasures. *Journal of Hunan Finance and Economics University*, Vol. 31, Issue 154, pp. 5–17.

exchanges, processing, and logistics and tourism for key ports on the border, in border cities and in economic cooperation areas. We should establish developing financial institutions, accelerate the construction of infrastructure connectivity with our neighboring countries and regions, and push forward the building of the Silk Road Economic Belt and the Maritime Silk Road, forming a pattern of all-around opening-up." At the opening of the Second Session of the 12th National People's Congress of China on March 5, 2014, Premier Li Keqiang pointed out in the *Report on the Work of the Government* presented to the State Council that "we should lose no time in planning the initiative of the Silk Road Economic Belt and the 21st-Century Maritime Silk Road, push forward the construction of the Bangladesh–China–India–Myanmar Economic Corridor and the China–Pakistan Economic Corridor, launch a batch of significant supporting projects, speed up infrastructure connectivity, and explore new room for international economic and technological cooperation." This means that the Belt and Road Initiative has become a state developmental strategy from a proposal for international cooperation at the beginning.

On November 4, 2014, the Leading Group for Financial and Economic Affairs convened a special meeting to examine the planning for the Silk Road Economic Belt and the 21st Century Maritime Silk Road, initiating the establishment of the Asian Infrastructure Investment Bank and the Silk Road Fund. President Xi Jinping stressed in his important speech that responding to the need of the era and the wish for the development of the countries involved, the initiative of the Silk Road Economic Belt and the 21st Century Maritime Silk Road provides a developmental platform with tremendous inclusiveness and with profound historical and cultural foundations, and it will combine the fast economic development of China with the interests of the countries along the Belt and Road. We should concentrate on this great undertaking under the principle of amity, sincerity, mutual benefit, and inclusiveness for peripheral diplomacy, and by building up our friendships and creating partnerships with our neighbors, so that the countries along the Belt and Road will develop a greater affinity toward, and be more supportive of, China. In 2014, the *Report on the Work of the Government* included the Belt and Road Initiative among the important tasks of the government. It was proposed at the Central Economic Working Conference, which was concluded on December 11, 2014, that the focus of the year 2015 should be laid on implementing the three regional development strategies for the construction of the Belt and Road Initiative, the integrated development of the Beijing–Tianjin–Hebei region, and the development of the Yangtze River Economic Belt.

On February 1, 2015, the Working Meeting for Accelerating the Construction of the Belt and Road Initiative was held in Beijing. Zhang Gaoli, Vice Premier of the State Council, pointed out that building the Belt and Road is a massive systematic engineering project; therefore, it is necessary for us to stick to the principle of joint consultation, building, and sharing as well as advance developmental strategies of the countries along the Belt and Road to coordinate with and complement each other. The building of the Silk Road Economic Belt marks a new era of China's reform and opening-up and a new stage of regional cooperation.

On March 28, 2015, the Chinese government launched the *Vision and Proposed Actions Outlined on Jointly Building the Silk Road Economic Belt and the 21st-Century Maritime Silk Road*, the guideline for the Belt and Road conception as initiated by China. Being dedicated to building a regional economic structure of openness, inclusiveness, balance, and mutual benefit, the initiative will push forward the all-round cooperation between China and many more countries and regions in the world.

It is fair to say that, having carried forth and developed the ancient Silk Road and the Maritime Silk Road, the Belt and Road Initiative is a significant strategic conception for China in strengthening cooperative development with relevant countries in a new international context. It proposes the new concepts of "the community of shared interests" and "the community with a common destiny" for equal benefits and win–win cooperation to be jointly built by the countries along the Land and Maritime Silk Roads[12]; it has drawn a new blueprint of a traffic route crossing Eurasia from the east to the

---

[12] Feng Zongxian. (2014, October 20). Strategic Significance of the Belt and Road Initiative. *Guangming Daily*, pp. 11. Retrieved from http://epaper.gmw.cn/gmrb/html/2014-10/20/nw.D110000gmrb_20141020_3-11.htm?div=-1.

west, coordinating between the China–Pakistan Economic Corridor and the Bangladesh–China–India–Myanmar Economic Corridor in the north–south direction, and connecting the Pacific Ocean, the Indian Ocean, and the Atlantic Ocean in the east–west direction. Additionally, 31 provinces and municipalities have proposed to participate in the significant decision-making of the Belt and Road conception. The year 2015 will become a new start for China in advancing the Belt and Road conception energetically.

2.1 *The Realistic Basis for Advancing the Belt and Road Initiative*

The reform and opening-up launched by China in 1978 mainly aimed at opening up to the outside world and bringing in foreign capital, advanced technologies, and management experience, the so-called "investment promotion." For this purpose, China has adjusted and straightened out its domestic relations to get itself connected to the world's economic rules according to the general regulations and trade rules of the world's economic development, thus taking in foreign capital, technologies, and management experience, for which China's joining the WTO is a significant sign. The implementation of this strategy has allowed for tremendous achievements and has won China worldwide attention.

The 35 years of reform and opening-up is the 35-year period when China's national economy realized development at full speed. Between 1979 and 2012, China's gross domestic product (GDP) annually increased by an average of 9.8%, while the average annual GDP growth of the world was only 2.8% for the same period. China's economic aggregate has been growing continuously, with its GDP increasing from RMB 364.5 billion in 1978 to RMB 51.8942 trillion in 2012. China's economic aggregate was ranked no. 10 in the world in 1978, while it came to no. 3 by replacing Germany in 2008 and no. 2 by replacing Japan in 2010. The per capita income increased to USD 5,680 in 2012 from USD 190 in 1978. By the practical international standard, China has risen to be among the middle-income countries. The over 30 years of reform and opening-up is the over 30-year period when China became increasingly conscious of the importance of adjusting its economic structure and transforming its developmental mode. Since more than 30 years ago, the three industries have made great progress during the process of adjustment, with the foundation of agriculture becoming increasingly strong, industry realizing continuous and fast development, and the service industry developing and growing fast. With the fast enhancement of industrial productivity, China has become a world manufacturer from a backward country relying upon agriculture.

For more than 30 years, China has mainly opened up the coastal areas to the outside world. The east of China shares around 90% of its imports and exports, 85% of the foreign investments, and 75% of the external investments, and the opening-up in the inland areas has obviously lagged behind. Opening-up westward and building the Silk Road Economic Belt will help to optimize the spatial layout of China's opening-up, transforming the west of China from a role of "backing up" to "forwarding" and forming an overall structure of opening-up with balanced development between the east and the west and between coastal and inland areas. It is known to all that the Third Plenary Session of the 11th Central Committee of the CPC held in 1978 launched the historical journey of China's opening-up. China established 5 special economic zones, including Shenzhen and four other cities; opened up and developed 14 coastal port cities and the Shanghai Pudong New Area; opened up 13 border cities, 6 river-side cities, and 18 capital cities of inland provinces; and built many zones and parks enjoying special policies. It is obvious that the focus of opening-up was laid on the coastal areas of the southeast during the early period, with Guangdong, Fujian, Jiangsu, Zhejiang, and Shanghai being the leaders in opening-up and reform and the first beneficiaries, while the central and western areas of China had been performing as the followers, which has to some extent caused an imbalance in economic development among the eastern, central and western areas. The Belt and Road, especially the Belt, starting from the west of China and traveling westward to Western Asia and Europe, will undoubtedly cause a significant change in the geographic layout of China's reform and opening-up. As the new pioneers who undertake the task of developing the area covering as much as 2/3 of the country's total land, the central and western areas of China share the task of "going global" with the eastern part of China. In addition, the eastern part of China remains an important engine for China's overall opening-up by further raising the level of China's opening-up through building "free trade zones" one next to another. At the same time, Central Asia in the hinterland of Eurasia and the western part of China were marginalized during the times when maritime power was in dominance; they became a "sunken area" between the Asia-Pacific and European economic circles, causing an imbalance in international development, providing the soil for the "three forces," including terrorists, and threatening peace among humankind. The bilateral economic cooperation between China and countries involved has developed rapidly, and China has become the no. 1 or no. 2 trading partner to many countries. For example, the value of trade between China and the five Central Asian countries increased to USD 50.3 billion in 2013 from USD 460 million in 1992, with an average annual increase of 25%. The countries along the Belt and Road generally hope they can develop along with China's rapid development; thus, they are becoming more willing to cooperate with China.

China's economy is going through a significant transformation from mere stress on "bringing in" to equal stress on "bringing in" and "going global," resulting in a new situation in which the market, resources, energy, and investment are deeply integrated with the foreign factors. In the early days of the reform and opening-up, with a low level of economic development, China was in urgent need of capital, technology, and a management mode. Therefore, opening-up at that time focused on bringing in foreign capital, advanced technologies, and a management mode. Statistics show that from 1979 to 2012, China brought in 763,278 foreign investment projects, with a total foreign capital of USD 1,276,108 million. It cannot be denied that these foreign investors and capital have played a great role in pushing forward China's economic development, technological advancement, and management modernization. It is right to say that this has been a great international transfer of industries led by developed countries. Currently, China has the capability of exporting factors despite the existing need for massive effective investments and technical transformation and upgrading. According to the statistics, as of the end of 2014, China's foreign investments had exceeded hundreds of billions of USD and had become a country of net capital outflow. The Belt and Road Initiative responds to the new trend of flow of factors in China. Through policy coordination, facilities connectivity, unimpeded trade, financial integration, and people-to-people bonds, the Belt and Road Initiative functions to deliver the productive factors of China, especially its high-quality excessive capacity, to the outside world, enabling the developing countries and regions along the Belt and Road to share the achievements of China's development. Sustainable development can only be achieved by sticking to opening-up and becoming deeply involved in the world's economy. The proposal of the Silk Road Economic Belt is foremost aimed at expanding and intensifying the opening-up. Building an open economy, connected to the world economy and integrated into world economic development, is one of the most important characteristics of China's 35-year-long reform and opening-up. Nevertheless, opening-up for the present is mainly practiced in coastal areas. Presently, faced with the historical task of intensifying the reform and the challenge of solving the structural problems and differences in regional development, China proposed the strategies of developing China's west and rejuvenating the economy of the northeastern part of China. It is more pressing for the provinces and regions on the boundary to achieve regional economic integration with their increasingly active economic activities. Therefore, it has become a trend of the era to realize all-round opening-up in the western and border areas in China and cooperate closely with regional economies. After gaining more and more experience in international cooperation, China's big businesses have an increasingly stronger wish to enter the global market. Therefore, from "bringing in" to "going global," transformation indicates the fact that China's reform and opening-up is growing more and more mature.

In the early days of China's opening-up, the developed economies, represented by European countries, the United States and Japan, had the advantages in capital, technology, and management, and China, which had been excluded from the outside world, now became the biggest receiver of their investments. Therefore, in the early period, China mainly opened up to developed countries and regions. In contrast, today, China's economy is faced with the bigger task of overall transformation and upgrading. Solutions must be found to use some of the capacity formed during the long-term construction, while many developing countries in the world are faced with the difficulties that China had previously. China's total volume of trade is ranked top in the world, and there are remarkable advantages in the areas of manufacturing, infrastructure, and information communications; however, China lacks arable land and energy resources in proportion to its big population. The countries along the Silk Road have bountiful energy resources and huge potential in agriculture and processing, which is highly complementary to China's situation. Only by using the advantages of both sides and the Chinese people's traits of being good at manufacturing and doing business, it will be possible to transform the respective advantages into practical results of development and benefit the people of each country. Therefore, the Belt and Road Initiative may facilitate these countries and regions in building infrastructure facilities such as roads, bridges and ports, help them develop some industries like textiles and garments, home electrical appliances and even automobile manufacturing, steel, and electricity supply, and enhance their capability for economic development and productivity, which also conforms to China's need in the upgrading of its industrial technology. In a report on the trade development of Central Asia, the United Nations Development Program announced that the exportation of the five Central Asian countries had become more dependent on raw materials and the exportation of energy, minerals, products, cotton, and metals from Kazakhstan, Turkmenistan, and Tajikistan accounted for 90% of their total exports. China and the five Central Asian countries are highly complementary in economic structure and in the structure of their goods destined for foreign trading. China's textile products, garments, light industrial products, and electrical products are more competitive in Central Asia, while for energy exports for the five Central Asian countries, China is their best choice in realizing the lowest transportation costs and the highest scale effect. China is complementary with the five Central Asian countries and even Iran and Russia along the new Silk Road in industrial structure, commodity structure, and trade structure. Therefore, it is beneficial for each party to push forward the trade with each other through international and regional cooperation.

2.2 *Eurasia Becoming an Important Growth Pole within the Global Economy*

The exchanges between the Asia-Pacific and the European economic circles, which are located at the two ends of the Silk Road, have been very active. In 2013, the volume of trade between China and Europe per se reached nearly USD 560 billion; thus, the two have become no. 1 partners to each other. There is also great potential in the trade among the inland countries in Asia and Europe. With the advancement in traffic technology, more convenient inland transportation, and reduced costs, trade by land will increase rapidly and will in part replace the sea route; moreover, it will possibly form the center for the trade between Asia and Europe following the Atlantic trade center and the Pacific trade center.

In terms of purchasing power parity, the proportion of Asia's GDP in the world will account for 42% in 2019, rising from 19.3% in 1980. However, the growth rate is different in the four regions of Asia. The proportion of East Asia's GDP in the world will rise to 25.6% in 2019 from 11.7% in 1980 and that of Southern Asia will rise to 9.4% in 2019 from 4.1% in 1980. It is fair to say that the growing proportion of Asia's GDP in the world is highly attributable to the growth of the GDP of Eastern Asia and Southern Asia. The proportions within Asia, however, remain basically unchanged: Eastern Asia's GDP will grow slowly to 61% in 2019 from 60.3% in 1980, that of Southern Asia from 21.3% to 22.4%, that of Southeastern Asia declining from 18.4% to 14.9%, and that of Central Asia from 2.3% in 1992 to 1.7% in 2019. In 1980, the GDP of Eastern Asia, excluding that of mainland China, accounted for 48.2% of Asia's GDP, of which Japan's GDP alone accounted for 40.4%, while that of mainland China accounted for 12.1%, less than 21.3% of Southern Asia and 18.4% of Southeastern Asia. In 1998, China's GDP accounted for more than that of Southeastern Asia, exceeding that of Southern Asia in 1993, and exceeding that of Japan in 1999. China's GDP in 1999 reached 25.9%, while Japan's GDP was 24.6%. In 2012, China's proportion reached 40.8%, having taken Japan's position in the economy of Asia in 1980, while the GDP of Eastern Asia, excluding China's, in the same year declined to even below 20%. It is predicted that, by 2019, China's GDP will account for 44.6%, while the GDP of Eastern Asia, excluding China's, will account for 16.4%.[13]

According to the report of *ASEAN, PRC, and India: The Great Transformation* jointly published by the Asian Development Bank and the Asian Development Bank Institute in 2014, the total GDP of the ASEAN countries, China, and India (ACI) will account for 28.8% in 2030 from 15.6% in 2010 at the market exchange rate, while the GDP of Japan will decline to 5.4% in 2030 from 8.8% in 2010. In terms of purchasing power parity, the GDP of ACI will account for 39.4% in 2030 from 23.6% in 2010, while the GDP of Japan will decline to 3.2% in 2030 from 5.9% in 2010.[14]

For China, the economic center is also shifting. Although the economy of the coastal area in the east of China is still leading, the proportion of the central and western parts of China is growing. According to the practice of dividing China into eastern, central, and western areas, the total GDP proportion of the eastern area declined to 55.4% in 2013 from 59.2% in 2004, while the proportion of the GDP of the central part grew from 23.5% to 24.6% and the western part from 17.2% to 20%. In terms of the proportion of imports to exports, the proportion of the east declined to 66.6% in 2013, according to the statistics provided by the National Bureau of Statistics of China. The east of China remains the economic center, but its position has somewhat declined in the past decade while that of the central and western parts of China has risen. In particular, the proportion taken by the west has grown faster than that taken by the central part by two times. In this sense, the Strategy of the Grand Development of Western China and the China-ASEAN Free Trade

[13] Zhong Feiteng. (2014). Beyond the Myth of Geopolitics: The New Asian Strategy of China. *Foreign Affairs Review*, Issue 6, pp. 16–39.
[14] The Asian Development Bank/The Asian Development Bank Institute. (2014). *ASEAN, PRC, and India: The Great Transformation.* Tokyo, Japan: The Asian Development Bank Institute, p. 28, Table 2.1 & p. 29, Table 2.2.

Area (FTA) have achieved substantial results. The statistics of the Secretariat of the WTO show that, in 2013, the value of China's export goods was USD 2.21 trillion, and the value of its imports was USD 1.95 trillion, with the exports and imports valuing USD 4.16 trillion in total (equivalent to RMB 25.83 trillion), and it has thus become the world's no. 1 trader of goods.

China has become the most important growth pole in Asia, and the geographical structure of Asia has also begun a new historical period. China proposes to deal with the peripheral relationships under the concept of "amity, sincerity, mutual benefit, and inclusiveness," it stresses the balance between trust and benefit, and extends the "Chinese Dream" in China to the "Asian-Pacific Dream," to see the benefit and loss of the present in the long run. Essentially, a concept or a value is livelier and travels faster than a policy for a certain period, and their influence on society is more far-reaching.

Since the EU-China Comprehensive Strategic Partnership was established in 2004, China and the EU have been becoming increasingly closer to each other and the scope for cooperation has been expanding. The EU became China's no. 1 trading partner, and China has remained the EU's no. 2 trading partner. The value of trade between China and the EU has exceeded that between China and Japan and China and the United States, meaning that the China–EU economic and trade relationship has become the most important trade relationship in bilateral relations. Currently, Germany, the Netherlands, the United Kingdom, France, and Italy are China's five biggest EU trading partners, and the investments by the United Kingdom, Germany, France, and the Netherlands are the top four from the EU in China; thus, the value of trade between China and the EU is continuously breaking through. Therefore, there exists the basis for the areas and scope for bilateral economic and trade cooperation between China and Europe to be explored deeper and to push forward the economic and trade operations in an all-round way.

The trade between China and the EU grew each year from 2004 to 2007 and reached a peak in 2008. Shocked by the global financial tsunami in 2008, China–EU trade had a slide in 2009, but it began to increase again after that, and the value of China–EU trade reached as high as over USD 729.9 billion in 2013. From 2009 to 2013, the value of trade between the two parties increased by 71%, and the EU remains China's no. 1 partner.

Similar to the value of China–US trade, the value of China–EU trade has undergone an increase and a decrease, but the latter has gone beyond the former. Since 2008, the value of China–EU trade accounted for 19% of China's total value of imports and exports, while the value of China–US trade accounts for 13%, with a difference of 6% points between the two.[15]

With Europe stepping out of the sovereign debt crisis, the *Developmental Strategy of Europe 2020* carried out, and the strategic goal of comprehensively intensifying reform as defined at the Third Plenary Session of the 18th Central Committee of the CPC, both China and Europe have realized the importance of strengthening their all-round cooperation further and seeking new growth points. A strong Europe will facilitate the development of China, and a strong China will also do the same for Europe.

Against such a context, upon the invitation from Herman Van Rompuy, President of the European Council, and José Manuel Barroso, President of the European Commission, President Xi Jinping paid a visit to the EU headquarters located in Brussels from March 31 to April 1, 2014. China and the EU jointly published the *Joint Statement on Intensifying the EU–China Comprehensive Strategic Partnership for Mutual Benefit*, indicating that China and Europe are shouldering the important tasks of further pushing the world's economic growth and realizing common prosperity. It was stressed that the two sides would maintain an open world economy together by opposing protectionism and pushing forward all-round cooperation starting from economic and trade cooperation. Both China and Europe agree on building a peaceful, growing, reforming, and civilized partnership in the next 10 years. A highlight in the Statement is that "both sides decide to

---

[15] Huang Weiping. (2015). New Development of the New Silk Road Economic Belt and the China-EU Economic and Trade Pattern. *China Business and Market*, Issue 1, pp 84–90.

develop synergies between China's Silk Road Economic Belt initiative and EU policies and to jointly explore common initiatives along the Silk Road Economic Belt," and the Statement includes the cooperation in traffic and transportation between China and the EU as a strategic goal. Subsequently, the combination of the new Silk Road Initiative with the EU–China Comprehensive Strategic Partnership was set down in a legal document that was accepted by China and the EU. Dominique de Villepin, former French Prime Minister, also believes that only the Belt and Road Initiative can reflect the new trend of globalization; the developmental trend and the center of globalization have changed; and the policy that can reflect the new trend of globalization today is the Belt and Road Initiative as a prioritized strategy for economy and diplomacy proposed by President Xi Jinping of China. The initiative is aimed at representing the glories of exchanges between the east and the west in the Tang Dynasty, and at providing a flexible framework for China to settle a series of big challenges of its own: to advance the internationalization of China's economy, enhance the role of the RMB in global trade, develop inland provinces, expand domestic demand, and so on. The Belt and Road Initiative also provides an opportunity for the international community to rethink the problem of the absence of a plan for common development since the end of the Cold War. The initiative proposes to fill the vacuum of economy, politics, and people-to-people communication between Eastern Asia and Europe, the two "prosperity poles," and also benefit the Middle East and Africa, through a great number of construction plans for infrastructures, including roads, railways, ports, banking, and telecommunications.[16]

2.3 *Development of Traffic and Transportation Facilitating International Regional Economic Cooperation*

On the one hand, the Silk Road Initiative covers such areas as international trade, cooperation on international technology and international investments, and also international regional cooperation; on the other hand, it not only expects that China and the EU will establish trans-Eurasia regional economic cooperation in the long term, but it also

---

[16]Dominique de Villepin. (February 27, 2015). Participate in Building the New Silk Road. *Les Échos.*

hopes that China and the five Central Asian countries, Iran, and Russia will establish multilateral or bilateral international regional economic cooperation in a short term, forming an international framework of regional economic cooperation with multiple levels and modes. Oil and gas supply pipeline, trans-border expressways, high-speed railways, information networks, and flight routes are major carriers for the new Silk Road, of which the trans-Eurasia high-speed railway is an important icon for the new Silk Road with an important role.

The new Silk Road travels through the five Central Asian countries, Iran, Russia, and Turkey. The high-speed railway along the new Silk Road reduces the costs for the flow of people, money, and materials. The "line" of the high-speed railway drives the "plane" of regional economic development, forming a new Silk Road Economic Belt. With mature high-speed railway technology, China is qualified for the development and investment overseas on a considerable scale. China has been bringing in and developing high-speed railway technologies on a large scale since 2005. China has taken in the technologies of Alstom from France, Siemens from Germany, Bombardier from Canada, and Kawasaki from Japan, and self-developed the high-speed railway with a speed of over 350 km/h, representing China's strength in the high-tech and economy.

With a speed of over 350 km/h, China's high-speed railway has greatly reduced the cost of land transportation. For example, it takes transportation along the Zhengzhou–Xinjiang–Europe railway, with a total length of 10,214 km, only 16–18 days with two customs transfers and two railway changes, saving 20 days as compared to transportation by sea and 80% as compared to transportation by air. If the speed reaches around 100 km for the transportation of goods in the near future, the time of the journey will be cut by 2/3 and reduced to 4–5 days, which marks a greater potential in replacing maritime transportation. It is predicted by relevant authorities that, by 2018, the turnover of the global machinery manufacturing industry for rail transportation will have exceeded 190 billion Euros. The countries and regions in the Middle East, South Africa, Asia, and South America will become the main field for railway construction. The overseas market for China's railways will expand with the continuous implementation of the Belt and Road Initiative, and will develop larger and stronger connectivity with such neighboring countries as India, Thailand, and Myanmar, thus linking Western Asia, Central Asia, and even the European continent in a railway "Silk Road."

The 21st century will be the century for Eurasia. The first fact is that the global economic center has been shifting, that is, from the Atlantic to Asia-Pacific, and that, to be specific, Eastern Asia and China have become a new engine for the global economy. The second fact is that new-type economies are mostly in Eurasia. Of the five BRICS countries, three are in Eurasia, that is, China, India, and Russia. The total population of the three countries is over 2.7 billion, accounting for nearly 2/5 of the world's total population. Their total GDP approaches 90% as compared to the United States. The third fact is that the trend of regional integration in Eurasia is becoming more and more obvious. The Shanghai Cooperation Organization, the China-ASEAN FTA, the Conference on Interaction and Confidence-Building Measures in Asia (CICA), the Asia-Europe Alliance, the China–Central and Eastern Europe "16 + 1," the China–Europe All-Round Strategic Cooperative Partnership, and so on, form a developmental pattern that integrates multiple sides. The fourth fact is that China and Germany have proposed their own plans for innovation. China proposed "Internet +" and "Made in China 2025" and Germany proposed the "Manufacture 4.0" plan. China is leading in the areas of high-speed railways, nuclear power energy, intelligent grids, e-commerce, quantum communications, and green energy. The Silk Road Economic Belt has Eurasia as its center and the Maritime Silk Road circles around Eurasia, thus forming a blue economic ring. Meanwhile, the Belt and Road has its influence on South–South Cooperation regions, such as Africa, the South Pacific, and South America. The Asia Infrastructure Investment Bank proposed by China will be essentially serving Asian and European countries mostly.

3. The Belt and Road Guided by the "Made in China" Plan

On March 5, 2015, Premier Li Keqiang pointed out in the Report on the Work of the Government that China will implement the "Made in China 2025" plan and stick to being driven by innovation, intelligent transformation, reinforced foundation, and green development, thus speeding up the transformation from a big manufacturing country to a strong manufacturing country. By the "Made in China 2025" plan, it basically means that, in the area of manufacturing, China will become not only the largest country in the world but also a world power by 2025. It is fair to say that the "Made in China 2025" plan avails itself of a solid foundation and a development plan for the smooth implementation of the Belt and Road Initiative.

3.1 *Basis for and Conception of the "Made in China 2025" Plan*

Even though it is a manufacturing giant, China is not a manufacturing power, as it lacks a number of backbone enterprises with international competitiveness and is still awaiting breakthroughs for a good number of significant issues in technology and machinery. Besides, China still lacks crucial products that take up a considerable share of the international market. China plans to transform itself from a manufacturing giant to one of the world's manufacturing powers within the next 30 years or so by following three phase-by-phase strategies. Of these strategies, the "Made in China 2025" plan is the first 10-year action plan of the "three steps." It is called China's "Industry 4.0" strategy by the industry and shares some characteristics with Germany's "Industry 4.0" plan. The planned period is quite the same. It will take 8–10 years for Germany to fulfill the "Industry 4.0" plan, with the temporal span roughly overlapping that of the "Made in China 2025" plan. If we compare the two plans in terms of contents, similar to the deep integration of industrialization and informatization proposed by China before, Germany's "Industry 4.0" lays emphasis on the connection between intelligent devices and products via wires or wireless, that is, the concept of the Internet of Things or industrial Internet proposed by China. The differences, however, lie in the developmental phase and the level of development. Currently, Germany is advancing from "3.0" to "4.0" generally, while Chinese enterprises have to go through the period from "2.0" to "3.0" before they advance toward "4.0."

The "Made in China 2025" plan stresses innovation-driven development, quality first, green development, structural optimization, and being talent-oriented. By aiming high, it plans to develop high-end equipment manufacturing. High-end equipment manufacturing is one of the most important valuable industries, the main battlefield for building a manufacturing power in all rounds, and the cutting-edge tool for fulfilling the strategy of building a manufacturing power. To transform from a manufacturing giant to a manufacturing power, China must pay enough attention to the development of high-end equipment manufacturing, accelerate to push forward the structural adjustment of key industries, and strive to realize breakthroughs in some key areas. It is necessary to grasp the opportunity of developing emerging strategic industries. In the Report on the Work of the Government, it is stressed that emerging industries and emerging commercial activities are the highland for competition. We should implement significant projects for high-end equipment, information networks, integrated circuits, new energies, new materials, biopharmaceuticals, aviation engines, gas turbines, and so on, to develop a number of emerging industries into leading ones. We should formulate the "Internet +" action plan, push forward the combination between mobile Internet, cloud computing, big data, the Internet of Things and modern manufacturing, and boost the healthy development of e-commerce, the industrial Internet, and Internet banking, leading the internet enterprises to increase their presence on the international market.

China has established the largest manufacturing system with inclusive categories in the world, and has become a world factor. There are over 200 industrial products in China whose outputs and exports are ranked no. 1 in the world, and dozens of products whose export value accounts for over 70% of the world's total. People around the world are enjoying the products "Made in China" with favorable prices and high quality, such as large as ships, motors, and equipment and as small as buttons, suction tubes, and cartridges. Without the products made in China, the prices of industrial products on the international market would be doubled and there would often be a shortage. In 1990, the total manufacturing output of China accounted for less than 3%, while it approaches 25% today. Eighty percent of the air-conditioners, 70% of the mobile phones, and 60% of the shoes sold worldwide are made in China. The supply chain that has formed in China's feverish growth of the manufacturing industry has stretched into various areas of Southeast Asia. Presently, nearly half of the products in the world are manufactured in "Asian factories." As a low-end manufacturing industry, China's share of garment exportations has actually increased from 42.6% in 2011 to 43.1% in 2013. China is manufacturing more spare parts for finished goods. The World Bank has found that, of all China's export commodities, the proportion of exported assemblies has declined to around 35% presently from 60% in the 1990s, the time of its prime. China's economy, which was supported by manufacturing, weathered the Asian financial crisis in 1998 and the global financial crisis in 2008. After the crises, the manufacturing that had received the biggest blow and was more dependent on exportations restored its growth. It not only served as an important drive to push China's national economy back to a steady growth, but it also increased the other countries' confidence in restoring their economies. According to the statistics of the World Bank, in 2010, the added-value of China's manufacturing accounted for 17.6% of the world's total. By the international standard industrial categorization, of the 22 categories, China was ranked no. 1 in 7 categories, and the outputs of over 220 industrial products, including steel, cement, automobiles, and so on, were ranked no. 1 in the world. A number of big enterprises with international competitiveness have grown rapidly. Eighty-nine Chinese enterprises, including those in Hong Kong, were listed among the World's Top 500 in *Fortune* in 2013. The total number had grown by 78 as compared to 2002 and was ranked second worldwide, immediately following the United States.[17] If the quantity of exported and imported products had been used to measure against the completeness of the manufacturing system of a country, China would have been listed among the countries with the most complete industrial systems in the world, together with the United States,

---

[17] National Bureau of Statistics. (November 6, 2013). A New Chapter for Glorious Economic Development upon Reform and Opening-Up. *People's Daily*, retrieved from http://politics.people.com.cn/n/2013/1106/c1001-23444065.html.

Japan, and Germany a very long time ago. An analysis was made based on the quantity of export products (i.e., the quantity of export products whose export value is more than zero) for the period between 1992 and 2008. During those 17 years, the quantity of products exported by China was 4,742.12 types each year on average, only somewhat fewer than the 4,871.18 types exported by the United States and more than the 4,729.24 and 4,550 types exported by Germany and Japan, respectively. Based on the research conducted by Carelli, between 1988 and 2004, the quantity of export products of 159 countries and regions was only 2,492 types on average. In terms of the quantity of imported products and compared to the United States, Germany, and Japan, China's annual average (4,798.76 types) was ranked no. 3, only following the United States (4,881.88 types) and Germany (4,864.59 types), but higher than that of Japan (4,774.18 types), during the period from 1992 to 2008, In the field of economy, the influence of China on its neighboring regions has been rising. China is almost the biggest trading partner to almost all of its significant neighboring countries, including Russia, Japan, South Korea, India, Pakistan, Kazakhstan, and the whole ASEAN community, including Indonesia, Thailand, Malaysia, and Vietnam. Moreover, there is Australia which is farther.

China is now in the middle-and-later period of large-scale industrialization and urbanization. China is self-sufficient in steel, cement, and design for construction and development. As a measurement indicator, the value of biddings won by China has been no. 1 in tenders for international engineering outsourcing contracts for many years. This shows China's capability for international competition in the industries relating to engineering construction and the supporting facilities from one perspective. Meanwhile, China's systems of education and technology also provide support to the current development of industrialization and urbanization. China can build the best high-speed railway system, expressway network, airport, and stations with its most efficient design, construction techniques, and cost in the world, and it can also build the most beautiful bridges and tunnels in the world, creating miracles one after the other. In a word, China has been equipped with a strong foundation for materials, technologies, management, and talents for building a modernized country relying on its own efforts.

China has been integrated into the world's economy and the global community and has achieved fast development. From the middle-and-later period of the 1980s, especially from the 1990s, China has been successfully integrated into the Asian economic system or the world's economic system by utilizing the chance of industrial shift of the "Four Asian Tigers": On the one hand, China was connected to the "Four Asian Tigers" and Japan, the suppliers of intermediate goods and spare parts, and has maintained a huge amount of trade deficit with these economies for a long time; on the other hand, China was connected to the markets of developed countries in Europe and America, and has maintained a huge amount of trade surplus with these countries and regions for a long time. As an intermediary, China is the Asian factory as well as the world's factory. Through the network of global production with China as the core, China has included many resourceful countries into this kind of international system of production and consumption since 2003. China has, on the one hand, built and accumulated a strong capacity and network for utilizing the world's technology, management experience, talents, and international market, and on the other hand, has accumulated and set up a broad range of materials and solid materials as well as a financial foundation, making the country capable of resisting the impacts from the external markets. For example, the foreign exchange reserve might at least protect China from being hit by the impact of the financial crisis or turmoil that frequently strikes developing countries, and the massive manufacturing network system also enables the country to better sustain the impact from external economic fluctuations. Many countries do not have the capability of both being integrated into the world and effectively resisting external impacts. This is also one important condition that is totally different from the early years of the reform and opening-up more than 30 years ago. Besides, China has still much scope for development. China is still a developing country despite its fast growth for over 30 years. In 2012, the per capita income of China was only USD 6,000 plus, which was lower than the world's average. China is still in the middle-and-later period of industrialization; it will take more than 10 years for China to complete the construction of a great deal of hardware, such as public traffic networks, sanitary facilities, and public service systems in big cities, and it will take longer for second-tier and third-tier cities to complete their urban construction. In terms of the latest plan for urbanization, China is still faced with heavy tasks in the long run. In terms of software, the development of the service industry is lagging behind, and the reform of medical care and health, education, and some other areas should be energetically pushed forward. The *Decision of the CCCPC on Some Major Issues Concerning Comprehensively Intensifying the Reform* adopted at the Third Plenary Session of the 18th Central Committee of the CPC has already included the detailed requirements and measures for expanding the opening-up and intensifying the reform in these areas.[18]

However, on the whole, China is still at the middle-and-lower end of the global value chain, and is still backward in some areas, such as some small mines and workshops that solely rely on the labor of manpower, although China is now productive in the most advanced industries and fields, such as space aviation, high-speed railways, and nuclear power.

3.2 *Industrial Development Plans of Other Countries*

Today, the world is greeting a new round of the industrial revolution, which is mainly characteristic of deep integration of information technology and manufacturing technology, with the most important technology for the digitalized, network-based, and intelligence-oriented manufacturing industry. The global manufacturing industry will go through new changes, which is an irresistible historical trend. After the financial crisis, developed countries launched their state strategies and plans to boost their industrial economies. The United States launched its plans for its "reindustrialization" strategy, "manufacturing rejuvenation," and "advanced

---

[18] Song Hong. (2014). New Opportunities for China to Develop Independently in the Next 10 to 15 Years. *International Economic Review*, Issue 1, pp. 9–17.

manufacturing partners"; Germany launched the "Industry 4.0" plan; Japan began to implement its "revitalization strategy"; South Korea started its "newly increased impetus strategy"; and France proposed the "New Industrial France" plan, and so on. The points shared by these strategies and measures include: providing subsidies and support to emerging industries, support to the R&D of cutting-edge technologies (future technologies), support to medium-and-small-scale enterprises, optimization of the environment of competition, nurturing markets for new products, and reform for talent development. Developed countries wish to win back their competitive edges in manufacturing through technological advancement and the adjustment of industrial policies. It can be found that the most advanced countries have not given up manufacturing, but they have been making structural adjustment to transformation and upgrading of their manufacturing industries.

3.2.1 *The Proposal of Germany's "Industry 4.0" Plan*

Jointly funded by the Federal Ministry of Education and Research and the Federal Ministry of Economics and Technology formulated with the suggestions and advancement from academic and industrial organizations of Germany, including the National Academy of Science and Technology, the Fraunhofer Society, and Siemens, the "Industry 4.0" research program has been elevated to a state-level strategy. The federal government of Germany has invested 200 million Euros in it. With the proposal of the "Industry 4.0" strategy and the official launch of the plan at Hannover Messe trade fair in April 2013, the German government aims at enhancing the competitiveness of German industries and taking advantage of the favorable opportunities in the new round of the industrial revolution. This strategy has been widely recognized by the research institutes and industries of Germany. The Fraunhofer Society has introduced the concept of "Industry 4.0" into the research institutes in the 6–7 production areas under it, and Siemens has applied the concept to the development of industrial software and to the systems of production control.

3.2.2 *The "New Industrial France" Plan*

France formally announced the implementation of the "New Industrial France" plan in September 2013. This detailed plan gives priority to 34 industrial plans for development. The plan is so inclusive that it covers almost every part of an ideal plan, from the objective to the organizational structure and from each step to the expected effect. From this plan, we can see that the model adopted by France for rejuvenating its industry has three distinctive characteristics.

First, there is an emphasis on being practical and progressive. This characteristic is clearly reflected in the three standards for prioritizing the approval of projects: First, the project must be in a sunrise industry with a bright future; second, the relevant cutting-edge technology must be owned by France; last, French enterprises have been leading in relevant markets or have the potential to excel. In a word, the objective of the industrial rejuvenation of France is to make more progress on the basis of existing results rather than develop any subversive ones. The 34 prioritized projects have already shown these standards. For example, it is obvious that the new generation of high-speed trains and electric aircrafts has carried forth France's advantages in transportation, aviation, and spaceflight; France has been a global leader in the areas of energy-saving building and food processing for a long time. The practicality of the plan can also be found in the projects in even traditional industries such as intelligent textiles and wood processing.

Second, there is an emphasis on the balance between the "two hands." The concept of Francois Hollande, President of France, is that the "visible hand" of the government is responsible for setting up the stage and the "invisible hand" of the market plays its role. How do the "two hands" cooperate with each other? The framework for the preparation and implementation of the plan for the "New Industrial France" is as follows: In the early stage survey, the National Industrial Council of France invited the leaders of various industries and international consulting companies, like McKinsey & Co, to take care of the planning. Within the National Industrial Council of France, the proportions of government employees and nongovernment employees are about 1:1, and the number of the latter may even be bigger, which has greatly restricted the will of the government. At the later stage of implementation, project leaders are mostly experts in specific industries or principals of enterprises, seldom government officers. One important duty of those leaders is to get professionals, government officers, and financial institutions to work out a roadmap for carrying out the plan, and the roadmap has to be approved by a newly organized guiding committee. The members of that guiding committee are mostly professionals, and so there are fewer government officers than professionals. Therefore, it is certain that each link will be driven by the market and that the government will stick to its role.

Third, there is an emphasis on a prompt follow-up of financial supporting measures. The French are at home with the rule that "capitals go first." Centering around the "New Industrial France" plan, France has launched various supporting financial measures. The mechanism of "R&D for tax offset," one important measure of this kind, has effectively boosted the initiative of medium-and-small enterprises, especially small-and-micro enterprises, in taking part in industrial R&D and innovation by simplifying the method of calculation for tax offsets, reduction, and exemption and substantially raising the upper limit for tax offsets.

3.2.3 *The US proposed "Reindustrialization"*

In the early part of 2009, the United States began to adjust its economic development strategy. In December of the same year, it announced *A Framework for Revitalizing American Manufacturing*. In June 2011 and February 2012, the United States kicked off the *Advanced Manufacturing Partner Plan* and the *State Strategy Plan for Advanced Manufacturing* one after the other to implement its "reindustrialization." The "reindustrialization" of the United States mainly aims at adjusting the industrial structure, transforming the developmental mode, and developing the advanced manufacturing industry. For example, the 3D printing technology industry has become one of the "top ten fastest growing industries" of the United States. It is believed by some experts that 3D printing technology may feature an epoch-making significance of the steamer or the telephone and that it is very likely to anticipate the arrival of a new industrial revolution.

3.2.4 *Revitalization of Japan's Manufacturing*

Unlike European countries and the United States, who pay more attention to the information-based industries, Japan has never put less effort into developing its manufacturing. In the early days of restoring its machinery industry, Japan formulated the *Law of Revitalizing the Mechanical Industry* and made three revisions to it according to the implementation. In the 1970s and 1980s, when the United States regarded manufacturing as the "sunset industry" and was interested in putting the focus of technological development on high technology and military technologies, Japan invested its major energy in the development of and investment in advanced manufacturing technologies, thus catching up with the international competition and shaking America's status as the leader in technologies. Entering the 21st century, Japan still believed that manufacturing was the foundation on the basis of building up the nation, and was conscious of the fact that an information-oriented society cannot function without developed manufacturing industries, and the importance of manufacturing industries cannot be underestimated while developing information technology energetically. This has been stressed by the Informal Meeting for Manufacturing Technologies, a consulting institution for the Prime Minister of Japan, when it presented the report that manufacturing was the lifeline of Japan, and no information industry and software industry would exist to speak of without the manufacturing industry. The Japanese government believes that, even in an information society, the manufacturing industry will always be the basic industry that needs strengthening and boosting. Besides, Japan stresses strengthening the technological basis for manufacturing. Pushed by the politicians, entrepreneurs, and labor unions of Japan, the Japanese government drafted the *Basic Law of Revitalizing Basic Technologies for Manufacturing* in 1999. It is believed that through this law, product design and manufacturing is the basis for the support of Japan's development. The Ministry of Economy, Trade, and Industry (METI) formulated the "National Industrial Technology Strategy" in 2000, defining the developmental goals and strategic measures needed for realizing these goals for 13 industries, including biochemistry, information communications, machinery, chemistry, energy, materials, environmental protection, aviation, spaceflight, and so on. The most important part of the strategy is to research and manufacture new materials and develop new manufacturing techniques, mainly including researching and developing the technologies for processing and manufacturing advanced semiconductor components through ion beams, radiation delivered by synchrotrons, laser and electric rays, and pushing forward the development of the mechanical industry by means of micro-mechanisms. Japan has formulated the blueprint for a technology strategy on a massive scale. First, the government increased its financial investment in cutting-edge technologies such as 3D printing machines. In 2014, the METI continued to list the 3D printing machine as the item enjoying favorable policies, with a plan to invest 4.5 billion yen that year, carry out a massive R&D project named "the product manufacturing reform with 3D modeling technology as the core," and develop the 3D printing machines for metal powder modeling that would be the most advanced in the world. Second, the METI planned to swiftly upgrade manufacturing technologies and enhance the competitive edge for product manufacturing.

It can be noticed that the three phenomena emerged in the manufacturing industry in Japan. The first one is that there have been more enterprises with "small production lines": Honda has reduced 40% of its production lines by reducing the spraying times and heat treatment techniques by adopting new technologies, and it has reduced the techniques for welding lines to 9 from the previous 18 by changing the design of the structure of the bodywork, building the shortest high-end model production lines in the world. The second one is that there have been more enterprises using small machines: by rebuilding the production facilities and techniques for aluminum die casting, DENSO from Japan has reduced the production costs for the casting lines by 30%, the area for equipment by less than 80%, and energy consumption by less than 50%. The third one is to break through the cost bottleneck by using robots, unmanned handlers, unmanned factories, and "cell manufacturing": Canon has greatly improved its competitiveness in costs through "cell manufacturing" of "mechanical cells" and with the first unmanned factory for digital cameras in the world.

3.3 *Potential for Upgrading "Made in China"*

On March 14, 2015, the cover story published in *The Economist* held that, with high-efficient costs, more and more steady positions as the center of the supply chain of Asia, and China's rise as a supermarket, "Made in China" has some unrivaled advantages. The new stage that the "Made in China" plan has entered is the position as the "Asian factory" relying on "Made in China," which is also the reason that it is impossible for non–Asia-Pacific countries to simply copy the developmental mode of China.

Though China is now confronted with the problems of a sloweddown economic growth, excessive supply of real estate, and an increase in its debt, China's manufacturing industry will retain its advantages as follows, thus boosting the overall development of its economy.

First, even if China enters the high-end market in order to explore more value-added economic activities, it will still pay enough attention to low-cost manufacturing. China's share of the global market for the exportation of garments has actually increased from 42.6% in 2011 to 43.1% in 2013. Besides, China is manufacturing more spare parts for finished products. According to the World Bank, of all China's exported commodities, the proportion of imported assemblies has declined to around 35% today from a peak of 60% in the middle of the 1990s. This is to a certain extent because China features high-efficient supplier clusters that are difficult for other places in the world to copy.

China's second advantage lies in its status as the "Asian factory" *per se*. With the rise in salaries, some low-cost manufacturing enterprises have indeed removed from China, many of which have moved to Southeastern Asia to rely upon the low-income population there. However, this process has its downside. In 2014, an NGO found that nearly 30% of the workers in the electronics industry in Malaysia are of the forced labor type. However, some transnational enterprises such as Samsung, Microsoft, Toyota, and so on. reinforced their regional supply chain with China as the center while they reduced their production in China and moved to Myanmar and the Philippines.

The third advantage is the fact that China is becoming the center of demand. With an increase and upgrading of consumption in China, the "Asian factory" is capturing a bigger share of the high-profit marketing and customer service. Meanwhile, the demand from the Chinese reinforces Asia's supply chain. On the domestic market, China's manufacturing enterprises are far more competitive than its rivals.

By virtue of the three advantages listed above, the Belt and Road Initiative proposed by China in 2015 is making an effort in consolidating the production eco-system of the "Asian factory." The advantages of the "Asian factory" are hard to be shaken.

The development of technologies has reduced the number of workers in factories. Manufacturing may not bring back the glories of creating employment opportunities and handsome income as it used to do. China and its neighbors might be the last group of countries that are able to realize a leap in development merely through employing unskilled people to work in low-cost production.

Exportation remains the most reliable approach for emerging markets to achieve success. It is the best way to participate in the global market competition to enhance productivity. The governments outside the Asian factory have to rely upon several important engines for their development: It is not only manufacturing but also the agriculture and the service industry. Comparing to the competition in labor costs, the pattern of participating in the competition on the global market is more challenging for policymakers. It should become a critical task for South American and African countries to establish a freer global system for trade in services. The investments in infrastructure should not be confined to fiber cables, but should be extended to building ports and highways. Education is critical to development, because skilled workers are needed for the country that will make a way for itself to become a part of the global market. These are formidable tasks for a developing country. One reason why China was able to fulfill these tasks lies in the fact that China has a highly efficient supplier "colony." Besides, China has excellent infrastructure facilities that continue to progress: China plans to build 10 airports each year by 2020. Presently, Chinese enterprises are using automation to improve productivity to minimize the impact of higher labor costs on their development. This is the essence underlying the new plan of "Made in China 2025." *The Economist* says in one of its articles that no other country is able to replace China's role as the "Asian factory," and no country needs to do that. The ASEAN community, made up of 10 countries, has a total population of 630 million, less than half of China's population. The comparative advantages among different regions will become more important with the supply chain expanding transnationally. Asia enjoys rich labor and capital resources and has established its image of leader in manufacturing. She will only keep growing.

China plans to complete its transformation from a manufacturing giant to a manufacturing power by means of three 10-year action programs and roadmaps. "The implementation of the 'Made in China 2025' plan will become the first step for China in transforming itself from a manufacturing giant to a manufacturing power." China's blueprint of developing into an industrial power, centering around the "Made in China 2025" plan, is clear and distinct after we sort out the relevant key points in the 2014 Report on the Work of the Government, the "Made in China 2025" development plan, and the 2015 Budget Report of the Government:

The Chinese Government proposes to speed up the transformation and upgrading of traditional industries. It is pointed out in the Report on the Work of the Government that we should advance the in-depth integration of industrialization and informatization, develop and utilize the network-based digitalization and artificial intelligence-based technologies, and try harder in some key areas to seize the opportunities and achieve breakthroughs. It is pointed out in the report on the plan that, in 2015, we should "launch a three-year action plan to strengthen the most important competitive power for manufacturing" and pay special attention to achieving breakthroughs in the fundamental technologies of some key areas, including robots for industrial use, equipment for railway traffic, equipment for high-end vessels and maritime engineering, new-energy automobiles, modern agricultural machinery, and high-end medical equipment and medicine, thus pushing forward industrialization.

New-type industries will become leading industries. Significant projects such as high-end equipment, information networks, integrated circuits, new energies, new materials, biopharmaceuticals, aviation engines, and gas turbines are listed in the Report on the Work of the Government; it is the first time that the "Internet+" action plan has been formulated; the concept of "Industrial Internet" received public attention for the first time, which aims at pushing forward the combination between mobile Internet, cloud computing, big data, the Internet of Things, and modern manufacturing.

The Chinese Government proposes to strengthen the supporting role of the service industry. It is clearly pointed out in the Report on the Work of the Government that we should energetically develop the services for everyday life and producers, such as tourism, healthcare, provision for the elderly, creative design, and so on. Additionally, the report on the plan lists items of high-end services that have won support for development, including such producer services as industrial design and financial leasing, and such high-tech services as R&D and design, system integration, intellectual property, and inspection and testing, to advance the integration and development of the service industry and manufacturing.

To further implement the strategy of innovation-driven development. It is explicitly pointed out in the Report that China has set up an RMB 40 billion fund for guiding the investments made for starting up emerging industries. The report of the plan says that the proportion of the R&D expenditure in the GDP in 2015 reached 2.2%. It was proposed in the budget plan that we should actively push forward the optimization and integration of various technology plans, and establish the mechanism to subsidize significant national scientific and technological infrastructures and large research instruments to facilitate the open sharing of technology resources; moreover, we should speed up the implementation of significant national and special scientific and technological plans and invest more in government procurement of innovative products.

For a long time, China's economic development has followed the pace of the "Four Asian Tigers," such as South Korea and China's Taiwan region. Many people take it for granted that China will pass the "relay baton" to other countries due to a lack of a backup at some point. However, the factor of salary rise is far from letting China pass on the "relay baton." On the contrary, China is holding it even more tightly. The first reason is that, even though China is involved in high-end markets and explored high-value-added industries, she is always working on the low-cost manufacturing. In fact, China's exportations of clothing accounted for 43.1% of the world's total in 2013, an increase from 42.6% in 2011. Meanwhile, China has more "Made in China" raw materials. With the rise in salaries, some low-cost operations are being made obsolete. A big part of them has been transferred to those places with lower incomes, such as Southeast Asia, which has further reinforced the leading position in the world of this "Asian factory." Samsung, Microsoft, Toyota, and some other transnational enterprises have reduced production in China and transferred it to Myanmar and the Philippines, which has also reinforced the supply chain for Southeast Asia with China as the Center. The second reason is that China is gradually becoming a key link in the supply chain. With the rise of Chinese consumers' spending power and taste, the "Asian factory" is gaining a bigger share in the high-profit marketing and customer services. At the same time, demand from China's market has greatly reinforced a series of supply chains in Asia. On China's market, the suppliers from Asian countries are more competitive than those from other regions. For instance, if calculated in quantity, the proportion of shoes exported from China to the United States decreased to 79% in 2014 from 87% in 2009. The lost market share was taken by other Asian countries, like Vietnam, Indonesia, and Cambodia. In fact, there are many more things that can be done through the alliance of Southeast Asian countries, which has the capability of building a unified market aiming at providing products and services with higher quality. Regional trade, even global trade, is helpful for spreading the manufacturing system from China to its neighboring countries.

Chapter

2

The Strategic Game in the International Context

Since the 1980s, relevant international organizations and countries have proposed their silk road development plans and have made some progress. These plans have their own intentions and focus, but objectively speaking, they have provided a certain basis for the Belt and Road Initiative. There are many versions of the silk road or the modern silk road plans proposed by other countries. The first one is the New Silk Road Initiative of the United States. The United States proposed the Silk Road Initiative in 1999 and 2006 and the New Silk Road Initiative in 2011, aiming to connect Southern Asia, Central Asia, and Western Asia with Afghanistan as the hub, in order to make it possible to "transport energy southward and goods northward" and to "transform aid into trade," thus boosting their economic resilience and retaining their influence in the hinterland of Central Asia. The strong points of such an initiative lie in a strong leading force, support from the Western countries, balanced benefits, and the high proactivity of each party. The negative aspects include travel through unsafe areas, difficulty in moving toward the west by excluding Iran, and the suspected sustainability of the plan. The second one is the silk road plan of Russia and the Eurasian Economic Union (EEU). Russia referred to the First Eurasian Land Bridge and the Second Eurasian Land Bridge as the "New Silk Road" many times, and alleged that it would play a decisive role in the construction of the silk road. In fact, on the basis of the Customs Union, the EEU established among Russia, Belarus, and Kazakhstan is planned to be founded in 2015. Presently, India, Turkey, and Vietnam are also thinking about joining the Customs Union. The EEU has the advantages of a historical bond and strong institutionalization, but it lacks economic complementariness among the members and drives in the economy. Besides, doubts and worries arise in Central Asia and other countries because there is a suspicion of restoring an Empire. The third one is the silk road plan as the South–North Corridor. Russia, India, and Iran initiated the North–South Corridor plan in September 2000, which evolved to be a 14-nation initiative with the participation of China and all the countries in Central Asia. The Corridor initiative largely overlaps with the New Silk Road Initiative of the United States. In August 2012, Afghanistan, India, and Iran discussed the "Southern Silk Road" to connect Iran with Central and Southern Asia. Besides, there are other influential silk road plans, including Japan's Silk Road Diplomacy, the EU's New Partnership with Central Asia, and India's New Strategy of Connectivity to Central Asia. The fourth one is the Silk Road Regional Program of the United Nations (UN). The UN is the first international organization to propose the revitalization of the "Silk Road," and it launched the program of a "Comprehensive Study of the Silk Road, a Road for Dialogue" in 1988. From 1992 to 2005, the UN carried out several projects on the construction of infrastructures, trying to rebuild the "Silk Road." At the Eurasia Economic Forum in 2008, the United Nations Development Program initiated the decision of making another investment, of the value of USD 43 billion, in the revitalization of the silk road, and 19 countries responded to it. The International Road Federation proposed the "Silk Road Rejuvenation" plan.

In September 2013, Chinese President Xi Jinping delivered a speech at Nazarbayev University in Kazakhstan, proposing the strategic initiative of jointly building the Silk Road Economic Belt. This initiative was further expounded in the *Decision of the CCCPC on Some Major Issues Concerning Comprehensively Intensifying the Reform* adopted at the Third Plenary Session of the 18th Central Committee of the CPC that "we should speed up the opening up of the border areas, accelerate the construction of infrastructure connectivity with our neighboring countries and regions, and push forward the building of the Silk Road Economic Belt and the Maritime Silk Road Economic Belt, forming a pattern of all-around opening-up."[1] On February 6, 2014, when President Xi Jinping attended the opening ceremony of the Winter Olympics held in Sochi, Russia, Russia for the first time responded publicly to the initiative of building the Silk Road Economic Belt and the Maritime Silk Road as proposed by China, saying that Russia will be willing to dock the Eurasian railway with the Belt and Road and thus create bigger benefits. From the 20th to the 21st of May, 2014, Russian President Vladimir Putin made a state visit to China and attended the Shanghai Summit of the Conference on Interaction and Confidence-Building Measures in Asia (CICA), where the heads of the two countries signed the *Joint Statement between the People's Republic of China and the Russian Federation Regarding the New Stage for the Comprehensive Strategic Collaborative Partnership* and suggested that both sides should seek the feasible links between the projects for the Silk Road Economic Belt and the EEU.[2]

1. Power Game Along the Silk Road

1.1 *The New Silk Road Initiative of the United States*

The New Silk Road Initiative of the United States was explicitly proposed for the first time by Hillary Clinton, US Secretary of State in

---

[1] Du Shangze & Chen Xiaowei. (February 7, 2014). President Xi Jinping Met Russian President Vladimir Putin. *People's Daily Online*. Retrieved from http://politics.people.com.cn/n/2014/0207/c1024-24286244.html.

[2] Joint Statement between the People's Republic of China and the Russian Federation about the New Stage for the Comprehensive Strategic Collaborative Partnership. (May 21, 2014). *People's Daily Online*. Retrieved from http://sn.people.com.cn/n/2014/0521/c356416-21252479.html.

July 2011, when she attended the Second US–India Strategic Dialogue held in India. The plan was then immediately included in the international agenda. At the "new silk road" ministers' conference held during the UN General Assembly in September 2011, the Istanbul Conference about the Afghanistan issues in November, the Bonn Conference about the Afghanistan issues in December, and the North Atlantic Treaty Organization (NATO) Summit held in Chicago, USA in May 2012, one important topic was the New Silk Road Initiative, showing that the United States attached great importance to it. Ms. Clinton remarked in her speech "The New Silk Road Initiative" that "Let us envision a new silk road, a network with economic and traffic interconnectivity." In such a network, "the oil and gas fields in Turkmenistan will satisfy Pakistan and India's growing demand for energy and create considerable transborder income for Afghanistan and Pakistan. Tajik's cotton will be made into cotton cloth in India. The furniture and fruits of Afghanistan will appear in Astana, Bombay, and even further away." For the sake of this new silk road, the United States will fund "private sectors investing in railways, expressways, energy infrastructure facilities, and projected oil piping, which will run from Turkmenistan through Afghanistan, Pakistan, and on towards India." Not long afterward, *Foreign Policy* in November 2011 published the long article entitled "America's Pacific Century" written by Hillary Clinton, and it was pointed out in the article that "The future of politics will be decided in Asia, not Afghanistan or Iraq, and the United States will be right at the center of the action." Hillary said, "We are the only power with a network of strong alliances in the region." "We will create a rules-based order that is open, free, transparent, and fair." Hillary believed that the United States was the only country that was qualified to create a new order in Asia and act as the "Asian police."

The conception of the New Silk Road Initiative is considered to have been envisioned by Prof. Frederick Starr, Chairman of the Central Asia-Caucasus Institute at Johns Hopkins University in the United States. In 2005, Prof. Starr proposed the idea of a "Great Central Asia," which was popular for a time. The book entitled *The New Silk Road: Traffic and Trade in Greater Central Asia*, with him as the chief editor, was published in 2007. In 2009, the United States explored the Northern Distribution Network through the Baltic Sea, the Caucasus, Russia, and Central Asia and leading toward Afghanistan. Prof. Starr further proposed making the Northern Distribution Network into an economic bridge between Europe and Asia by relying upon the transportation and connections between Europe and Asia. Prof. A. Kuchins from the Center for Strategic and International Studies of the United States is another initiator of such conception. When the United States was ready to withdraw from Afghanistan and seek further arrangements for the country, Prof. Starr suggested that regional connectivity should drive the regional economy, in order to develop and reinforce the economy of Afghanistan. These ideas find a centralized expression in reports such as *Afghanistan beyond the Fog of Nation-Building: Giving Economic Strategy a Chance* by Prof. Starr and *Key to Afghanistan's Success: The Modern Silk Road Initiative* by Prof. Kuchins. The objective of the New Silk Road Initiative is to connect Central Asia and Southern Asia with Afghanistan as the center. The new silk road does not refer to any route, but an extensive network that connects regional transportation and economies. According to an official explanation by the United States, the construction of the New Silk Road Initiative includes the construction of software and hardware. The construction of software refers to free trade, reduced trade barriers, improved management policies, simplified transborder formalities, faster customs clearance, overcoming bureaucracy, eliminating corruption, and an improved environment of investment. The construction of hardware refers to building infrastructure facilities such as railways, highways, power grids, and gas pipelines to connect Central Asia, Afghanistan, and Southern Asia. It is expected that the free trans-regional flow of commodities, services, and people may be pushed forward through the construction of software and hardware.

1.1.1 *Strategic Orientation of the United States' New Silk Road Initiative*

Not long after the Soviet Union collapsed and the Cold War ended, the United States proposed the Silk Road Initiative, mainly presented in the *Silk Road Initiative Act of 1999* adopted by the US Congress in May 1999, in order to help the newly independent countries in Central Asia to get rid of the influence of Russia and Iran and develop democracy, while, at the same time, to achieve its own goal of diversified sources of energy importation by utilizing the rediscovered gas resources in the region of the Caspian Sea. After the end of Cold War, the United States made a policy design for the Central Asian countries and the South Caucasus countries as a whole, which stressed strengthening of the link between this region and the outside world through economic measures. The oil and gas resources of the Caspian Sea became a focused concern of the United States; thus, the target of the plan was to strengthen the economic and energy connection between Central Asian countries and the South Caucasus countries and Europe, rather than the Russia–Iran relationship in the north–south direction.

In July 2011, in order to withdraw its troops from Afghanistan successfully and prevent a sharp decline in the safety of Afghanistan after the US troops withdrew and the harm to its strategic benefits in Central Asia and Southern Asia, the United States proposed an updated New Silk Road Initiative, trying to strengthen the economic cooperation among the countries in Central Asia and Southern Asia with Afghanistan as the center.

The strategic orientation of the initiative mainly includes the following details:

First, by strengthening the Central Asia–Afghanistan–Southern Asia economic cooperation, the United States would help Afghanistan with its steady development after the withdrawal of the US troops to prevent the situation from becoming worse. It is estimated that, since the United States waged the Afghanistan war that lasted till 2011, the United States had provided aid valued at USD 18.8 billion to Afghanistan, more than the investment the United States had made in any other country. The substantial consumption and aid provided by the United States and its allies in Afghanistan produced a "wartime economy" in Afghanistan, deforming its economic growth pattern, which led to 97% of the GDP attributed to international consumption. It was estimated by the World Bank that it would be difficult for Afghanistan to continue with the current economic growth rate after 2014, and the withdrawal of the US troops and those of NATO would directly result in a decrease of 2–3 percentage points in the economic growth of Afghanistan. After 2014, it is not only that the consumption from the troops of the United States and NATO will decrease greatly, but that the aid from the United States and from the international community would also face a sharp decline, driving the economy of Afghanistan toward the brink of collapse. In the circumstance that the economy of Afghanistan lacks endogenous power and its situation regarding politics and security is increasingly uncertain, the United States hopes that the New Silk Road Initiative might open up the trade passageways among Central Asia, Afghanistan, and Southern Asia to provide energy to Afghanistan and create jobs and explore the market for products.

Second, the United States hopes to strengthen its strategic partnership with India. With the rapid growth of India's economy and its expanding regional influence, the United States has great expectations in the US–India relationship, hoping that the United States may check China and the Islamic world by making use of India's power. India has a close connection with Afghanistan in history and reality and has been trying to play a more important role in the reconstruction of Afghanistan. However, the United States keeps a low profile in the cooperation with India in terms of issues regarding Afghanistan because it is worried about the attitude Pakistan might assume. With the continuous deterioration of the relationship with Pakistan, the United States began to try to impose pressure on Pakistan by elevating the position of India. Leon Edward Panetta, the US Secretary of Defense, remarked during his visit to India that "the USA will regard India as a security provider for the area covering the Indian Ocean and other places." Moreover, officials from the United States Department of Defense also said that the United States welcomed India to participate in the training of the national defense force and the police force of Afghanistan. The New Silk Road Initiative attempts to push forward the energy cooperation between Central Asia and Southern Asia, which is a great attraction to India that lacks energy; the initiative advances the construction of infrastructures with Afghanistan as the center, and this largely overlaps with the goal of

India, which has made a huge investment in Afghanistan for the reconstruction of the community; the initiative pushes forward regional cooperation to stabilize the economy of Afghanistan, which also conforms to the interests of India. Therefore, the New Silk Road Initiative will bring practical benefits to India and also provide a platform to enlarge India's influence, through which the United States wishes to get closer to India to serve its strategic interests. This is also the reason why the US Secretary of State Hillary Clinton officially announced the New Silk Road Initiative in India.

Third, the initiative aims to prevent Russia and China from monopolizing the affairs in Central Asia. It has been the strategy of the United States to prevent Russia from monopolizing Central Asian affairs; with China's rapidly increasing influence in Central Asia, the United States also regards China as a target of its strategic defense, believing that a stronger China–Central Asia relationship would hamper Central Asian countries in developing in the liberal and democratic direction. The United States believes that, unlike the "great game" in the Central Asian region in the 19th century, the game among big countries in Central Asia presently is multilevel and multidimensional and involves diverse agents, including Central Asian countries. After the United States withdrew its troops from Afghanistan, Central Asian countries feared that they would be faced with double threats: one fear was that the Islamic terrorist organization allied with the Talibans might come into power in Afghanistan; the other fear was that the United States' withdrawal would put them under pressure from Russia and China and get them forced into the sphere of influence of either one of them. Based on the above concerns, the United States is attempting to seek a new direction for Central Asian countries to export energy through the New Silk Road Initiative, in order to prevent them from relying too much on Russia and China, and also to prevent the United States from losing the "great game" to Russia and China after it withdrew its military influence from Central Asia on a large scale.

Lastly, the initiative aims to prevent Iran from interfering in Afghanistan. Iran and Afghanistan share a borderline running nearly 1,000 km. In each historical period of Afghanistan as an independent country, Iran has been strengthening its influence on its neighbor, taking Afghanistan as one part of its scope of influence. After the United States overthrew the Taliban sovereign, Iran played a big role in the Afghanistan issues. According to a comment that Ambassador James Dobbins, special representative of the United States in Afghanistan, made in 2001 at the international conference held in Bonn, Germany, about issues regarding Afghanistan, the Iran team of delegates proposed that Hamid Karzai should be the leader of Afghanistan. When discussing the issues regarding Afghanistan at the Tokyo Conference in 2002, Iran announced that it would provide aid in the sum of USD 540 million to Afghanistan. Iran is the country that has provided the most aid among the member states of the Economic Cooperation Organization and that aid has been basically allocated. Although Iran used to play a somewhat proactive role in the Afghanistan issues, which was once acknowledged by the United States, the United States still insisted that Iran had to give up its nuclear plan and imposed economic sanctions on Iran. Besides, the United States has the need to check Iran from becoming an overlord in the region on account of the United States' Middle-East strategy. Therefore, the United States is against regional energy cooperation with the Iran–Afghanistan–Pakistan relationship as a major regional force. Hence, the United States is pushing forward its New Silk Road Initiative as a major inter-regional kind of cooperation.

1.1.2 *Implementation of the United States' New Silk Road Initiative*

The New Silk Road Initiative has four major aspects. The most important one is the construction of infrastructures, mainly including the construction of highways in Afghanistan, the railway network, and the building of a power grid between Afghanistan and its neighboring countries. The second is to lower the trade barrier so as to push forward trade communication among the countries in the region. The third one is to construct the Turkmenistan–Afghanistan–Pakistan–India (TAPI) natural gas pipeline. The last one is to push forward the sharing of water resources in the region.[3]

---

[3] Shao Yuqun. (2014). Evaluation of America's New Silk Road Initiative. *South Asian Studies*, Issue 2, pp. 58–70.

The US government announced its New Silk Road Initiative in July 2011; to date, no progress has been made on any of the four aspects. First, in terms of infrastructure, some progress has been made in building transnational railways. On June 5, 2013, the track-laying ceremony for the Turkmenistan–Afghanistan–Tajikistan railway was held in Lebap, Turkmenistan. The leaders of the three countries jointly expressed that the three countries showed great enthusiasm for the project, and would jointly invest in the first-phase construction; thus, the project was not only closely related to the economic and trade relations among the three countries, but it was also important to build a transnational transportation corridor in the region. Turkmenistan felt that it would not have any financial problems. Compared to this project, the Central Asia–Southern Asia high-voltage power transmission line project, that is, the CASA-1000 project, was progressing slowly. The goal of the project was to transmit the high-voltage power from Tajikistan and Kyrgyzstan to Afghanistan and Pakistan, in order to alleviate the energy shortage in these two countries and also help to consume the excessive power from Tajikistan and Kyrgyzstan during the summer. Although the World Bank has repeatedly claimed that this project only aimed at transmitting the excessive power of Tajikistan and Kyrgyzstan in the summer to Afghanistan and Pakistan and there was no such problem of enlarging the generating capacity by building the Rogun Dam, the Tajikistan government insisted that the CASA-1000 project was directly related to the Rogun Dam, which was firmly objected to by Uzbekistan. The conflict between Tajikistan and Uzbekistan is one of the reasons for the long delay in the project. Besides, there is a disagreement between Tajikistan and Kyrgyzstan on the demarking of the borderline, and relevant investors considered withdrawing from the CASA-1000 project because they were worried that the project might facilitate the "illegal power sale" in this region. The latest update is that it is likely that the Asian Development Bank may withdraw from the project, which further makes the future of the project bleaker.

Second, no substantial development has been achieved in the trade exchanges between Central Asia and Southern Asia. Because of various disputes over history, politics, and economic benefits, the five countries in Central Asia are not active in trade within the region, and the volume of trade has remained at a low level since the collapse of the Soviet Union and has not changed at all, even today. The export growth of each country is mainly driven by the two large markets of China and Russia. To be specific, each country is developing on different levels, and the dispute over water resources between Kazakhstan and Kyrgyzstan and between Uzbekistan and Tajikistan has not come to a settlement through negotiations; furthermore, the situation of Kyrgyzstan is becoming uncertain, and these are the major reasons for the impossibility of realizing integration in Central Asia in a short period of time. In Southern Asia, pushed by the United States and some other countries, Afghanistan and Pakistan signed the Afghanistan–Pakistan Transit Trade Agreement (APTTA) in 2011. The agreement aimed at pushing forward the trade exchanges between Afghanistan and Pakistan, at helping Afghanistan export its goods to India, China, and even to other sea ports and airports via Pakistan in particular, thus to increase the income from taxes of the two countries and create more jobs in the two countries. After the APTTA was implemented, the tax income of Pakistan decreased and its economy was undermined because a great number of goods were smuggled from Afghanistan to Pakistan, which caused many complaints from Pakistan. The governments of the two countries have tried to reduce the trade barriers between them with the advancement by the United States, but the interference from the political disagreements between them makes the border trade fail to reach the expected development. The trade between India and Pakistan also fails to achieve development in the long run, and the level of economic and trade cooperation within Southern Asia is very low. In such a situation, it is impossible for the trade exchanges between Central Asia and Southern Asia to make any substantial progress.

Third, the TAPI projects progressed very slowly. Many years after conception and negotiation, the TAPI piping project is gradually making some progress. In particular, Turkmenistan and Afghanistan signed an agreement on natural gas trade in July 2013. Even so, there are still many substantial uncertainties in the future development of the project. One uncertainty is whether the four participating countries will be able to reach an agreement on the price of natural gas. Before the agreement is reached, the trade between Turkmenistan and Afghanistan was based on the memo; the second uncertainty is whether there will be continuous investment funds available in the future. It is estimated that the project will need a total fund amount of USD 10–20 billion, but the Asian Development Bank has committed itself to invest only USD 7.5 billion to date. The third uncertainty lies in the great difficulty of the project. It needs the participation of the major international oil and natural gas corporations, but the Turkmenistan government has refused that; besides, solar energy corporations such as Chevron, Exxon Mobil, and British Petroleum are not willing to join in the project due to the impossibility of gaining any profit in the upper stream of the project. The fourth uncertainty lies in the unstable security situation in Afghanistan, and there are many worries about the safety protection of the pipeline. The pipeline runs as long as 1,735 km, of which 735 km is within Afghanistan. The Afghan government has promised to send 9,000–12,000 policemen to guard the safety of the project, but whether Afghanistan's police force is able to fulfill the task remains unknown. According to the existing plans, it will take 4–5 years to complete the design and construction of the project, but the period will be lengthened based on the actual progress.

Lastly, the construction of the Rogun Dam in Tajikistan has been delayed for a long time beyond the set schedule. The project was started in the period of the Soviet Union, and the construction was not completed due to the collapse of the Soviet Union in the 1970s. Weathering the civil war in the 1990s, Tajikistan was faced with the challenges of restoring its economy and improving the situation of its energy shortage. The Tajikistan government started to rebuild the dam in 2006, hoping to transform the abundance of water resources into electric power through the restoration of the dam to not only satisfy the domestic demand for power but also to export power to other countries. However, Uzbekistan, located downstream on the Vakhsh River, believed that the design and application technologies for the dam were obsolete, and humanitarian disasters such as an earthquake can damage the dam. Besides, they believed that the construction of the dam might affect the water supply and environment of the Central Asian region. In order to prevent the construction of the dam, the Uzbekistan government has been trying to obtain international financial support by various diplomatic and economic means, which were strongly objected to by Tajikistan. The contradiction between the two countries has been almost raised to the height of "national pride." In order to settle the conflict, the World Bank, as the third party, provided an independent technical evaluation of the project. However, because the project has been imbued with too many political factors by both Tajikistan and Uzbekistan, it will be very difficult to have much progress on the project in a short period of time.

1.1.3 *Comparison between China's and the United States' "Silk Road" Initiatives*

The New Silk Road Initiative proposed by the United States includes the building of a thoroughfare starting from Eurasia and moving to the Indian Ocean. The thoroughfare has Afghanistan as the center and has an influence on the countries and regions next to Afghanistan. It pushes forward the transnational trade relationship among Afghanistan, Pakistan, and India to the south of Afghanistan, and advances the transnational trade relationship between Afghanistan and the Central Asian countries in the north. A series of transportation networks and constructions of infrastructures has brought Central Asia, Afghanistan, and the Southern Asian regions into a closely linked regional economy, developing a regional economic circulation. It is aimed at forming a Central Asia–South Asia geographical economic section led by the United States.

The Silk Road Initiatives proposed by China and the United States both involve the Central Asian region. In comparison, China's Silk Road Initiative covers more countries and regions. First, the Silk Road Economic Belt involving the Central Asian region facilitates China in carrying out extensive economic and trade exchanges and cooperation with the five Central Asian countries by utilizing the market resource complementariness with the central and western provinces of China as the backbone. Second, the 21st Century Maritime Silk Road links the coastal port cities in China and Southeast Asian countries through the construction of the China-Association of Southeast Asian Nations (ASEAN) free trade area (FTA). The whole idea of the strategy will connect China and the countries in Central Asia, Southeastern Asia, and the other countries along the route more closely, thus advancing the cooperation between China and the countries along the route, realizing the integration and improvement of the economic and trade relations within the region.

Through the silk road, China develops an economic and trade relationship with its neighboring countries by economic and diplomatic means; it establishes a strategic partnership, creates a favorable peripheral environment and the strategic rear for China's security, and prevents some powers outside the region from deploying themselves inside China's neighbors and carrying out strategic containment toward China while checking China's development. The strategy will establish new mechanisms of cooperation and a new model of economic cooperation for regions and cities that need connectivity on land and sea; it will make the link of mutual benefits for China, Central Asia, and Southeast Asia even tighter; it will imbue the drive and source for China's sustainable economic development, better maintain the stability and development of the western area of China, and guarantee the safety of domestic energy. Taking the strategic cooperative form in all rounds, China further upgrades its strategy by using the function of two existing organizations, that is, the Shanghai Economic Cooperation Organization and the China-ASEAN FTA. Through the construction of FTAs and economic and trade cooperation zones along the silk road, each side will carry out diversified economic cooperation and exchanges in the areas of construction of infrastructures, energy cooperation, agriculture, electric power, telecommunications, transportation, finance, investments, and the development of tourism. Meanwhile, China will introduce technologies, equipment, and manufacturers to Central Asian countries to settle the local problem with employment and improve the construction of the industrial system. In a series of construction projects, China is playing the role of planner and leader by relying upon its strong capital and market advantages. The US strategy also involves the construction of infrastructure, including that for transportation, such as railways, highways, and oil and natural gas pipelines; it is engaged in free trade among the countries in the region; and it is reducing trade barriers and simplifying the cross-border formalities, to realize regional economic opening-up. Besides, China helps each country overcome its bureaucracy and corruption and improve the environment for investment. Owing to the geographic restrictions, the United States plays the role more of leader and driver in diplomacy in terms of implementing the projects, trying hard to win support from the international community, especially its Western allies, to provide substantial help for the initiative. The United States is not willing to invest in the projects; instead, it hopes that India, Pakistan, and Afghanistan will undertake greater responsibilities and encourage development banks, overseas investors, local governments, and private sectors to actively invest in these regions.

China's Belt and Road Initiative has a more solid cooperation foundation and enjoys higher regional recognition. Russia has expressed its will to provide favorable regional environmental security and power support to China's building of the silk road. China has established a strategic partnership with the five Central Asian countries and has no direct confrontational interest conflicts in geopolitics, and so, there is a bright future for cooperation. The strategy could bring huge benefits to the participating countries' economic development, which is obviously multiwin. In terms of the relationship with Southeast Asian countries, China's influence in Southeast Asia is much greater than that of the other countries by relying upon the China-ASEAN FTA. As the no. 1 trading partner to the ASEAN community, China features a sound political and economic foundation for further cooperation. In terms of the advantage of timing, the New Silk Road Initiative proposed by the United States was launched earlier; thus, it has won more time in converting relevant agreements into practical actions. Financially, China is able to exert an important influence by using its strong economic strength, China is greatly complementary with the economy of the countries of Central Asia and Southeast Asia, and Chinese enterprises' overseas investments also join with these countries and regions.

In comparison, the United States depends on contributions and support from the Asian Development Bank and overseas; consequently, the United States lacks the financial support in implementing the strategy. Geographically, the United States is far away from Asia. Meanwhile, there appeared a voice pointing out that "the silk road will be built by Asia but not led by the West." In comparison, the opening up of the western area and the southeastern coastal areas of China to the countries and regions involved in the Silk Road Initiative is the frontier for economic opening-up and cooperation; thus, China has a geographical advantage. In terms of cooperation, China has accumulated rich experience in cooperating with Central Asian countries and ASEAN countries, having formed a preliminary basis for comprehensive high-level cooperation. However, China has to face the challenges from the dispute between China and Vietnam and the Philippines over the sovereignty of the South China Sea. The feasibility of the United States' New Silk Road Initiative is in doubt, and many efforts have to be made due to the situation of regional security and the backward economic and social development.[4]

1.1.4 *The Inclusive Development of the New Silk Road Initiative and the Belt and Road Initiative*

The Belt and Road Initiative has similarities and dissimilarities with the United States' New Silk Road Initiative. The two initiatives can be pushed forward without contradicting each other through cooperation and then realize inclusive development.

The land and maritime silk roads in history were never a single route, but instead, multiple routes. In the present time, when science, technology, and transportation are highly developed, it is less possible for the Belt and Road to be a single route. It comprises land, water, and air routes. Taking the advantages of high-speed railways and highways, supersonic aircrafts, ocean-going vessels, and the Internet,

---

[4]Zhang Xiaotong. (October 24, 2014). Comparison between the Silk Road Initiatives of China and the USA. *China Industrial Economy News*. Retrieved from http://opinion.hexun.com/2014-10-21/169510555.html.

the Silk Road Economic Belt and the 21st Century Maritime Silk Road will cover a range as extensive as all of Eurasia, Africa, Oceania, and even the whole world. The silk road in history boosted the communication between different countries, nations, and cultures and advanced regional cooperation, while today's Silk Road Economic Belt and the 21st Century Maritime Silk Road will play a bigger role in this sense. Therefore, the Belt and Road Initiative will compete with and also cooperate with other regional cooperation mechanisms. Furthermore, it is inclusive to achieve the goal of win–win. The other regional cooperation mechanisms include the United States' New Silk Road Initiative and the EEU energetically pushed forward by Russia.

The inclusive development of the Belt and Road Initiative and the New Silk Road Initiative is beneficial to the stable development of the China–US relationship. In the situation wherein the strategic focus of the United States moves eastward, and terrorism and extremism form a new wave of threats, the stable development of the western part of China shows a more obvious strategic significance. In terms of economic strength, China is the strongest in the regions covered by the Belt and Road; therefore, China's active participation is indispensable, about which the United States is very clear. Meanwhile, the US government is faced with serious economic weariness and fiscal pressure, and the economic strategy aiming toward Afghanistan and the "Great Central Asia" lacks the domestic support; thus, it is pressing for the United States to seek cooperation with other countries. Therefore, the United States pays great attention to China's attitude, which may be the reason why the United States changed the name of its strategy in consideration of China's objection. In brief, the cooperation and complementariness between the Belt and Road Initiative and the New Silk Road Initiative and their inclusive development may help China play an active and constructive role in settling the issues of rebuilding Afghanistan and regional development, which may not only enhance the friendly cooperative relationship between China and the countries in Central Asia, Southern Asia, Western Asia, and the other relevant countries, but may also urge China and the United States to develop new areas for cooperation on issues such as rebuilding Afghanistan. It will also facilitate the construction of a new type of a major-power relationship. It is helpful for China to create a favorable international environment, particularly, in maintaining peripheral security.[5]

President Xi Jinping pointed out that, "The history of communication for over two thousand years has proved that countries of different races, beliefs and cultural backgrounds have all the means necessary for sharing peace and common development as long as we insist on solidarity and mutual trust, fairness and mutual benefit, inclusiveness and mutual learning, and cooperation for win–win. This is the valuable enlightenment that the ancient silk road left to us." It is fair to say that this understanding and judgment is the guiding principle for dealing with the relationship between the Belt and Road Initiative and the New Silk Road Initiative.

1.2 *The Eurasian Economic Union Led by Russia*

1.2.1 *Progress and Problems*

During the first decade after the collapse of the Soviet Union, Russia pushed forward the integration of the Commonwealth of the Independent States (CIS), but it did not make any substantial progress in this respect owing to the sharp decline in its own economic strength. In 1994, the CIS FTA agreement, the primary document for integration adopted by 12 CIS states, had lost its functionality. At the turn of the 21st century, Russia realized that the deep integration of the post-Soviet Union space is an important task for it to restore its position as a world power; therefore, Russia began to adjust its policies toward the CIS, explicitly pointing out that the CIS is the priority for its diplomatic policies and regional development, thus restarting the process of integration.

In 2000, Russia, Belarus, Kazakhstan, Kyrgyzstan, and Tajikistan established the EEU on the basis of the Customs Alliance founded in 1995, in order to establish a customs alliance and form a common

---

[5] Pan Guang. (April 9, 2015) Origin, Evolvement and Developmental Vision of the US New Silk Road Initiative: A Dialogue with S. Frederik Starr, Proposer of the New Silk Road Initiative. *People's Daily Online*. Retrieved from http://world.people.com.cn/n/2015/0409/c1002-26820843.html.

economic space among the member states and deepen the economic, cultural, and people-to-people integration. In 2006, Uzbekistan joined the EEU and withdrew in 2008. Apart from the five member states, the EEU also includes three observer states, that is, Ukraine, Armenia, and Moldova. However, the economic integration of the countries at different levels of development turned out to be rather fruitless; therefore, Russia decided to push forward integration allowing for different paces and levels within the framework of the CIS in 2007. In October 2007, the Russia–Belarus–Kazakhstan Customs Alliance was established under the common framework of the EEU, and the Customs Alliance Committee was founded as the only standing supervisory organization. In November 2009, the leaders of Russia, Belarus, and Kazakhstan signed nine fundamental documents, including the *Customs Code of the Customs Alliance*. On January 1, 2010, the Customs Alliance was implemented officially and the three countries established common external tariffs, including the common trade policies for the third country and eliminating the barriers of customs tariffs and noncustoms tariffs within the alliance, to further increase the free flow of commodities within the alliance.

On January 1, 2011, one year after it was implemented, the Customs Alliance formed the Single Economic Space in its area. Based on the *Schengen Agreement* of the EU, the Single Economic Space implemented coordinative policies and actions in many areas. The main difference between Single Economic Space and the Customs Alliance is that, despite the free flow of goods, the member states would also achieve the free flow of capital, labor, technologies, and services. The Single Economic Space aimed at achieving not only trade integration but also the integration of production and at constructing a single infrastructure for transportation and telecommunications and for coordinating the macroeconomic policies. On May 29, 2014, the leaders of Russia, Belarus, and Kazakhstan signed the *Treaty on the Eurasian Economic Union*, which took effect officially on January 1, 2015. As defined by the treaty, the EEU is an international organization for regional integration and has a subjective status according to international laws. The EEU does not fall into contradiction with the CIS, but instead complements it. In addition, the EEU is an open organization that welcomes other partners to join. Priorities will be given to the states of the CIS. Russia, Belarus, and Kazakhstan promised that they would achieve the free flow of commodities, services, capital, and labor by 2025 and try to coordinate the policies for major industries, represented by energy, processing, agriculture, and traffic and transportation. Its ultimate goal is to establish an economic alliance similar to the EU, a single grand market to cover a total area of 20 million square kilometers, involve a total population of 170 million, and produce a total GDP of USD 3 trillion. Presently, the original Soviet Union member states that are preparing to join the EEU include Armenia, Kyrgyzstan, and Tajikistan. Beyond the original Soviet Union regions, India, Vietnam, and Turkey also expressed their interest to join the Customs Alliance. In addition, the Customs Alliance countries are actively carrying out negotiations on an FTA agreement with organizations and countries outside the region, including Vietnam, New Zealand, Israel, Syria, Macedonia, and the four EU countries that did not join the European Free Trade Association, that is, Iceland, Liechtenstein, Norway, and Sweden.

The establishment of the EEU will be a major achievement for the advancement of integration in the post-Soviet Union space after Putin came to power in Russia. It is a strategic arrangement through which Russia hopes to explore the potential for the common economic foundation of the Soviet Union and enhance the capability for trade and investments among various nations by developing regional cooperation and striving for long-term diversified economic development. In the official operation of the Russia–Belarus–Kazakhstan Customs Alliance in 2010 for the signing of the *Treaty on the Eurasian Economic Union* in May 2014, Eurasian economic integration completed its first three steps, that is, the Customs Alliance, the Single Economic Space, and the EEU, before the fourth step of the Eurasian Alliance within a short period of four and a half years. On October 3, 2011, Putin published a signed article in the *Izvestia*, emphasizing that to establish the EEU "is not to rebuild the Soviet Union in any form, and any attempt to restore or copy the past is naïve." The new alliance will be built based on totally different values and political and economic principles. "What we have proposed is a strong model supranational alliance.

It will become a pole of today's world, and play its role as a 'tie' connecting Europe and the Asia-Pacific." It will be a supranational union, with a major role of "coordinating the economic and monetary policies of the member states." Putin also believed that the EEU may have its presence together with the European Union, the North America FTA, China, APEC, and the ASEAN community.[6]

The Russia–Belarus–Kazakhstan Customs Alliance lasted for three years, from when the decision of its establishment was made in August 2006 to January 1, 2010. During this period, the action plan for establishing the Customs Alliance was officially approved in 2007 and the Customs Alliance Committee was organized in 2009, thus formulating and approving a uniform customs code. Meanwhile, there was also the arrangement of the mechanism for the organization and settlement of disputes of the Customs Alliance, stipulating that the Customs Alliance Committee is the only standing coordinating organization with the power to manage all the affairs related to the operations of the Customs Alliance. The proportions of the voting rights of the three countries are as follows: 56% held by Russia, 22% held by Belarus, and 22% held by Kazakhstan, with Russia in the leading position. In addition, the Customs Alliance has specific regulations regarding the mechanism for the payment and collection of import tariffs, VAT, and consumption tax; the mechanism for the distribution of benefits for the three taxes and for the payment and collection of the internal taxes relative to the member states and a third country. The EEU to be established will consist of four organizations, that is, the Eurasian Highest Economic Council, the Eurasian Inter-Governmental Commission, the Eurasian Economic Commission, and the EEU Court. According to the treaty, the alliance is an international organization for regional integration and has a subjective status under international laws. Russia, Belarus, and Kazakhstan promised to achieve the free flow of commodities, services, capital, and labor by 2025 and try to coordinate the policies for major industries, represented by energy, processing, agriculture, and

---

[6] Li Jianmin. (2014). The Silk Road Economic Belt, the Eurasian Economic Union and China–Russia Cooperation. *Academic Journal of Russian Studies*, Issue 5, pp. 7–18.

traffic and transportation. The ultimate goal of the alliance is to establish an economic alliance similar to the EU and develop a uniform market.

The four-year operation of the Customs Alliance has not created a remarkable effect in the creation and transfer of trade. After the Customs Alliance was launched on July 1, 2011, the trade within the member states increased by 37% from the previous year, but this situation did not last long. From 2012 to the first half of 2014, the value of trade within the member states of the Customs Alliance declined. Measured by the indicators of trade compactness and trade complementariness over a longer period, from 1998 to 2012, although the trade compactness indicator was high for trade among Russia, Belarus, and Kazakhstan, it was on the downward trend. In terms of the indicator for commodities complementariness, from 1998 to 2012, the value of the indicator of trade complementariness in trade among the three countries was lower than 1. The decline in the indicator of the trade compactness shows that there is low trade complementariness in trade among the member states; thus, the potential for trade is limited. However, trade among Russia, Belarus, and Kazakhstan expanded much faster than the internal trade of the member states. The countries outside the region, the EU in particular, and China are the major trading partners of the Customs Alliance member states. For a long period of time, the value of trade between Russia and the EU accounted for over 50% of Russia's total value of trade. Since 2010, China has been Russia's largest trading partner, and the value of China–Russia trade accounting for 12% of Russia's total. The member states of the EEU are all in a period of transformation, and each country has big differences in economic scale and political system. In terms of economic scale, for example, the GDP of Russia was 30 times that of Belarus and 10 times that of Kazakhstan in 2012 according to the International Monetary Fund (IMF) data. There is an imbalance of development within the Customs Alliance, and it is hard to imagine that there will be "fairness" within the alliance. In the structure of exportations of Russia and Kazakhstan, resource and energy products are always the major export goods, and importation focuses on electromechanical products, which shows that, within the Customs

Alliance, the member states fail to provide needed products and a market to each other. As the leading state, Russia does not have a strong enough economy, and its economic investment is limited. Russia's economy lacks enough attractive traits because it lags behind in market reform. The Eurasian Economic Commission is a supranational organization but the stipulations made by it for some industries have not been carried out, so it lacks substantial transnational political power.

The process of Eurasian integration is faced with a lot of competition and challenges, and the loose internal economic connection will become a major impediment for the development of the EEU in the future. Against a background in which the sanctions on Russia are intensified due to the Ukraine crisis, the EEU will be affected in exerting its potential.

1.2.2 *The Belt and Road Initiative and the EEU*

On the existing basis, the Belt and Road Initiative and the EEU may focus on the following areas for prioritized project cooperation.

The area of interconnectivity. From 2010 to 2011, with the support of the Eurasian Development Bank, the Eurasian Economic Community formulated a comprehensive plan for the development of infrastructures for highways and railways. The plan is to implement 142 projects by 2020, including 51 projects for improving highways; 42 for developing railways; and 45 for building logistics centers, of which 10 will be transnational logistics centers. Regarding interconnectivity, the total value of 23 super large projects reaches USD 68 billion, but both domestic projects and developmental strategies for transportation and international projects and plans are faced with the problem of insufficient internal financing. The tasks cannot be fulfilled by the EEU alone; it will need to attract international financial institutions and development institutions to join in. To a larger extent, the plan for a Eurasian railway passageway, proposed by the Railway Transportation Organization in 1996, is being pushed forward as scheduled. The plan includes 13 Eurasian railway passageways, with the major ones including China–Kazakhstan–Russia–Europe,

China–Mongolia–Russia–Europe, Russian Far East–Europe, and Europe–Russia–the Caucasus. All these passageways need to utilize the existing infrastructure facilities, which are to be integrated with uniform technical standards. On the passageways for Asia–Europe railways, several railways in Europe and the CIS member states have recently been rebuilt.

On July 8, 2014, the engineering project for modernizing the Baikal–Amur Railway, a branch of the Siberian Railway in Russia, was launched. In the future, it is hoped to realize a Eurasian integrated railway network with the Asian railway network, the CIS railway network, and the European railway network as the main structures and the interconnection between Eurasian railways such as the Siberian Railway and the New Eurasian Land Bridge, which is in harmony with the road interconnectivity as included in the Belt and Road Initiative. In recent years, during the period of fast development, China's railway group has energetically pushed forward original innovations, integrated innovation, and re-innovation after importing and taking in technologies; relevant enterprises have developed a strong capability in design, construction, equipment manufacturing, and operations management, and they have accumulated rich experience. Together with China's financial advantage, the Belt and Road projects may cooperate with the EEU at bilateral or multilateral levels regarding the construction of railway connectivity.

The area of power supply cooperation. The EEU decided to build the EEU single power market in 2019. First, the concept of building a uniform electric power market of the EEU was formulated and submitted to the leaders of the three countries for examination on July 1, 2015; the three countries then developed a guideline for building a uniform electric power market according to this concept by June 1, 2016, and officially complete the uniform electric power market for the three countries in 2019. Presently, the connectivity of power grids among the countries and regions is a general trend for the global power system. The development of interconnected synonymous power grids will bring huge benefits: First, it will guarantee the development and utilization of high-capacity machine units, large hydraulic power units, nuclear power, and renewable energy, and it will improve the efficiency and reduce the operational costs; second, it will reduce the backup capacity of the system and boost the complementariness of different sources, thus saving engines; third, it will achieve the optimized allocation of energy resources on a large scale, facilitating the expansion of the competitive energy and power market; and fourth, it will improve the efficiency of the overall grid and safety reliability. Currently, China's State Grid is the worldwide leader on a general scale, voltage classes, extra-high voltage technologies, and to a large extent, the capability for resource allocation, as well as the construction of intelligent grids. On May 20, 2014, the State Grid Corporation of China signed a strategic cooperation agreement with Russian Grids. The two parties planned to carry out long-term technical exchanges and cooperation for mutual benefits in the research and application of the technologies of extra-high AC/DC voltage and intelligent grids, the construction and rebuilding of power transmission and supply facilities, and the feasibility of building a Eurasian power bridge. In the future, if China is able to participate in building a uniform power market of the EEU, electric power may be supplied to it through transnational connectivity, and China may supply power to the countries lacking power along the Belt and Road, such as Afghanistan and Iran, which will help to boost the coordinated development of regional economy and foresee a bright future for cooperation.

Cooperation in agriculture. According to the treaty of the EEU, after the union is founded, it will implement agricultural policies; in order to guarantee a balanced development among agricultural products and cereal production and market, it will provide equal conditions for competition in agricultural market access, will unify the conditions for the flow of agricultural products and cereals, and will protect the benefits for the producers of the member states in domestic and overseas markets. Besides, the EEU will formulate common cereal policies to coordinate the policies for crop planting, cereal market interference, cereal reserve warehousing, price setting, the state support of agriculture and exportations. Russia, Belarus, and Kazakhstan feature excellent conditions for agricultural development and have achieved a leap in agricultural development in the past

10 years. From 2007 to 2011, the market shares held by the Single Economic Space, that is, Russia, Belarus, Kazakhstan, and Ukraine are 36.3% for barley, 21.5% for wheat, and 7.7% for corn. Presently, Russia is the world's third largest wheat exporter, Kazakhstan is a major flour exporter, and Belarus enjoys high agricultural productivity. All the three countries have adopted agriculture as a new economic growth point. China is a world giant for cereal production and consumption. It is now in the middle of accelerating its industrialization and urbanization process; the problems of shortage in the basic resources for agricultural production, including land and water resources, are conspicuous, and the pollution of the agricultural environment is becoming more severe. For China's agriculture to go global, as a strategic choice, China needs to actively participate in the international labor division and cooperation and continuously explore the space for existence and development, in order to respond to the current trend of world economic development. Agriculture will be an important area in which China can push forward the Belt and Road Initiative to dock with the EEU. In addition to expanding cooperation in the area of trade in agricultural products, China and the EEU will have vast potential for cooperation in areas such as the development of industrialization, organic agriculture, agricultural machinery trade, and cereal transportation. Presently, because of the Ukraine crisis, the West and Russia are continuing with the sanctions and anti-sanctions, which provides an opportunity for China to export vegetables, fruit, and pork to Russia. Compared to short-term opportunities, it is more important to create conditions and lay the foundation for long-term cooperation.

Cooperation in the financial area. Financial cooperation has a good foundation available between China and the EEU member states. In 2009 and 2011, China signed currency swap agreements with Russia and Kazakhstan, respectively. In August 2014, China and Russia reached a currency swap agreement, and the agreement is being examined and set for approval. Currency swap is not a step included in currency internationalization in a strict sense, but is a breaking point for pushing forward the internationalization of the RMB. Currency swap will necessarily greatly reduce the financing and exchange costs for the currencies of both countries. Before, China and Russia had made significant progress in domestic currency settlement for trade and settlement of payments via the China UnionPay card. Today, 75% of the transnational settlements of trade between China and Russia is paid in US dollars. Because Russia and the United States are trapped in a quasi "Cold War" state due to the Ukraine crisis, Russia is very determined to withdraw from the US dollar mechanism. China and Russia expressed explicitly in the "5·20 Joint Statement" in 2014 that they would closely coordinate in the financial and banking area, including the expansion of the scale for direct settlement with the domestic currencies of China and Russia during China–Russia trade, investment, and loans, in order to protect the two countries from being affected by the fluctuation of the exchange rates of the major worldwide currencies. VTB of Russia and the Bank of China signed an agreement to develop a partnership in various areas, including cooperation on the clearing of roubles and renminbi, investment banking, interbank loans, trade financing, and capital market trade. During the docking between the Belt and Road Initiative and the EEU in the future, the financial area will play a role of booster to deepen the cooperation within the following aspects: First, to actively push forward the bilateral domestic currency settlement and establish the multilateral settlement system for China and the EEU when the conditions are ready; second, to gradually expand the scale of the currency swap with EEU state members; third, to actively explore a new model for capital operations with joint investments and joint benefits; fourth, to boost the steady opening-up of the financial market, set up a transborder financial service network, practically enhance cooperation on international financial governance and financial supervision, and improve the coordination of financial policies.

1.3 *Japan's and Mongolia's Silk Road Plans*

1.3.1 *Japan's Silk Road Diplomacy*

As early as July 24, 1997, Ryutaro Hashimoto, the former Prime Minister of Japan, proposed to carry out diplomacy with Eurasia,

Central Asia, and the Caucasus region placed in a critical position, in a speech delivered at the Association of Corporate Executives. Since then, Japan's diplomacy with Central Asia has been called the Silk Road Diplomacy. The most important reason for Central Asia to have drawn the attention of Japan is its rich energy reserves, especially oil and natural gas in the offshore area of the Caspian Sea. Japan's current supply of oil and natural gas is seriously dependent on the Middle East. Therefore, it is quite natural for Japan to pay attention to Central Asia for the sake of diverse energy supplies. Besides, in the bilateral relations between Japan and Russia, the resources in Siberia and Sakhalin have been Russia's trump card. If Japan could join hands with Central Asia for energy development, it will be holding more aces at the negotiation table with Russia.

The most critical point is that the development of its relationship with Central Asia may become a card for Japan to play in the game with China. The restriction on the exploration and importation of important resources such as oil may detain China's economic development and check China's progress on the whole. Besides, it may also contain the Shanghai Cooperation Organization (SCO) if it succeeds in establishing a close relationship with Central Asian countries. It was reported by the Associated Press that, on August 26, 2004, Hatsuhisa Takashima, Japan's Foreign Ministry Spokesman, stated that Japan wished to be an SCO observer state.

Japan is also very much concerned about the relationship between Central Asia and Xinjiang of China. Recent years have witnessed the rapid economic growth of Xinjiang. Xinjiang also enjoys an important location, as the Eurasia Bridge, which starts from Lianyungang in China and goes through the area of Xinjiang. Some Japanese scholars have also pointed out that Central Asia is the backyard of China; thus, it is more than helpful to keep an eye on China's backyard. Japan has been increasing its aid to Vietnam and Mongolia and building a close relationship with India, while it has been reducing its aid for the development of China, posing a strategy of checking China's progress by building relationship with China's neighboring countries.

Besides, Japan is developing itself into a political power, which means that it has to expand its influence in international politics.

Japan hopes that those pro-Japan Central Asian countries may become reliable partners. The Central Asian countries supported Japan in becoming a standing member of the Security Council, which was highly appraised by Japan. When Japan's Foreign Minister Yoriko Kawaguchi paid a visit to Tashkent, the capital of Uzbekistan, in August 2004, she pointed out that the core of Japan's aid to Central Asia lies in energy and the environment and that Japan was ready to provide a 16.4 billion yen loan with interest to build the railways in the south of Uzbekistan. Additionally, Japan will receive students from Central Asian countries for them to continue with their studies in Japan, and there will be a total of 1,000 students in the next 3 years. Japan will also provide financial aid to the countries in Central Asia to help them obtain estuaries. Therefore, after suggesting that the Central Asian countries should speed up the construction of the regional railway network, the Japanese government built a railway network through Afghanistan.

At present, the achievements that Japan has made in its Silk Road Diplomacy are mainly because of the developmental aid to the governments of some Central Asian countries. From 1991 to 2000, the Japan government provided a total of 188.248 billion yen as development aid to Central Asia. From 1999 to 2000, Japan remained the largest donator to Kazakhstan, Kyrgyzstan, and Uzbekistan and the second largest donator to Turkmenistan. After the September 11 attacks, it provided complementary aid of 240 million yen to the support program for the Afghanistan refugees in Tajikistan, complementary aid valuing 185 million yen to the "mother and son health improvement plan" of Tajikistan, and complementary aid valuing 355 million yen to the "health improvement plan for dry areas" of Uzbekistan.[7]

1.3.2 *Mongolia's Grassland Silk Road Plan*

To advance the economic development of the country and improve the people's living conditions, the Mongolian government started the

---

[7] Lan Jianzhong. (September 2, 2004). Japan: The Silk Road Diplomacy Intended to Contain China and Russia. *Reference News.* Retrieved from http://www.canka oxiaoxi.com.

construction of its highway facilities in 1990. In 2000, the Mongolian government proposed the plan for the construction of the "millennium highway" project. In April 2004, Mongolia signed, with the United Nations, the agreement between the member states of the UN Economic and Social Commission for Asia and the Pacific, and took part in the construction project for the network of Asian expressways. The network of Asian expressways, from Japan to Turkey, has a total length of 141,000 km. Mongolia is responsible for building the AH3, AH32, and AH4 highways. Mongolia built the highways that connected five provinces in 2013, hoping to achieve the connectivity between the expressways of China and Russia and boost the construction of facilities for natural gas, oil, and other energy sources.

In 2012, the Mongolian government proposed the building of the Grassland Silk Road to connect the transborder roads of transportation between Russia and China. The goal of the Grassland Silk Road formulated by Mongolia was to build an expressway, stretching 997 km from Altanbulag toward Ulan Bator and connected Dzamiin-Üüd. Besides, there was a goal of completing the laying of 1,100 km cables and the construction of the pipeline for natural gas and oil supply, which lasted 2–3 years. There were about 1,000 Mongolian companies and 30 foreign companies that took part in the construction, thus planning to create 300,000 to 400,000 regular jobs and interim jobs. According to the prediction made by the Ministry of Economic Development of Mongolia, once the construction project of the Grassland Silk Road plan is kicked off, it will increase investments and enlarge the space for developing the energy and mining industry throughout Mongolia, and will also increase Mongolia's GDP. The GDP of Mongolia will have increased by USD 10 billion each year by then, while its GDP is presently USD 10 billion. On September 2, 2014, the Mongolian government officially organized a special working team for the Grassland Silk Road, which will take care of pushing forward the implementation of the project and including important projects such as the Grassland Silk Road in its strategic plan for national development.

In 1999, China became Mongolia's largest trading partner by transcending Russia. The economic and trade cooperation between China and Mongolia has been making rapid progress, particularly since 2000. In 2008, the two governments signed the *Guidelines for the Mid-term Development of Economic and Trade Cooperation between China and Mongolia*. According to the statistics of China's customs, Mongolia's exports valued USD 4.38 billion in 2013. The products that are mainly exported to China include copper, coal, gold, livestock, animal by-products, wool, leather, and so on. China has become its largest export destination, and the exports to China account for 92.6% of the total value of exports. In 2013, the imports to Mongolia valued USD 6.738 billion, and the main products of importation include machinery, fuels, food, industrial consumer goods, chemicals, building materials, sugar, tea, and so on. China is Mongolia's largest partner in terms of imports, and its imports from China account for 27.6% of the total value of importations (Table 2.1).

Moreover, the economic and trade cooperation between China and Mongolia has been expanding through economic cooperation such as trade, investments, loans with favorable terms, and aid. In 2012, China's investments in Mongolia reached USD 280 million, accounting for 49.4% of the total foreign investment in that country. In recent years, faced with economic problems such as a decline in foreign investments, intensified inflation and an increased unemployment rate, and so on, Mongolia is expecting new cooperation with China on investments in transportation, energy and mining. According to the statistics of the authority for foreign investments, there are 12,640 state-owned investment companies, and the 6,169 Chinese investment companies account for 48.81% approximately. In 2012, there were 5,639 Chinese companies investing in Mongolia. From

Table 2.1 Total Value of Trade between China and Mongolia (2004–2014) (Unit: USD 1 Million)

	2004	2005	2006	2007	2008	2009	2010	2011	2012	2013	2014
Total	671.1	821.5	1,414.4	1,980.3	2,534.6	1,914	3,437.3	6,463.8	6,600	6,400	7,310
Exports	413.9	514.2	1,049.4	1,411.4	1,635.9	1,389	2,466.3	4,439.9	3,900	3,356	2,220
Imports	257.2	307.3	365	568.9	898.7	525.0	971.0	2,023.9	2,700	3,044	5,090

Source: Ministry of Commerce of the People's Republic of China.

2008 to 2012, the investment companies increased by four times and the total amount of investments increased by 3.7 times. A total of 67.3% of the Chinese investment capital is focused on the areas of geology and mining, and 20% on trade and the catering industry. Besides investments, China has also been pushing forward the development of economic cooperation between China and Mongolia by means of loans and aid, having provided loans with favorable terms for the amount of RMB 200 million from 2001 to 2005. For 2008, the amount of loans totaled 46.1 million roubles, an equivalent of RMB 330 million, and of aid totaled USD 41 million. Since 2003, the leaders of China and Mongolia have had many bilateral meetings; the two countries have been strengthening their bilateral economic and trade relations. The two parties have focused on mining and exploitation and the construction of infrastructures during the meetings. For China and Mongolia, it is wise to realize the diversification of their bilateral partnership. The relationship between the two countries has transcended the meaning of economic development; they are making more efforts in political and military exchanges.[8]

President Xi Jinping visited Mongolia in August 2014, seeking a stronger partnership with Mongolia in terms of economy and trade, politics, and security. The two countries decided to elevate the China–Mongolia relationship with a comprehensive strategic partnership and reached a consensus on extensive cooperation in military and culture. This coincides perfectly with Mongolia's objective of playing a bigger role in regional foreign affairs. The building of the economic belt of the Grassland Silk Road is not only the construction of the economic belt itself, but also more of a comprehensive platform for the construction of a corridor, industrial cooperation, and trade development. China and Mongolia share cultural origins and customs, and besides, the two countries have some differences regarding their endowed elements, their level of economic development, industrial structure and income that serve as the basis for industrial cooperation between the

---

[8] Yu Hongyang, Oudeka and Badianjun. (2015). An Analysis of the Basis and Obstacles for the China–Mongolia–Russia Economic Corridor. *Northeast Asia Forum*, Issue 1, pp. 96–106.

two countries, mainly presented in the mutually beneficial cooperation of resources and energies, agriculture and planting, animal husbandry, development of light industry, and industrial manufacturing. As neighbors to each other and complementary in the economy, there is a great potential for the development of trade between China and Mongolia. In particular, with the building of the economic belt of the Grassland Silk Road, China and Mongolia, despite large differences in economic development, will carry out extensive industrial cooperation and boost the development of trade. In terms of conditions for development, the docking ports Reecho and Dzamiin-Üüd between China and Mongolia have the most complete facilities and enjoy the best location of all docking ports. They are a perfect choice for building an economic cooperation area on the border between China and Mongolia. Through these docking ports, the area of economic cooperation may utilize the favorable policies granted by the government to achieve free development of the economic and trade relationship within the scope of regional cooperation. In particular, it is possible for them to realize the internationalization of Chinese products by taking advantage of the preferential treatments, such as tax exemption and reduction, to be enjoyed by Mongolia in many countries through the transborder economic cooperation area.

There is not only a borderline running 4,710 km between China and Mongolia, but also several docking ports. These natural advantages, however, have not found their sufficient play in the economic and trade cooperation between China and Mongolia. Therefore, the two countries will build a cross-border economic cooperation area to innovate the cooperation mode and deepen the economic and trade relationship between them by taking advantage of their neighborly relationship. In the development of the economic and trade relationship between China and Mongolia, Inner Mongolia has its unique advantages in sharing not only the 3,139 km borderline with Mongolia, but also more than ten ports opened between China and Mongolia. The advantages were highlighted in June 2013 when Erenhot was listed as the second national experimental zone for development and opening-up in Mongolia, immediately following Manzhouli. The implementation of this policy in the largest land port opened to Mongolia is significant for the development of the China–Mongolia economic and trade relationship.

Although the proposals of different countries contained their own details and plans for building the silk road and they also reflect the different concepts of each country in revitalizing the silk road, they do not exclude one another. On the contrary, these plans may strengthen each other with concerted efforts. They may exert the role of "strength multiplier" to support economic growth and employment which are to be driven by private economy and advance the economic integration of the countries in Eurasia and even on a wider scope. It is obvious that, through building up the people-to-people connection and strengthening resource integration, it is possible to push forward the stable and healthy development of the economy of Asia and Europe and the other countries in the world as well.

2. Creating an External Environment for Peaceful Development

Although hegemonies, power politics, and neo-interventionism are rising presently, diversified forms of protectionism are being restored, and traditional and nontraditional threats toward security, such as arms race, terrorism, and network security, are interwoven with each other, "with the world's multi-polarization, further development of economic globalization and cultural diversification, and the continuous advancement of social informatization, human beings today are better equipped to march toward the goal of peace and development than in any period in history before, and cooperation for mutual benefit is a realistic approach to this goal." The era when very few countries or power groups monopolized the world affairs and governed the destiny of other countries is forever gone. China's President Xi Jinping pointed out that, at present, with the deepened multi-polarization of the world, the balance between international powers is becoming favorable for maintaining world peace. With the continuous multipolarization of the world and economic globalization, countries are becoming more dependent on each other. The economy of a country will advance if it is connected to other countries, and will fall back if disconnected. Therefore, the critical tasks that China is now facing with include being concerned with and improving today's China–US and China–Europe relationships, developing the international presence of the BRICS countries, making the China-ASEAN cooperation bigger and stronger, pushing the economic development of the Belt and Road Initiative to a higher level, and establishing the worldwide influence of China's culture throughout the globe.

2.1 *China–US Relationship toward In-depth Competition and Cooperation*

In November 2011, then US Secretary of State, Hillary Clinton, published "America's Pacific Century" in *Foreign Policy*, an American magazine. After its release, the media and academia of China named it as a high-profile declaration of "America's pivot to the Asia-Pacific." In an interview in 2010, Barack Obama expressed his opinion that the United States will increase its influence in East Asia. The declaration made by Hillary Clinton delineates the strategy and introduce most complete version of it. Clinton pointed out in the article that an open Asian market provides the United States with unprecedented opportunities for investment, trade, and cutting-edge technologies. At the 2012 summit meeting of APEC, the United States energetically pushed forward the establishment of the *Trans-Pacific Partnership Agreement* (TPP). Under the existing *Trans-Pacific Strategic Economic Partnership Agreement* led by New Zealand, Singapore, Vietnam, and Brunei, the United States reached a comprehensive free trade agreement with them that was inclusive of all commodities and services by breaking the conventional FTA mode with the signing countries. The fact that the United States did not invite China, one of the largest economies in East Asia, to join the TPP shows that the United States has the goal of excluding China's influence in East Asia and building a mechanism of cooperation for the economy of East Asia, which centers around the United States and integrates ASEAN and APEC resources.

With the advancement of globalization, as the two largest economies in the world, China and the United States are becoming increasingly dependent on each other in trade and the economy. China and the United States are for the most part relying upon each other, especially in East Asia, which is mainly presented as follows. First, China and the United States are becoming increasingly dependent on each other in trade, investment, and finance. In the area of bilateral trade, China and the United States are the second largest trading partners to each other. The statistics of the Ministry of Commerce show that, in 2013, the value of bilateral trade in goods between China and the United States reached a record-breaking value of USD 521 billion. By the end of 2013, the aggregate of the two-way investment value between China and the United States exceeded USD 100 billion. The two countries are the second largest trading partners to each other. China is the no. 1 exporter to the United States and has been the fastest-growing export market for the United States for 10 years straight. Obviously, the United States is increasingly more dependent on China's market. In the financial area, the United States' national bonds held by China are continuously increasing, having exceeded USD 1.27 trillion, thus providing strong economic support to the restoration of the US economy. In investments, China retains its irresistible attraction for American enterprises.

In the past few years, the economy of the United States was affected by wars and the financial crisis in 2008, and remained in depression for quite a long time. The big fiscal deficit once again brought the White House to the awkward situation of "shut-down," and the unemployment rate as high as 9%–10% caused by the economic downturn even made the American society question their institutions and values that they had so long been proud of and popularizing energetically around the world. Some American elites also believed that it was abnormal for the United States, with only 5% of the world's population, to possess 30%–40% of the economy of the world, and it was normal for the United States' economic strength to decline relatively. They believed that the declining strength of the United States was not zero-sum, but the low economic growth, lasting financial crisis, and substantial fiscal deficit intensified Americans' sense of crisis.[9] In 2011, the number of unemployed reached over

---

[9] Men Honghua. (2012). The Critical Moment: China, America and the World in the Eye of American Elites. *Social Sciences in China*, Issue 7, pp. 186–188.

13.3 million and the semi-unemployed 10 million. That is to say, one out of six Americans was in poverty. The United States had an increase of 1.6 million jobs that year, but far from enough for the huge unemployed population. The fiscal deficit was as high as USD 1.234 trillion and the debt balance reached USD 14.34 trillion, above the upper limit of USD 14.29 trillion established by the US Congress in an act passed in 2010. In 2014, the unemployment rate of the United States was as high as 6.2%.

China's total GDP is ranked the world's second after surpassing Japan in 2010. The most important is that China successfully weathered the impact cause by the 2007 global financial crisis and has maintained its stable economic development. The strength balance between China and the United States is undergoing major changes. The comparison of shares acquired by the United States and China in the comprehensive national strength in the world's total shows that, in the past 20 years, China's comprehensive national strength has been growing and developing on an upward spiral, while the United States' comprehensive national strength has been declining and is developing on a downward spiral. The comprehensive national strength of China's proportion of the world's GDP had grown to 16.57% in 2013 from 4.03% in 1990, by 12.54 percentage points; for the same period, that of the United States had declined to 16.32% in 2013 from 22.71% previously, by 6.39 percentage points. The relative difference between the comprehensive power of China and that of the United States has greatly changed, narrowed down to 0.98 times in 2013 from 4.03 times in 1990 (Table 2.2).[10]

In the past more than two decades, in particular the recent decade, the comparison of the comprehensive national strength between China and the United States has fundamentally changed. This forms a strong basis to establish a new type of relationship between these two powers. Although China's comprehensive strength is approaching that of the United States, China is still in the preliminary period of socialism in terms of the level of development, in particular

---

[10] Hu Angang, Zheng Yunfeng, and Gao Yuning. (2015). Evaluation of the Comprehensive National Strength of China and the United States (1990–2013). *Journal of Tsinghua University (Philosophy and Social Sciences)*, Issue 1, pp. 28–41.

Table 2.2 Proportions of Comprehensive National Strength of China and the United States in the World's Total (1990–2013) (Unit: %)

	1990 China	1990 The United States	1990 The United States/China	2010 China	2010 The United States	2010 The United States/China	2013 China	2013 The United States	2013 The United States/China
Economic resources	4.05	21.17	5.23	13.90	17.17	1.24	15.86	16.49	1.04
Human resources	24.49	10.21	0.42	24.82	7.72	0.31	25.18	7.61	0.30
Natural resources	10.55	12.85	1.22	11.14	11.53	1.04	12.07	11.45	0.95
Capital	1.48	26.58	17.96	15.54	21.84	1.41	19.14	22.00	1.15
Knowledge and technology	0.86	39.90	46.40	15.55	21.34	1.37	22.20	22.45	1.01
The Government	0.74	20.54	27.76	8.33	18.26	2.19	10.65	15.14	1.42
The Military	8.20	21.27	2.59	10.97	21.04	1.92	12.56	18.16	1.45
International	1.09	13.48	12.37	8.67	11.20	1.29	10.01	10.98	1.10
Comprehensive	5.64	22.71	4.03	13.84	16.86	1.22	16.57	16.32	0.98

Source: Hu, Zheng, and Gao (2015).

the per capita indicators. China has a long way to go and much to do before she catches up with developed countries such as the United States.

Fundamentally, the development of China and that of the United States are not conflicting with each other, but should be achieved through cooperation for mutual benefit and a win–win situation. The foundation for the cooperation between China and the United States lies in, on the one hand, the immense common benefit that China and the United States are facing for the first time: Globally, the two countries are dedicated to the peace and stability of the world and both expect a favorable environment for peaceful development; regionally, as the two big countries on the two sides of the Pacific Ocean, China and the United States are dedicated to the development and prosperity of the Asia-Pacific region; for the two countries *per se*, the bilateral cooperation between them has brought huge benefits to themselves, which is the biggest motivating force for their cooperation. On the other hand, the foundation for that cooperation lies in the commitment shared by the two countries. Presently, it is impossible for many global issues such as global warming, pervasive terrorism, and the transformation of the global system to be solved by one country single-handedly. Only through the joint cooperative efforts and the spirit of win–win of China and the United States, more efficient solutions may be obtained for these global issues.

In recent years, the China–US relationship shows a trend toward a rebalance. A trend has been seen in which the factors in the economic exchanges of the two countries shift from a one-way flow to a two-way flow, which makes the economies of the two countries more dependent on each other. In the trade relationship, it seems that the absolute value of the trade deficit of the United States with China keeps growing, up to USD 295.3 billion in 2013, but the fact is that, comparing the situation before the financial crisis, the growth rate of that trade deficit has declined notably. The annual average growth rate of the trade deficit was 7.8% from 2009 to 2013, lower than the annual average growth rate of 13.5% from 2004 to 2008, in which the deficit for 2013 increased only by USD 100 million from 2012. From 2009 to 2013, the United States' exports to China increased at a rate of 16.6% annually, obviously higher than the annual export growth rate of 10.5%, and as compared to the data for the years 2004–2008, the difference between the annual average export growth rate and the import growth rate increased to 6.1% from 5.2%. In the past few years, the United States has been continuously climbing up to new levels in exports to China, with a value of USD 115.5 billion in 2010 and USD 160.5 billion in 2013. The abovementioned data clearly show the trend of a rebalance of the trade relationship between the two countries during the two-way flow of the China–US trade. In terms of investment relationship, China's direct investment in the United States has been growing rapidly as it has always been, with USD 8.07 billion of stock assets in the United States in 2013, increased by seven times from the USD 1.1 billion in 2008. For the same period, the United States kept a steady increase in its direct investments in China. The United States' stock assets in China were USD 61.53 billion in 2013, an increase of 14.1% from USD 53.92 billion in 2008. The result is that, although the United States' stock assets remained more than China's in the United States, the gap was narrowed down rapidly, with the proportion from 49:1 for 2008 narrowed down to 7.6:1 for 2013. Moreover, the investments by both parties tend to flow in both directions. In 2012, China for the first time exceeded the United States in investment flow to the opposite country, and the rebalance between the investment relationship between the two countries became quite obvious. Regarding the financial relationship, from the outbreak of the crisis to date, the USD assets held by China have been increasing on the whole, but the pace for consumption has slowed down remarkably, especially in purchasing the national bonds of the United States. The US national bonds held by China accounted for 21.9% in 2013, a decline from 23.6% in 2008, of the total amount of those that China held overseas. Since 2013, the monthly US national bonds held by China fluctuated around USD 1.27 trillion. In addition, the United States is accelerating in purchasing China's financial assets. China's securities assets held by the United States increased to USD 119.3 billion in 2012 from USD 53.2 billion in 2008, with an increase as large as 124%. Therefore, on the whole, although the US national bonds held by

China is still 10 times China's assets held by the United States, the financial relationship between the two countries is developing toward a balance from an imbalance as the investments made by the two countries in financial assets of the opposite side increase at different paces.[11]

In the future, the structure of the economic growth of China and the United States will remain in the process of reaching a rebalance jointly affected by cyclical factors, structural factors, and policy factors. China will become more driven by consumption, while the United States will be more driven by exports and investments, which will reduce China's imbalanced growth pattern that is highly dependent on exports and investments, and the United States' imbalanced growth pattern that is highly dependent on consumption, to develop in a more balanced way. In terms of the trade relationship, China attaches more importance to consumption and to earnestly developing the service industry, which is highly complementary to the United States that is more concerned with exports. This will be focused on the United States' exportation of consumer goods to China and trade in services with China.

For a long time, consumer goods have assumed a small proportion of the United States' exports to China; instead, the United States' exports were previously focused on aircraft, machinery, and minerals that would meet China's demand for further investments and exports, besides agricultural products. With the continuous increase in the aggregate of the domestic consumption and upgrading of the quality of consumption in China, it is hopeful that the United States' exportations of consumer goods will increase greatly. The United States' long-time strict restriction on high-tech exports to China has seriously impeded the development of the trade relationship between the two countries and artificially intensified the imbalance of trade between them. Against this background, the Chinese government has appealed to the American government on many occasions to relax restrictions on its exportation of high-tech products

---

[11] Zhang Jiye. (2014). An Analysis of the Rebalance of the China–US Economic Relationship. *Contemporary International Relations*, Issue 12, pp. 44–51.

to China. Besides, the United States has outstanding strength in the service industry and the exportation of trade in services remains one of its biggest exports to China. In 2013, the value of service exports to China was as high as USD 37.7 billion, accounting for 23.4% of the total value of trade with China in 2013, as compared to 16.9% in 2007. It is very likely that the United States will increase its exports to China substantially. Regarding the investment relationship, China will be less dependent on investment increases, and the investments that overflow from China will seek new targets overseas; in the process of achieving a rebalance of its economy, the United States, to be more driven by investments, will have a bigger demand for attracting overseas investments. Therefore, the two countries are highly complementary. This will be shown mainly in China's investments in the high-tech industry and in the construction of infrastructures in the United States. Presently, China's overseas investments are experiencing a transition period, that is, from investments in the areas of energy and resources to diversified investments. In the future, with the continuous upgrading of China's economy, its overseas investments in the high-tech industry will undoubtedly increase, and the United States, with its advantages in technologies, brands, labor quality, and market scale, will become a major target for investments by Chinese enterprises. Moreover, the infrastructure facilities for transportation, energy, water supply, and so on, that were built in the 1950s in America will enter a period of upgrading in the next 20 years, and the investments in this respect are predicted to be as high as USD 8 trillion. This is a huge attraction for Chinese manufacturers with industrial competing edges and financial strength to invest in the United States.

2.2 *New Opportunities for China–Europe Economic and Trade Cooperation*

In 2004, China and Europe established a comprehensive strategic partnership, boosting increasingly frequent exchanges in trade and expanding the areas for cooperation between the two parties. The EU became China's no. 1 trading partner, while China remains the EU's no. 2 trading partner. The value of China–EU trade has transcended that of China–Japan and China–US trade, and the China–EU trade relationship has become the most important bilateral trade relationship. Currently, Germany, the Netherlands, the United Kingdom, France, and Italy are China's first five trading partners, and the investment from the United Kingdom, Germany, France, and the Netherlands are ranked the first four in the EU's investments in China. The value of the trade between China and the EU has broken the historical record. Obviously, China and the EU are developing their bilateral economic and trade cooperation in more areas and advancing toward all-round cooperation.

The trade between China and the EU had been growing between 2004 and 2007, and reached its summit in 2008. The China–EU trade slid in 2009 as it was struck by the global financial tsunami in 2008. It restored its growth and reached a value as high as USD 729.9 billion in 2013. From 2009 to 2013, the trade between the two parties increased by 71%, causing the EU to remain China's no. 1 trading partner. Since 2008, the value of China–EU trade has accounted for 19% of China's total import and export value on average, while the value of China–US trade has accounted for 13% of China's total import and export value on average, with a difference of 6 percentage points between the two.[12]

After reviewing the history of communication between China and Europe, the two sides share a dream that "China will develop westward and Europe eastward, to be connected to the Eurasian corridor." For China, the silk road means prosperity, stability, civilization, and advancement. The New Silk Road initiative brings China and the EU for the establishment of a comprehensive initiative partnership, accelerating the expansion of international and regional economic cooperation, and establishing and pushing forward the New Silk Road Initiative with the joint efforts by both. The connection between the land traffic in Eurasia is not only helpful in raising the China–EU trade to a new level from where it is now, but it may also

---

[12] National Bureau of Statistics, The Grand Blueprint of the Eurasian Land Corridor. Retrieved from http://finance.china.com.cn/news/20180831/4748207.shtml.

facilitate the regional cooperation among the countries along the Silk Road Economic Belt; the new silk road is the road toward the rejuvenation of the long-established civilizations of China and Europe. The New Silk Road initiative conforms to the common interests of China, Europe, and the countries along the belt.

In the latter half of the 20th century, the China–EU relationship went through three stages: the China–EU relationship led by ideology (from the 1950s to the 1970s), the China–EU relationship under comprehensive development (from the mid-1970s to the end of the 1980s), and the China–EU relationship toward a "comprehensive cooperative partnership" (from the early 1990s onward). It is a general trend for both sides to carry out institutionalized collaborative cooperation on a wide scope and at a higher level that is above pure economic trade.[13] On April 2, 1998, the leaders of China and the United Kingdom, including British Prime Minister Tony Blair, then Chairperson on duty of the EU; Jacques Santer, President of the European Commission; and Premier Zhu Rongji of China met in London and explicitly showed, in the *China–EU Summit Joint Statement*, that both sides would be jointly devoted to building "a constructive partnership that would be able to face the 21st century with long-term stability." In October 2003, the EU clearly defined the China–EU relationship as a "strategic partnership" in its *Towards a Mature Partnership: Common Benefits and Challenges in the EU–China Relationship*, indicating that the EU had acquired a better understanding of the importance of the China–EU relationship. In September 2012, Herman Van Rompuy, President of the Council of Europe, and Jose Barroso, President of the EU Commission, pointed out that "The China–EU relationship is strong and continuously expanding. The EU and China are two of the three largest economies in the world. We are important trading partners to each other. The EU is China's largest trading partner, while China is the EU's second largest trading partner with the fastest growth. China's trade with the

---

[13] Huan Qingzhi, Gai Yuqiang. (2012). The China–EU Comprehensive Cooperative Partnership against the Background of Globalization. *Journal of Shandong University*, Issue 4, pp. 114–120.

EU makes up 1/10 of the world's total. We will be in a close relationship in the future. Despite various challenges, we are certain that our cooperation will greatly facilitate our success."[14]

The China–EU relationship has become one of the most important international relations in today's world. It is also a strategic relationship and a cooperative one. Regarding the former, the China–EU relationship affects the whole world, for its total population and the GDP of the world's largest developing country and the largest group of developed countries account for 1/4 and 1/3 of the world's total, respectively, and the two economies serve as important poles in the world; for the latter, China and the EU are highly complementary for further development, such as China's "12th Five-Year Plan" and the EU's "2020 Strategy"; thus, the cooperation between the two sides could still be win–win for mutual benefits (far beyond the combination of "Europe's design" and "Made in China"). The statistics prepared by the Secretariat of the World Trade Organization show that, in 2013, the value of China's exports was USD 2.21 trillion, the value of its imports was USD 1.95 trillion, and the total value of its imports and exports was USD 4.16 trillion (equivalent to RMB 25.83 trillion), having become the world's no. 1 trader of goods. The *Trans-Pacific Strategic Economic Partnership Agreement* led by the United States excludes China intentionally. While continuing to hold an open attitude toward the *Trans-Pacific Strategic Economic Partnership Agreement*, China proposed the New Silk Road Initiative to push forward the international and regional economic cooperation between Asia and Europe, which is not only a wise decision for breaking through the United States' policy of "pivot to the Asia-Pacific," but also an inevitable approach for China to realize the transformation from a trading giant to a trading power and push forward the strategy of all-round reform and opening-up. The New Silk Road Initiative's significance to Europe is not limited to economy alone. After the two world wars, the role of Europe as the overlord of the world's economy was replaced by the United States and declined to be a foil to the

---

[14] European Council, Press Statement by Herman Van Rompuy and Jose Manuel Barroso Following the 15th EU–China Summit (Brussels: EUCO 172/2, 2012).

prosperity of the United States for quite a period. Therefore, it is only possible for Europe to revitalize its economy and restore its glories by exploring its own road to revitalization and viewing and advancing the cooperation with China at a strategic height. Comparing to maritime transportation, passenger transportation on land will be replaced by air transportation due to a smaller quantity and a higher cost, leading to the slow development of trade through the Eurasian Bridge for a long time. This situation of international transportation, however, has been changing with the development of high-speed railway technologies. The speed and load featured by the high-speed railway break the bottleneck for the development of land transportation, and its competing edges are becoming increasingly notable in international transportation. The high-speed railway imposes the replacement effect on air transportation in terms of medium- and short-distance passenger and freight transportation, and has a complementary effect on maritime transportation in long-distance freight transportation. Moreover, Eurasia is home to most of the world's inland countries. The five Central Asian countries at the center of Eurasia are more dependent on land transportation than other countries, and the East European countries, which are distant from the Atlantic Ocean, also wish for a land transportation route from the Middle East to the Far East. Therefore, the new Silk Road Economic Belt between China and Europe has an immense potential demand for high-speed railway transportation. When observed from a comprehensive perspective of economy, history, culture, geopolitics, and global structure, the New Silk Road Initiative responds to the trend of China's and Europe's economies and to that of the development of their trade and conforms to the fundamental interest of both sides; the New Silk Road Initiative is China's national strategy for it to be engaged in developing trade with the other countries in Asia and with European countries, which fully shows that China is concerned with elevating the comprehensive strategic partnership between China and the EU to a higher level of cooperation. The high-speed railway will greatly improve the efficiency of the flow of people and property and materials; it will reduce the cost for resource allocation, and will definitely lead to a new investment upsurge and drive economic development. In addition, the trans-Eurasia high-speed railway will launch a new mode of carrying out China's foreign investment and cooperation. Stretching the high-speed railway overseas displays China's wish to share its achievements in high-speed railways and cooperate with other countries, which is helpful for China in expanding new areas for foreign investment and boosting in-depth cooperation between China and the countries through which the high-speed railway runs.[15]

The status quo of the development of trade between China and the EU. The EU and China are important economies in the world; thus, the economic and trade relationship is the foundation for the China–EU relationship. Since 2004, the EU has been China's largest trading partner. The EU has been China's no. 1 export destination since 2007, and China has become the EU's no. 2 trading partner. After China joined the WTO, the value of imports and exports between China and the EU from 2001 to 2008 grew at an average annual rate of 25%, from USD 76.6 billion in 2001 to USD 425.6 billion in 2008. Subsequently, the value of China–EU trade underwent a slight year-on-year decline in 2009 and 2012 mainly due to the impact of the financial crisis. In 2012, the total value of China's imports from and exports to the EU was USD 546 billion, of which the value of exports was USD 334 billion, a decrease of 6% from the previous year, and the value of imports was USD 212 billion, a decrease of 0.4% from the previous year (Table 2.3).

The economic and trade cooperation between China and the EU has developed rapidly toward reaching a balance after being actively pushed forward by both sides. The EU has remained China's no. 1 trading partner for 10 years straight. The value of China–EU trade for 2014 was USD 615.1 billion, accounting for 14.3% of the total of China's import and export value for the same period and with a year-on-year increase of 9.9%, the highest in the past three years. Through visits between the high-level leaders of China and the EU and the

---

[15] Huang Weiping. (2015). The New Silk Road Economic Belt, the New Development of the China–EU Economic and Trade Structure, and the Strategic Values of the Trans-Eurasian High-speed Railway. *China Business and Market*, Issue 1, pp. 84–90.

Table 2.3   China's Imports and Exports to the EU During the Period 2001–2013 (Unit: USD 100 Million, %)

Year	Balance of Trade	Imports	Increase/ Decrease from the Previous Year	Exports	Increase/ Decrease from the Previous Year	Imports and Exports	Increase/ Decrease from the Previous Year
2001	52	409	7	357	16	766	11
2002	97	482	18	385	8	868	13
2003	191	722	50	531	38	1,252	44
2004	370	1,072	37	701	29	1,773	33
2005	701	1,437	34	736	5	2,173	23
2006	917	1,820	27	903	23	2,723	25
2007	1,342	2,452	29	1,110	22	3,562	27
2008	1,602	2,929	20	1,327	20	4,256	20
2009	1,085	2,363	−19	1,278	−4	3,640	−14
2010	1,428	3,112	32	1,685	32	4,797	32
2011	1,448	3,560	14	2,112	25	5,672	18
2012	1,219	3,340	−6	2,120	0.4	5,460	−4
2013	1,189	3,390	1.5	2,201	3.8	5,591	2.4

Source: Ministry of Commerce of the People's Republic of China.

work done by the China–EU Economic and Trade Joint (Mixed) Committee, the China–EU cooperation on finance, energy, vessels, and ecological parks has been broadened, and more efforts are being made in negotiations on investment agreements between China and the EU. The nonfinancial direct investments made by Chinese enterprises in Europe are also "rocketing" as high as USD 9.848 billion. This historical record is 1.44 times the EU's investment in China, an increase of 117.7%, the fastest growth rate in the last five years.[16]

It is worth noting that, since 2012, there have been more frictions in the trade between Europe and China. A substantial decrease in demand from Europe due to its economic downturn, a relative rise in labor costs in China, and the rise in the value of the RMB as

---

[16] Ministry of Commerce. New Progress in Economic Diplomacy Carried out by the Ministry of Commerce in 2014 (February 6, 2015). Retrieved from http://www.mofcom.gov.cn/article/i/dxfw/gzzd/201502/20150200890104.shtml.

compared to the euro are the main reasons for the stagnation of China's exports to Europe, and the difficulties in the trade between China and the EU have been intensified by the rise of trade protectionism. Against the background of further development of the world's multipolarization and economic globalization, the China–EU relationship has become one of the most important bilateral relationships in the world. It is not only consistent with the fundamental interests of China and of Europe to further expand and deepen the comprehensive strategic partnership between China and the EU, but it is also helpful to maintain peace, stability, and development of the world. China should further strengthen its cooperation with the EU in high-tech and emerging industries, explore new growing points for trade, enhance the construction of the platform for high-tech cooperation between China and the EU, and participate in the EU framework plan by integrating its domestic advantageous resources in an organized way.

Bai Ming, Deputy Director of the Department of International Markets of the Ministry of Commerce, remarked that the Belt and Road Initiative will facilitate not only China's opening-up westward, but also the EU's opening-up eastward, which is an ideal arrangement for mutual benefit and a win–win situation in a true sense. By virtue of the Belt and Road Initiative, Europe may have more commercial opportunities in Asian countries, and the initiative may help the EU to expand the scope of its resources and customer allocations. Currently, the drive for economic growth is not strong enough within Europe, and the game on financial retrenchment within the eurozone is becoming more intensified. Zhu Dan, Chairman of the Human Resources Association of EUCCC, believed that, "Suffering various problems with the economic development of Europe, all parts of Europe pay more attention to the policy dividend to be created by the Belt and Road Initiative." On the one hand, China and Europe are highly complementary in economic structure. The strong points of European enterprises are products and technologies, while China's advantages lie in human resources and the broad market, thus providing a solid foundation and space for the development of the two countries to enlarge their economic and trade cooperation. On the other hand, the Belt and Road Initiative provides more convenient conditions for Chinese enterprises to "go global." Because of the economic downturn in Europe, European enterprises are more eager to accept investments from China. Obviously, the Belt and Road Initiative is beneficial at home and abroad: It is a plan for China's external development in the ASEAN community, Central Asia, Southern Asia, and Europe, and also an internal strategy with an immense scale, covering heavy tasks such as boosting domestic investments, shoring up China's economy, and improving the weak points in the development of the western areas of China.[17]

2.3 *The BRICS Countries, China and the ASEAN Community, and the SCO*

2.3.1 *The Economy and Trade of the BRICS Countries*

In 2001, Goldman Sachs, based in the United States, proposed the concept of BRIC for the first time, including the four emerging countries: China, India, Brazil, and Russia. In October 2003, Goldman Sachs published the global economic report entitled "Dream with the BRIC." It is estimated in the report that, by 2050, the world economic structure will undergo a drastic shuffling of the cards, and the six largest economies will be China, the United States, India, Japan, Brazil, and Russia. In June 2009, the leaders of the BRIC countries met for the first time at the summit meeting held in Russia and published the *Joint Statement of the BRIC Leaders Meeting in Yekaterinburg, Russia*. In April 2010, the second BRIC summit meeting was held in Brazil. After the meeting, the leaders of the four countries published a *Joint Statement* to express their views and standing points on issues such as the world's economic situation, and decided to push forward the implementation of the measures for cooperation and coordination among the BRIC countries. By then, the BRIC cooperation mechanism had been basically shaped. In November 2010, the G20 Summit

---

[17] The Belt and Road Will Become the New Starting Point for the Relationship between the Two Poles of Eurasia. (February 12, 2015). *Xinhuanet*. Retrieved from http://www.xinhuanet.com/world/2015-01/15/c_127387966_2.htm.

was held in Seoul, where South Africa submitted its application for joining the BRIC countries. In December 2010, China, as Chairman on duty for the BRIC cooperation mechanism, negotiated with Russia, India, and Brazil and decided to take in South Africa as an official member of the BRIC cooperation mechanism, thus to transform BRIC to BRICS that includes five countries. China held the third leaders' meeting in Sanya, China in April 2011, published the *Sanya Statement*, and started the domestic currency settlement for trade for the first time. Strengthening the cooperation on finance became an important result of the BRICS leaders' meeting this time. In the presence of the leaders of the five countries, the *Agreement on a Framework of Financial Cooperation for a Mechanism of Cooperation for BRICS Banks* was officially signed. On March 28 and 29, 2012, the fourth meeting of the BRICS leaders was held in New Delhi, the capital of India. After the meeting, the *New Delhi Declaration* and the action plan were published. This meeting, on the one hand, greatly pushed forward practical cooperation among the BRICS countries and reinforced the characteristic of the mechanism for BRICS cooperation of maintaining the benefit of emerging and developing countries, and on the other hand, the active participation in global economic governance further explored the areas for cooperation among the BRICS countries. In the presence of the leaders attending the meeting, the development banks of China, Brazil, Russia, India, and South Africa jointly signed the *General Agreement of Credit Extension for Multilateral Domestic Currencies for the BRICS Bank Cooperation Mechanism* and the *Service Agreement of Multilateral Confirmation of L/C.*

BRICS cooperation is an objective demand for developing international relations. The development of BRICS will multipolarize the growth point of the world's economy and become a natural drive for the democratization of international economic relations. The BRICS countries share the same concern for and appeal to reforming and improving global economic governance. It is a general trend to strengthen coordination and cooperation. Besides, it has been a new characteristic of international relations since the outset of the 21st century. To establish the BRICS Development Bank, a consensus was reached at the fourth meeting of the BRICS leaders in 2013. The financial ministries of BRICS officially kicked off the negotiations over establishing the BRICS Development Bank in August 2013. There were altogether seven rounds of negotiations. The agreement reached on July 16, 2014 mainly includes the following: The objective of the bank is to support the BRICS countries and other emerging markets and developing countries in the construction of infrastructures and sustainable development; the assessing capital of the bank is USD 100 billion, and the preliminary capital for subscription is USD 50 billion that is to be averagely shared among the BRICS countries; the founding members of the bank are the five BRICS countries, and the bank will take in new members after it has been established. The BRICS countries also signed the *Agreement on the Arrangement of Emergency Stock for BRICS*, specifying that the swapping scale for the BRICS emergency stock should be USD 100 billion.

On April 15, 2015, the countries that applied to join the Asian Infrastructure Investment Bank (AIIB), including South Africa, completed the procedure of seeking advice from multisides, and became an original member of intention of the AIIB. By then, the BRICS members, including Brazil, Russia, India, and South Africa, had all been listed as members of intention of the AIIB, which meant that all BRICS countries had become the original members of intention of AIIB.

After entering the 21st century, the economy of the BRICS countries has grown faster, which has laid the financial basis for the countries to carry out cooperation. During the 10 years from 1999 to 2008, the annual growth rate of the economies of the BRIC countries (Brazil, Russia, India, and China) was 3.33%, 6.99%, 7.22%, and 9.75%, respectively, much higher than the world's average of 3.07% and 2.58% for the United States.[18] In 2011, the GDP of the BRICS totaled USD 11.43 trillion based on the annual average exchange rate, accounting for 18.2% of the world's total, of which China was ranked no. 2 in the

---

[18] Chen Fengying. (2011). Recent Economic Situation and Policy Coordination of the BRICS. *The Contemporary World*, Issue 5, pp. 28–30.

world, accounting for 9.3% of the world's total; Brazil no. 7, accounting for 3.3%; India no. 9, accounting for 2.6%; Russia no. 11, accounting for 2.4%; and South Africa no. 28, accounting for 0.6%. According to the Total Economy Database (TED) published in January 2012, the GDP of the BRICS countries totaled USD 22.352244 trillion for 2011, an increase of 7.58% from the previous year. In 2013, the total GDP of the BRICS countries accounted for 28% of the world's total, while it only accounted for 8% in 2001. With the economic development of the BRICS countries, the bottleneck in the depth and breadth of their external financial cooperation is becoming conspicuous and gradually becoming an obstacle for the five countries to raising their position in the world. Economic growth lays a solid foundation for each country and makes it a necessary choice to carry out financial cooperation. In addition, the population of the BRICS countries accounts for 42% of the world's total (3 billion) and their GDP accounts for 28% of the world's total (USD 16 trillion). From 2000 to 2007, for Morgan Stanley Capital International, the market index of emerging markets, with the BRICS as the major ones, increased by 270%, while that for developed markets was only 12%. According to the report published by the Boao Forum, the world's economy grew by 3% in 2013, that of developed economies by 1.3%, that of emerging markets and developing economies by 4.7%, and that of the BRICS countries by 5.7%, of which China's economy grew by 7.7%, Brazil's by 2.3%, Russia's by 1.5%, India's by 4.4%, and South Africa's by 1.8%. According to the *2013 OECD Report*, the total GDP of China and India for 2025 will exceed the total of the OECD. The accumulation of this economic hard strength is the basis for the BRICS countries to realize institutional innovation and a breakthrough in their soft strength.[19]

In the early part of 2013, the BRICS's total assets of foreign exchange reserve account for 75% of the world's total, of which

---

[19] Guo Shuyong, Shi Mingtao. (2015). The Possibility of Building New-Type International Relations: To View the Change to World Order from the BRICS Development Bank and Emergency Reserve Arrangement. *International Review*, Issue 2, pp. 15–29.

China's foreign exchange reserve accounts for 30% and that of Russia and India is also huge. Statistics show that, presently, the total of foreign exchange reserves of the BRICS countries has reached USD 4.4 trillion, about six times the funds in the IMF. Therefore, it is an aspect of importance to the world's economy.

Trade between China and the other BRICS countries. From 1999 to 2009, the total value of trade between China and India increased from USD 1.981 billion to USD 51.94 billion, with a trade surplus of USD 19.07 billion in 2009; the total value of trade between China and South Africa increased from USD 1.717 billion to USD 19.249 billion, with a trade deficit of USD 1.611 billion in 2009; the total value of trade between China and Russia increased from USD 5.703 billion to USD 46.395 billion, with a trade deficit of USD 4.447 billion in 2009; the total value of trade between China and Brazil increased from USD 1.85 billion to USD 35.413 billion, with a trade surplus of USD 11.827 billion in 2009. China's exports to the other four BRICS countries focus on labor-intensive products such as textiles, garments and shoes, and suitcases and bags. The exports from the other four countries to China focus on resource-intensive products such as raw materials, steel, and minerals.

In foreign trade, the BRICS countries have developed much faster than developed countries. In the early part of the 1990s, the total value of imports and exports of the G7 countries was 8.5 times and 9.7 times those of the BRICS's total, respectively, while the total value of imports and exports of the G7 were 2.0 times and 2.5 times the BRICS's total, respectively, showing a remarkable narrowing down of the difference between the two. Meanwhile, the total value of imports and exports of the G7 countries account for 32.22% and 36.56%, respectively, of the world's total in 2010, a decrease from 47.25% and 46.73% in 1992; the total value of imports and exports of the BRICS countries accounted for 16.39% and 14.89%, respectively, of the world's total in 2010, an increase from 5.5% and 4.8% in 1992. In 2012, the value of exports of the BRICS countries increased to USD 3.2 trillion, accounting for 17% of the world's total value of exports, from USD 494 billion in 2001; the import value of the BRICS countries increased to USD 2.8 trillion from USD 417 billion in 2001.

China is the largest trader among the BRICS countries, accounting for 62.5% of the total value of trade of the BRICS countries.[20] Statistics show that the total value of trade of the BRICS countries accounts for around 17% of the world's total, and 11% of the world's outward foreign direct investment (OFDI) flows to the BRICS.

As a representative of emerging economies, the BRICS countries, that is, Brazil, Russia, India, China, and South Africa, play an outstanding role in global investment, but their mutual investments are small and unbalanced. In 2013, the foreign direct investment (FDI) flow to the BRICS reached USD 322 billion, an increase of 21% from 2012, accounting for 22% of the global FDI flow. The BRICS OFDI also increased to USD 145 billion in 2012, accounting for 10% of the global FDI flow, from USD 7 billion in 2000. However, the mutual investments among the BRICS countries are rather limited. The two-way investments between China and the other BRICS countries have lagged behind. They are not major investment partners to each other, and the potential for cooperation has not been fully released. In the recent decade, the general two-way investment between China and the other BRICS countries has been small in scale and has featured a remarkable fluctuation. From 2004 to 2013, China realized a total investment of USD 12.056 billion in the other BRICS countries, accounting for 2.35% of China's OFDI for the same period. In view of the other four BRICS countries' investment in China, their accumulated actual investment in China was USD 2.05 billion from 2004 to 2013, only accounting for 0.23% of the total FDI that China took in for the same period. In 2013, the investments made by Chinese enterprises in the other BRICS countries totaled USD 1.39 billion, while their actual investments in China were only USD 85 million. The investments made by Chinese enterprises in the other BRICS countries were 16.4 times the latter's investments in China.[21]

---

[20] Ministry of Commerce of the People's Republic of China. (March 31, 2013). *China and other BRICS countries jointly seek trade growth with Africa*. Retrieved from http://www.mofcom.gov.cn/article/i/dxfw/gzzd/201303/20130300073139.shtml.

[21] Li Jihong. (2015). Characteristics and Problem Analysis of Two-way Investment between China and the Other BRICS Countries. *Practice in Foreign Economic Relations and Trade*, Issue 4, pp. 22–26.

Currently, the areas of China's investments in the other BRICS countries focus on energy, mining, communication services, and engineering machinery, and the investments are spreading to other areas such as automobiles, home appliances, agricultural products, finance, garments, and building materials. For each country, China has different focus. China's investments in Brazil are expanding from traditional areas such as energy, mining, and agriculture to communications, finance, and infrastructure. China's investments in Russia mainly focus on agriculture, forestry, husbandry, fishery, leasing and business service industry, mining, manufacturing, and real estate. China's investments in India mainly focus on infrastructure, power supply, and communication services. China's investments in South Africa are moving from early projects such as textiles, garments, and light industry to finance, energy, mining, manufacturing, architecture, and agriculture. Likewise, the other four BRICS countries have their own investment focus in China. Brazil's investments in China focus on trade, trade consultancy, procurement, and sale. Russia's investments in China focus on manufacturing, architecture, and transportation and traffic. India's investments in China focus on the IT service industry and have the trend of developing toward the two ends of knowledge-intensive industries and low-tech labor-intensive manufacturing. South Africa's investments in China are moving from areas such as light textiles, beverages, and building materials to projects requiring higher technologies within the scope of manufacturing.

China and the other BRICS countries share the same extensive benefits and basis for cooperation in establishing the world's new order of politics and economy. From June 2009 to July 2014, the BRICS leaders held six summit meetings, during which they reached an extensive consensus on finance, trade, and investments. China should make full use of the BRICS cooperation mechanism and multilateral cooperation mechanisms such as the G20 summit meetings and the China–Russia–India cooperation mechanism, in order to strengthen cooperation and coordination with the other BRICS countries in multilateral areas. In terms of bilateral areas, President Xi Jinping visited India in September 2014 and Premier Li Keqiang visited Russia in October of the same year, and those visits have enhanced the understanding and trust between China and the other BRICS countries and they have achieved fruitful results. China should be more active and proactive in strengthening the bilateral cooperation and dialogues with the other BRICS countries in politics, economy, and people-to-people exchanges; deepen mutual trust and advance cooperation; and realize inclusive growth in sustainable development, in an attempt to eliminate some of the BRICS countries' anxieties about the rise of China. Against the background of global economic integration and regional economic integration, China and the other BRICS countries should also accelerate their studies on establishing bilateral or multilateral FTAs, with the purpose of driving the investment growth of each side forward by exerting the active effect of the FTAs.

2.3.2 *Trade between China and the ASEAN community*

The ASEAN includes Indonesia, Malaysia, the Philippines, Singapore, Thailand, Brunei, Vietnam, Laos, Myanmar, and Cambodia. The precursor of the ASEAN community was the Association of Southeast Asia established by Malaya (now Malaysia), the Philippines, and Thailand in Bangkok on July 31, 1961. On the 7th and 8th of August, 1967, the ministers of foreign affairs of Indonesia, Thailand, Singapore, and the Philippines and the Deputy Prime Minister of Malaysia held a meeting in Bangkok and published the *Bangkok Declaration* (or, *The Declaration of Establishing the Association of Southeast Asian Nations*), an official announcement of the establishment of the ASEAN. This organization covers the whole region of Southeast Asia, forming a 10-country group with a total population of 500 million and a total area of 4.5 million square meters. Papua New Guinea is an observer state. The 10 dialogue states of ASEAN are as follows: Australia, Canada, China, the EU, India, Japan, New Zealand, Russia, South Korea, and the United States. The objective and goal of the ASEAN community is to boost the economic growth, social advancement, and cultural development of the region with concerted efforts, in a spirit of fairness and cooperation; to lay a foundation for establishing a prosperous and peaceful community of countries in Southeast Asia; and to push forward peace in and the stability of the region.

In the early part of the 1990s, the ASEAN group initiated a process of regional cooperation in Eastern Asia, developing a series of regional cooperation mechanisms with ASEAN as the center. The ASEAN community and China, Japan, and South Korea (10+3), and the ASEAN group and China (10+1) cooperation mechanisms have been developed into the major channels for cooperation in Eastern Asia. Besides, the ASEAN community has also developed dialogue partnerships with the United States, Japan, Australia, New Zealand, Canada, South Korea, China, Russia, India, and the EU. The ASEAN FTA was officially launched on January 1, 2002. The goals of the FTA are as follows: to push ASEAN to be a competitive base to attract foreign investments; to eliminate the tariff and nontariff obstacles between member nations and make regional trade freer; to enlarge the scope of trade for the mutual benefit among member nations and boost the trade within the region; and to establish an internal market. On August 15, 2009, China and the ASEAN community signed the *Investment Agreement* for the China-ASEAN FTA, signaling the completion of the main negotiations for the China-ASEAN FTA; the China-ASEAN FTA is the first FTA over which China negotiated with foreign businesses and also the first FTA over which the ASEAN group as a whole negotiated with foreign businesses. This is an FTA made up of developing countries with a total population of 1.9 billion, with a total GDP of nearly USD 6 trillion, and a total trade value of USD 4.5 trillion.

In September 2013, President Xi Jinping paid state visits to Turkmenistan, Kazakhstan, Uzbekistan, and Kyrgyzstan, and proposed the building of the Silk Road Economic Belt jointly. On October 3, 2013, President Xi delivered the speech entitled "Jointly Building the China-ASEAN Community with a Common Destiny" at the Congress of Indonesia, expressing that "China is willing to strengthen maritime cooperation with the ASEAN, make good use of the China-ASEAN maritime cooperation fund set up by China, develop good maritime cooperative partnerships, and jointly build the 21st Century Maritime Silk Road." He stressed that "China will stay firmly committed to the path of peaceful development, the policies of peaceful diplomacy with independent sovereignty, and the strategy of opening up for mutual benefit and a win–win situation." He sincerely hoped "to explore the bright future of the China-ASEAN community with a common destiny, and make bigger contributions to the noble cause of world peace and development." From October 24 to 25, 2013, at the Peripheral Diplomacy Symposium, Xi Jinping emphasized that doing a good job in peripheral diplomacy is necessary for achieving the goal of "two one-hundred years" and the Chinese Dream of realizing the great rejuvenation of the Chinese nation. He stressed that the basic guideline for China's peripheral diplomacy is to stick to the philosophy of making friends and partners with the neighbors, living harmoniously with the neighbors and providing them with security and wealth, highlighting the idea of relationship, sincerity, benefit, and inclusiveness. The Maritime Silk Road will become the artery and bridge for China's peripheral diplomacy. China is actively pushing forward the Maritime Silk Road Initiative.[22] The Third Plenary Session of the 18th Central Committee of the CPC, the Central Economic Working Conference after that, and the 2014 Work Report of the Government all recognized the construction of the Maritime Silk Road as an important part of China's peaceful developmental strategy.

The China-ASEAN economic and trade relationship has developed rapidly, particularly since China officially proposed the conception of organizing the China-ASEAN FTA (CAFTA) in November 2001; agreed to reduce and exempt tariffs; and signed the *Comprehensive Economic Cooperation Framework Agreement* the following year. The trade volume has increased rapidly between China and the ASEAN community since the two sides announced the establishment of "the strategic partnership facing peace and prosperity" in 2003. In 2002, the total bilateral trade value realized between China and the ASEAN community was USD 54.767 billion in 2002, while as of 2012, the total bilateral trade value had reached USD 400.093

---

[22] Gao Lan. (October 31, 2013). Maritime Silk Road: Artery and Bridge for Peripheral Diplomacy. *Wenhui Daily*. Retrieved from http://wenhui.news365.com.cn.

billion. The annual average growth rate reached 22% and the value of trade was 7.3 times that of 2002. In 2013, the total value of bilateral trade between China and the ASEAN community continued to grow at a high rate. The total amount of imports and exports between China and the ASEAN community was USD 443.61 billion, a year-on-year increase of 10.9%, 3.3 percentage points higher than the national growth rate of foreign trade. The growth rate is high among China's major trading partners. Currently, China is the ASEAN community's no. 1 trading partner, while ASEAN is China's no. 3 trading partner, its no. 4 export market, and its no. 2 source of imports (Table 2.4).

After the launch of the CAFTA, China's importation of agriculture-intensive and energy-intensive products has been declining from the ASEAN community, while the importation of capital-intensive products is on the increase; the share of primary commodities has continuously declined, while the bilateral trade of high-tech products such as integrated circuits, cell phones and spare parts, computers, and their spare parts is on the increase. The bilateral trade is changing from traditional inter-industry trade to trade within industries; there has been a remarkable progress in the labor division within the industries of both sides, and the labor division within the industries in the region is becoming more detailed.

With respect to trade in services, China is opening up the 26 sectors under five service departments of building, environmental protection, transportation, sports, and commerce to the markets of ASEAN countries, and the ASEAN community is opening up the industries of finance, telecommunications, education, tourism, building, and medical care to China's market. The total value of bilateral trade in services for China and ASEAN increased to USD 26.8 billion in 2010 from USD 12.6 billion in 2006. Those five years witnessed a growth rate of 113% and the bilateral trade in services doubled. As of 2012, the total value of trade in services for China and the ASEAN community had reached USD 31.7 billion. This achievement has made China the ASEAN community's fourth largest trading partner country, and the ASEAN community leaped to become China's no. 4 trade in services partner. In recent years, the areas that have gained a

Table 2.4 China-ASEAN Trade and Investment Development (2002–2012) (Unit: USD 100 Million)

	2002	2003	2004	2005	2006	2007	2008	2009	2010	2011	2012
Total value of trade	547.67	782.55	1,058.8	1,303.7	1,608.4	2,025.08	2,311	2,130.1	2,927.8	3,628.5	4,000.9
China's investment in ASEAN	0.81	1.89	2.26	1.58	3.36	9.68	24.84	26.98	44.04	59.05	61.00
ASEAN's investment in China	32.6	29.3	30.4	31.1	33.5	43.9	54.6	46.8	63.2	70.0	70.7

Source: China Statistical Yearbook.

rapid increase in trade in services between China and the ASEAN community include direct investments in various service industries, international engineering outsourcing, and international labor cooperation. The ASEAN countries also make full use of their advantages to strengthen international cooperation with China in transportation and traffic, tourism, air transportation, and building engineering. ASEAN's cooperation with China in areas such as sea transportation, financial services, and building engineering services has become an important component of China's service imports; in areas such as investments in the service industry, engineering outsourcing, and labor cooperation; the ASEAN community has become an important export destination for China's trade in services. In November 2011, China and the ASEAN countries signed the *Agreement on the Second Lot of Detailed Commitments to Implementing the China-ASEAN FTA (Trade in Services Agreement)*, which would make trade in services freer.

Regarding investments, the FTA has effectively boosted the development of direct investments within the area. China and the ASEAN countries mutually provide each side's investors with citizen treatment and most-favored-nation treatment. With greatly accelerated development in trade in goods and services, the two-way investment of both sides is on the fast-track of growth. At the end of 2002, the two-way investment between China and the ASEAN countries totaled USD 30.1 billion. For over a decade of growth and high-quality development, the two-way investment between China and the ASEAN countries increased by over USD 70 billion, with a total of USD 100.7 billion, of which the ASEAN's investments in China reached USD 77.1 billion in aggregate, and China's investments in the ASEAN community reached USD 23.6 billion in aggregate. Of the two-way investment valued at USD 11.489 billion between China and the ASEAN community in 2012, China's proportion was increased to 38.5%. In terms of investment areas, China's FDI in ASEAN countries focuses on business services, retail and wholesale, power engineering, industrial manufacturing, financial services and support, and metallurgy and mining, while the ASEAN's large amount of investments in China focuses on real estate, manufacturing, and transportation and traffic. The two sides are negotiating over projects in various fields, including the construction of infrastructures, agricultural industrialization, processing manufacturing, restaurants and tourism, and business services, or they are building a series of large cooperative projects with an unprecedented total investment. Presently, China has become the no. 4 foreign investment source for the ASEAN community, and the ASEAN community has become China's no. 3 source.[23] The signing of the *Investment Agreement* has effectively facilitated the direct investments made by China in ASEAN's infrastructure facilities, and Chinese enterprises are paying more attention to the ASEAN group. Bilateral investment cooperation has achieved remarkable results.

Singapore is an ASEAN country that invests the most in China and attracts most of the Chinese investments. As of the end of 2012, the first three countries that had made the most direct investments in China were Singapore, Malaysia, and Thailand; the first three countries in which China had invested the most were Singapore, Cambodia, and Laos, from no. 1 to no. 3 respectively; the first three countries in which China had increased its investments the fastest were Vietnam, Cambodia, and Laos. This shows that China communicates very closely with only five countries of the ASEAN community, while the other five countries carry out very little trade with China. In terms of industrial layout, in recent years, with the more accelerated OFDI made by China, China's direct investments made in the construction of infrastructures in ASEAN member countries have grown remarkably. Even so, China is still lagging behind in investments in those competitive entity industries in ASEAN countries. For example, the mining, automobile, and textile industries of Indonesia are developed, but it is obvious that Chinese enterprises lack investments and cooperation in these areas. The investments and participation in entity industries are an important area for future investment and cooperation to be made by China and ASEAN member states.[24]

---

[23] Yu Miao. (2014). An Analysis of Challenges and Countermeasures for China-ASEAN Economic Integration. *Journal of Chifeng College*, Issue 10, pp. 11–13.
[24] Lin Lin, Wang Xin. (2015). A Study of China-ASEAN Trade and Investment Cooperation Development, *Dongyue Tribune*, Issue 1, pp. 149–152.

Since the reform and opening-up, the economic and trade cooperation between China and the countries along the Maritime Silk
Road[25] has grown on an increasingly large scale. In 2012, the total
value of trade between China and the countries along the Maritime
Silk Road was USD 690 billion, accounting for 17.9% of China's total
overseas trade; the nonfinancial direct investments made by Chinese
enterprises in the countries involved in the silk road were USD 5.7
billion, accounting for 7.4% of foreign investments made by Chinese
enterprises; the turnover of engineering outsourcing undertaken by
Chinese enterprises along the silk road was USD 42.2 billion,
accounting for 37.9% of the total turnover of engineering outsourcing undertaken by Chinese enterprises overseas.[26] The three groups of
data are much larger than those produced from the Silk Road
Economic Belt. Therefore, unlike the China-ASEAN (10+1) FTA,
the Maritime Silk Road will create substantial growth in trade in
goods and services as well as investments from the two sides once it
is launched, which may be taken as an "upgraded version" of the
comprehensive economic cooperation between China and the ASEAN
community. After entering the 21st century, the value of trade within
Asia has increased to USD 3 trillion from USD 800 billion previously,
and the value of trade between Asia and other countries in the world
has increased to USD 4.8 trillion from USD 1.5 trillion, which has
fully proved that the regional cooperation in Asia tends to gather and
attract the strong aspects of various sides. Although some Asian countries have joined the TPP negotiations, they will by no means give up
the regional cooperation within Asia. The *Regional Comprehensive
Economic Partnership* (RCEP), led by the ASEAN community, is very

---

[25] The 21st-century Maritime Silk Road will link the market chains of the economic
sections of ASEAN countries, South Asia, West Asia, North Africa and Europe. We
will develop the strategic cooperative economic belt facing the South China Sea, the
Pacific Ocean and the Indian Ocean, taking the integration of economy and trade of
Asia, Europe and Africa as a long-term goal of development.
[26] "Because the ASEAN community is located at the crossroads and a must-pass-
through area for the maritime silk road, it will be the foremost developmental target
for the new maritime silk road initiative." Shen Danyang, spokesperson for the
Ministry of Commerce of China, April 18, 2014. Retrieved from http://stock.
hexun.com/2014-04-18/164070931.html.

different from the TPP controlled by the United States, but the two protocols reflect their intention of reinforcing or transcending the value orientation of the WTO, and the different economic scale and structure and cultures of member states have determined the complexity and benefit diversification for different member states to join. The Asian regional economic cooperation and the Asia-Pacific regional economic cooperation are after all two different regional concepts; therefore, it is unreasonable to take the Asian regional economic cooperation as the Asia-Pacific regional economic cooperation. China takes the strategy for regional economic cooperation through which it will properly carry out the three negotiations for the China–South Korea FTA, the China–Japan–South Korea FTA and the RCEP.[27] On June 1, 2015, the China–South Korea FTA protocol was signed. This is a milestone, which will inject a strong driving force for the economic growth of China and South Korea, and will contribute more to the economic integration of Eastern Asia and even global economic development.

The roadmap of China's industrial exportation includes three aspects: the first one is the Silk Road Economic Belt mainly serving China's industrial exports to Central Asian countries; the second one is the 21st Century Maritime Silk Road and the Beibu Gulf Strategy mainly serving China's industrial exportation to Southeast Asian countries; and the third one is the industrial exportation between China and Africa and Latin America. During the period when the United States provided aid to Europe, the United States was at the top end of the global industrial chain, and its industries were exported by taking advantage of an opportunity, while China's situation is immensely different from that of the United States before, as China was at the low end of the global industrial chain. The future of the Silk Road Economic Belt lies in the complementary operations of the industries between China and Central Asian countries, but the complementariness is not yet notable at present. The status quo of some central Asian countries is rich resources and underdeveloped industries. China is

---

[27] Gu Yuanyang. (2014). Powers Gathered in Asia and China's "Operating in Its Neighbors": Construction of the 21st-century Maritime Silk Road. *Asia & Africa Review*, Issue 5, pp. 46–56.

characteristic of a lack of resources generally and the "world's manufacturer". The industry of Central Asian countries remains at the low end of the global industrial chain, and China's industries are also at the low end of the global industrial chain, with the western part of China even lower. China needs to launch a "westward movement" before it realizes the development of its western area. The ASEAN community has become China's no. 3 trading partner, no. 4 export market, and no. 2 source of imports. In 2013, the value of the trade between China and the ASEAN community was USD 443.6 billion, with a trade surplus of USD 8.45 billion. The most typical is the trade between China and Vietnam. The value of the bilateral trade between China and Vietnam reaches USD 50.2 billion, with the value of China's exports to Vietnam reaching USD 36.94 billion and the value of Vietnam's exports to China reaching USD 13.26 billion. Vietnam has a trade deficit of USD 23 billion with China, which makes it to feel pressured during the new round of competition. Asia is an engine for global economic growth, and China is the largest country in Asia; thus, China needs to show enough confidence in Asia. As an economic giant with a colossal of low-end industries, China has a huge obstacle that prevents it from trading better with the countries in Southeast Asia. The trading of the two sides is restricted by the similarity between their industrial structures. Therefore, it is critical for both sides to carry out the transposition of industries for a big leap in trade, for which the key lies in China's lead in fulfilling its industrial upgrading. Meanwhile, China also needs to change from a production giant to a consumption giant. Once China becomes a consumption giant, it will become a huge overseas market for the countries in Southeast Asia.

2.3.3 *The Important Role of Central Asia*

The definition of Central Asia, that is, the central part of Asia, was first proposed by Alexander Von Humboldt, a German geologist, in 1843. The scope covered by it is defined in various ways. A broad definition of Central Asia is "the area that stretches eastward to the eastern border of Mongolia and the eastern part of Inner Mongolia; its south includes Iran and the north of Afghanistan, India, the northwest of Pakistan, and the northwest of China, including Xinjiang and the Hexi Corridor in Gansu Province; its western side starts from the Caspian Sea and covers Kazakhstan, Uzbekistan, Kyrgyzstan, Turkmenistan, and Tajikistan; it stretches northward to Minusinsk and Krasnoyarsk in Siberia." The narrowest definition comes from the Soviet Union, that is, Kazakhstan, Kyrgyzstan, Uzbekistan, Tajikistan, and Turkmenistan. The five countries cover an area of 4,003,400 square kilometers. According to the statistics for 2013, their population was over 66 million, and the five countries have a total GDP of RMB 2.1 trillion, equivalent to USD 338.796 billion, with a per capita GDP of USD 5,099.

China's cooperation with Central Asian countries. The cooperation between the two parties has made remarkable achievements with over 20 years of efforts. Presently, the relationships between China and the five Central Asian countries have all become strategic partnerships. China adheres to the principle of not interfering with the internal affairs of other countries, supporting the Central Asian countries in choosing the developmental road that conforms to their own situation out of their own will, supporting the sovereign independence and territorial completeness of Central Asian countries, and appealing to consultation and peaceful negotiations on an equal footing for settling the problems that involve bilateral relations, and it will not impose any additional conditions on Central Asian countries for providing aid and investments to them. China has settled the boundary problems with Kazakhstan, Kyrgyzstan, and Tajikistan.

China has established a mechanism for economic and trade deliberations at the deputy-minister level with all of the five Central Asian countries, that is, the Economic and Trade Cooperation Committee. Each country holds an annual meeting in turn. There are subcommittees and expert work teams under the Economic and Trade Cooperation Committee, through which both sides may communicate and coordinate with each other in detail about the economic cooperation.

During more than 20 years after the independence of Central Asian countries, the value of bilateral trade between China and them has increased by 100 times. The FDI China has made in Central Asian countries is over USD 20 billion. China has become a major investor and trading partner to Central Asian countries. Take the China–Kazakhstan relationship as an example; in 2013, China's investment in Kazakhstan was USD 19.51 billion. According to the statistics published by Kazakhstan in 2013, the China–Kazakhstan trade value reached USD 22.527 billion. China is Kazakhstan's no. 2 trading partner. There are seven ports between the two countries. The China–Kazakhstan Khorgos Port International Border Cooperation Center was launched in 2011. In the same year, the central banks of China and Kazakhstan set up a special account for domestic currency swaps. Presently, large cooperation projects carried out by the two sides include the project of expanding the China–Kazakhstan oil and gas pipelines, the project of building the Beineu-Bozoy-Shymkent natural gas pipeline, and the project of crude oil deep processing at the Atyrau Refinery. The construction of the Double-West Road (the transborder road from China's west to the West of Europe) is under a tight schedule, and it is predicted that it will be completed by 2015. The Second Eurasian Land Bridge (the railway entering Kazakhstan from Lianyungang through Khorgos and the Alataw Pass, and traveling westward to Europe) will play an important role in pushing forward the economy and trade between China and Kazakhstan. Huawei, ZTE, and China Telecom have their telecom network constructions in Kazakhstan. Besides, China and Kazakhstan have built a logistics yard in Lianyungang, and Xi'an has become a center for freight transportation between China and Kazakhstan. The China-Central Asia natural gas pipeline system is under continuous expansion and improvement. Currently, China and Central Asian countries have formed a three-dimensional traffic and telecom network covering ports, highways, railways, pipelines, and cables. Furthermore, China, Kazakhstan, Uzbekistan, Kyrgyzstan, and Tajikistan are making incessant efforts to carry out multilateral economic cooperation within the framework of the SCO.

Besides economic cooperation, China and Central Asian countries have also achieved much in terms of security cooperation and people-to-people cooperation. In the area of security, China and Central Asian countries have made remarkable achievements in safe law enforcement and defense cooperation under the bilateral framework and the multilateral framework of the SCO. Regarding people-to-people communication, China has founded eight Confucius Institutes in Central Asia; the number of overseas students from both sides is growing fast, and there has been continuous cooperation and communication in the arts, media, and tourism, having energetically advanced the mutual understanding between the people of the two sides. Central Asian countries have all formulated their developmental strategies and hope that they may realize their developmental goals through expanding external cooperation. Kazakhstan formulated the "Strategy by 2025," aiming to be among the Top 30 developed countries in the world. The Tajikistan government defined the *National Plan of Investment, Financial Aid and Major Construction 2014–2016.* Kyrgyzstan formulated the *Steady Development Strategy 2013–2017*, proposing a series of economic developmental goals; the GDP had risen to USD 13.5 billion by 2017, with an average annual increase of 7%; per capita GDP had risen to USD 2,500; the poverty rate had decreased to 25% from 37%; and the average salary had risen to USD 553 from USD 193. Uzbekistan formulated its plan for the transformation of its economic system by 2030 through cooperation with the World Bank, aiming at becoming a middle-income country by the middle of the 21st century. Turkmenistan formulated the *Developmental Strategy for Economy, Politics and Culture by 2020 of Turkmenistan*, a national development guideline, aiming at raising the living standard of its people to that of developed countries throughout the world, thus making sure that the people will be living a happy life.

Each country in Central Asia has proposed their own plans for developing transportation and traffic in their strategies for development, because they all have difficulty in traffic due to their location in the hinterland of Eurasia. The collapse of the Soviet Union fragmented the original system of regional traffic and communications. It is very difficult for each country to make huge investments in maintaining and rebuilding infrastructure facilities for traffic because of the long time and heavy tasks for them to reestablish the country and restore their economy. It is common to see very old and damaged roads and bridges in those countries. Since their independence, Central Asian countries have been hoping that their geographical disadvantages would be changed to advantages, that is, the traffic hub would later be the trading hub that links Asia and Europe.

Kazakhstan proposed developing infrastructure and building central cities in the region, developing its cross-border transportation potential, and building an east–west transportation artery, including the construction of the Double-West Road, the Kazakhstan–Turkmenistan–Iran railway, and Aktau Port. Tajikistan hopes to sign the inter-government highway transportation agreement with China, in order to improve the conditions of international highway freight transportation; simplify the issuing of visas and border procedures; customs and traffic supervision; gradually push forward the construction of the China–Tajikistan highway; improve the infrastructure for the Karasu-Kuolemai Port and realize the all-year-round opening of the port; advance the utilization of border terminals; build new traffic corridors and railway hubs; and build transborder free areas, warehouses, and logistics centers in the border areas. In addition, Tajikistan actively participates in and pushes forward the construction of the transnational railway in Central Asia, including the Russia–Kazakhstan–Kyrgyzstan–Tajikistan railway and the Turkmenistan–Afghanistan–Tajikistan railway. Kyrgyzstan plans to build and repair over 450 km of roadway with asphalt concrete pavement each year, not only to connect the traffic between the north and the south of the country but also to settle the problem of the transportation of mineral products out of the mining areas. Meanwhile, Tajikistan is laying emphasis on developing air and railway transportation, with an expectation to become a regional transportation hub. Uzbekistan is engaged in the transformation of railway electrification in the country, planning to raise the railway electrification rate of the country to 54% by 2017 from 35% currently. Moreover, Uzbekistan is actively pushing forward the construction of transnational railways, including the China–Tajikistan–Uzbekistan railway.

Besides traffic development, the Central Asian countries also hope to bring in foreign investments; accelerate the construction of infrastructures in the country; develop their agriculture; and innovate industries, medium- and small-sized enterprises, and social sectors. Kazakhstan is planning to build a grain transfer station at the border, establish a joint agricultural work team, develop the processing of agricultural products, and increase the exportation of produce. Tajikistan hopes to push forward the projection and exploitation of resources jointly with China; expand the cooperation on energy exploitation and the development of wind energy, solar energy, and recycled resources; and expand the cooperation on power infrastructure and creating the conditions for Tajikistan to export power to the western part of China. Tajikistan hopes that both parties may join in its plan of restoring and modernizing the energy industry, carry out the rebuilding and modernization of power enterprises in Tajikistan, and conduct research on the enterprises that set up and repair energy equipment in Tajikistan. Besides, Tajikistan also wishes to establish enterprises with joint production in agriculture, light industry, and food industry with China, and expand their cooperation on the manufacturing of agricultural equipment, agricultural produce processing, soil improvement, nurturing fine sprouts, fishery, and information exchange among agricultural technicians. Kyrgyzstan anticipates that China may set up a demonstration center for agricultural technologies in Kyrgyzstan, establish cooperation on the planting of corn with China, bring in China's fine seeds and advanced planting technologies, improve the efficiency of agricultural production and output, and export dairy and meat products and other agricultural products. Uzbekistan and Turkmenistan plant to bring in advanced technologies for processing agricultural produce from China, in order to establish an industrial chain inclusive of raw material production–finished good production–exportation. Central Asian countries hope to develop their own processing and technology-intensive enterprises, while China has its advantageous industries with international competitiveness in these areas. China's investments in these countries can help them to establish some competitive processing and technology-intensive enterprises, which will be helpful not only to the transformation of the industrial structure of Central Asian countries but also to the improvement of the bilateral economic and trade relationship and structure. China is an important destination for exportation for Kazakhstan's, Turkmenistan's, and Uzbekistan's oil and natural gas. The stronger bilateral cooperation will help the three countries to obtain steady income from oil and natural gas, and then provide stronger guarantees for the financial budget of the central government of the three countries to cover the expenditures in livelihood and weak areas. Currently, Kazakhstan expressed its interest to increase its oil exportation to China to 20 million tons each year in the next two years. Some Chinese enterprises have entered the special industrial zones in Uzbekistan to build factories there. Turkmenistan hopes to possess several passages for exporting natural gas, thus creating a seller's market for natural gas. At present, China and Turkmenistan have reached an agreement on building the China-Central Asia natural gas pipeline, Line D. The two parties have agreed to ensure the gas supply via Line D by 2016, in order to realize the goal of exporting 65 billion cubic meters of natural gas to China each year.

China is close to Central Asian countries in terms of location, sharing a total borderline of over 3,300 km. The two sides are close to each other in terms of people-to-people connections and tend to share close relationships with each other. The Kazaks, the Khalkhas, the Ozbeks, the Tajiks, and the Salars in China share many similarities in language, religion, customs, mentality, and culture with the Kazaks, the Kyrgyz, the Ozbeks, the Tajiks, and the Turkmen in Central Asia. The Uyghur, the Russian, the Tartar, and the Donggan people in Central Asia have some similar historical origins and connections with the Uyghur, the Russian, the Tartar, and the Hui people in China. All these aspects provide natural advantages for China and Central Asian countries to expand and deepen their economic cooperation in the future.

Despite the difficult advancement of the world's economy, the economic performances of China and Central Asian countries are not as bad as one might think, having provided favorable realistic conditions for enhancing mutual economic cooperation. In 2013, China's economy grew by 7.7%. With the continuously growing economy of China, China's foreign currency reserve has been growing and the capability for foreign investments has been strengthened. In September 2013, when President Xi Jinping paid a visit to Central Asia, China signed economic and trade agreements valuing USD 48 billion with Kazakhstan, Uzbekistan, and Kyrgyzstan. During the next five years, China's foreign investments will likely reach USD 500 billion, and it is very likely to become the world's largest market for consumer goods within the next five years. China believes that the stability and development of Central Asian countries are closely related to its interests; therefore, China encourages its enterprises to go global. In 2013, Central Asian countries achieved high economic development. Kazakhstan's economy grew by 6%, Uzbekistan's by 8%, Tajikistan's by 7.4%, Kyrgyzstan's by 10.5%, and Turkmenistan's by 10.2%. In addition, in order to attract for more foreign investments, Central Asian countries have made great efforts in creating a favorable investment environment, employing professional and high-quality officials, making stringent attacks on corruption, establishing special economic zones, and implementing many slack policies in tax reduction and customs clearance. In the future, Central Asia will become an important investment destination for China and China's market will greet more enterprises and products from Central Asian countries.

The importance of Kazakhstan. With the fact that China released its plan for the Silk Road Economic Belt in Kazakhstan, China hopes to take Kazakhstan as the breaking point. There are sufficient reasons for this. If it is fair to say that Central Asia is the main gate for China in developing westward, then Kazakhstan is exactly such a main gate. Of the over 3,300 km borderline shared by China and Central Asia, the China–Kazakhstan borderline runs over 1,780 km, most of which is traveling along advantageous locations. Of the 10 Class-I land ports opened by China to Central Asia, there are seven ports opened to Kazakhstan, and the other three opened to Kyrgyzstan and Tajikistan. The natural environment for the ports is harsh and allows the transportation of small freight, but smooth traffic cannot be guaranteed in winter. China's two trains connected to Central Asia will travel through Kazakhstan. Although preparation for the China–Kyrgyzstan–Uzbekistan railway that travels through Kazakhstan has been going on for many years, it has not been completed yet. Meanwhile, Kazakhstan is an important pass on the modern silk road. Road connectivity can only be via the air route without the participation of Kazakhstan. Besides, Kazakhstan has another geographical advantage by which a trip can be made directly to the Caspian Sea and Russia without traveling through other countries.

Among the five Central Asian countries, Kazakhstan has the closest economic ties with China. Kazakhstan is China's largest trading partner in Central Asia. The volume of trade between China and Kazakhstan is more than the total volume of trade of the other four countries. In 2012, the total value of trade between China and Central Asia reached USD 45.9 billion, of which that between China and Kazakhstan was USD 25.7 billion, more than half of the total. Kazakhstan's position in trade is more conspicuous in Xinjiang. In 2012, Kazakhstan's trade in Xinjiang accounted for around 44% of Xinjiang's total value of trade and accounted for around 70% of the total amount of trade between Xinjiang and Central Asia.

Kazakhstan's economy weighs the most in Central Asian countries. According to the statistics of the World Bank, the GDP of Kazakhstan is more than two times the total of the other four countries in Central Asia (the GDP of Kazakhstan for 2012 was USD 201.7 billion and the total GDP of the other four was USD 98.2 billion). The differences would be bigger if comparisons were made between Kazakhstan and one of the other four countries alone. With a large economic scale, its influence is bigger and it will create a more remarkable effect of demonstration in building the Silk Road Economic Belt.

China and Kazakhstan also share a profound foundation for political relations. Kazakhstan is China's earliest strategic partner in Central Asia. When the relationship between China and the other Central Asian countries also rose to that of strategic partners, China and Kazakhstan were already marching toward the "comprehensive strategic partnership", which does not mean that there are no problems between China and Kazakhstan. For example, there is some force in Kazakhstan that exaggerated the so-called economic expansion of China. However, the appeal for deeper cooperation is the major voice. Besides, Kazakhstan also has a grand plan to develop cross-border transportation by making use of its geographical advantages. In 2012, President Nazarbayev pointed out that, by 2020, the cross-border traffic volume in Kazakhstan will have been doubled and increased by 10 times by 2050. Therefore, it is necessary for Kazakhstan not only to build more highways and railways, but it also needs more material flow. This proceeds in the same developmental direction as the Silk Road Economic Belt.

The fact that China, Russia, and the United States all have strategic considerations in Central Asia reflects the high attention they pay to the region. Russia has been operating in Central Asia for half a century. Despite the collapse of the Soviet Union, Russia still has various connections to Central Asia. It is quite natural that Russia wants to revive its embrace. The United States' strategic presence in Central Asia was caused by a special circumstance, namely, the War in Afghanistan. With the outbreak of the War in Afghanistan, the US troops rushed to Afghanistan and set up military bases in Central Asia. What followed was the huge amount of political and material investment made by the United States. The United States gained influence as large as that of Russia and China in this region, and it became one of the powers that have a great influence on Central Asia. From a broader perspective, regional economic cooperation is the world's trend involving China, Russia, and the United States, who are all trying to be active players. The United States is pushing forward regional economic integration across the semi-hemisphere. The most significant project is the *Trans-Pacific Partnership Agreement* (TPP) and the *Transatlantic Trade and Investment Partnership*. At the time of proposing the building of the Silk Road Economic Belt, China also proposed the plans for the Maritime Silk Road, the China–Pakistan Economic Corridor, and the Bangladesh–China–India–Myanmar Economic Corridor. During his visit to South Korea in November 2013, the President of Russia Putin once again proposed the building of the Eurasian corridor that will travel through South Korea and North Korea and then link up with the Trans-Siberian Railway, which was named by some media as the "Steel Silk Road." In addition, the FTA projects negotiated by Russia, India, and Vietnam all feature considerable scales.

2.4 *The Belt and Road Initiative and the Spread of China's Culture*

In the *Decision of the CCCPC on Some Major Issues Concerning Comprehensively Intensifying the Reform* as adopted at the Third Plenary Session of the 18th Central Committee of the CPC, it was proposed that "China should be more open to promoting the culture, and the cause should be led by the government, organized by enterprises, operated through the market and participated in by the whole society. We should expand cultural exchanges with foreign countries, and enhance our capability for publicizing our culture throughout the world and constructing a system of external discourse, thus pushing Chinese culture to go global."

China has a long history and an extensive and profound culture. The culture of China had a far-reaching influence on the culture of the world several times in the course of history. In the Han and Tang dynasties, China was the world's economic and political center and enjoyed unprecedented prosperity in cultural exchanges with other countries. Traditional Chinese culture, including the philosophies of Confucianism, Taoism, and Buddhism, and various techniques and technologies were spread to East Asia and West Asia via the silk road, Monk Jianzhen's sea trip to Japan, Japan's diplomats to the Tang Dynasty, and so on. In the Song and Ming dynasties, China's economic and cultural position remained top in the world. Many Western travelers, merchants, and missionaries visited China and spread China's excellent culture to Europe, which facilitated the formation and development of the capitalist society of the West; through seven voyages across the oceans, Zheng He brought China's silk, porcelain, coins, policies and art to the world once again. From the 17th century, a number of Chinese works on science and technology, such as *Basics on Physics* and *Exploitation of the Works of Nature* (*Tiangong Kaiwu*), and Confucian classics such as *The Analects, The Great Learning*, and so on, were translated and carried over to Europe and Japan. In addition, there emerged a good number of works studying Chinese culture (Hanxue) on the European Continent, such as *On Confucius's Morality, China's Philosophy, China's Moral Philosophy and Legal Philosophy*, and *Morality of the Chinese Philosopher Confucius*. Incomplete statistics show that, between 1570 and 1870, there were over 70 kinds of books about China's officialdom and political system written in English.[28]

Since the reform and opening-up, China's economy has kept growing at a high speed. Its comprehensive power and international

---

[28] Chen Yamin. (2010). An Analysis of the Developmental Strategy for Overseas Confucius Institutes from the Perspective of Cultural Geography. *Journal of Shandong Normal University (Humanities and Social Sciences)*, Issue 4, pp. 151–156.

influence are becoming stronger, and the exchanges between China and other countries are becoming frequent and extensive. Many countries are seeing a strong demand for learning the Chinese language; thus, there is a wave of "zest for the Chinese language." More and more people are becoming enthusiastic about learning the Chinese language and culture, but there is a serious shortage of teaching resources for the learning of Chinese overseas. In this situation, the Chinese government expands its publicity of Chinese culture worldwide in response to the "zest for the Chinese language," enhances foreign exchanges, grasps opportunities actively, carries out an overall plan, and pushes forward the publicity of the Chinese language and culture at the level of a national strategy. The Chinese government has set up the National Leading Group for Teaching Chinese as a Foreign Language in 1987 to have a centralized guidance for the teaching of Chinese to foreigners nationwide. In 2004, after learning from the experience of France, Spain, and Germany with publicizing their own languages, China established the first nonprofit organization aiming at publicizing the Chinese language and spreading the Chinese culture overseas, that is, the Confucius Institute. The development of the Confucius Institute fits into the demand of other countries worldwide for learning Chinese, helps the peoples from all over the world to understand China's language and culture better, enhances the exchanges and cooperation in the fields of education and culture between China and other countries, develops friendly relations between China and other countries, and boosts the development of diversified cultures in the world.

Since it was founded, the Confucius Institute has been embodied with the significance of "making it possible for people from all over the world to understand the Chinese language and culture better, developing friendly relationships with other countries, and providing learners from all over the world convenient, excellent conditions for learning Chinese." The Confucius Institute is a nonprofit public organization with the basic tasks of popularizing the language and culture of China and supporting the local Chinese teaching. Its most important job is to provide standard and authoritative modern Chinese teaching to Chinese language learners worldwide. The first

Confucius Institute was opened in Seoul, South Korea, in 2004. As of December 2015, 500 Confucius Institutes and 1,000 Confucius Classrooms, totaling 1,500, have been opened in 134 countries and regions on the five continents. There are over 1.9 million registered learners, having preliminarily formed a multilevel and diversified structure with an extensive coverage. The first Radio Confucius Institute was established in Beijing on December 6, 2007. With wireless radio and online radio as the carriers, it teaches the Chinese language in 38 languages to learners around the world. The Online Confucius Institute hosted by the Confucius Institute Headquarters was put into trial operation on March 20, 2008. The fast growth and increasingly extensive coverage of the Confucius Institutes have sufficiently proved that the Confucius Institute has become an important platform and glorious brand for accelerating the process of pushing the Chinese language and culture to become global.[29]

Holding the philosophy of "prizing harmony and peacefulness" and "harmony in diversity," the Confucius Institute is dedicated to push forward the building of a harmonious world with lasting peace and common prosperity.[30] Overseas media have high praised the Confucius Institute. In November 2006, the *New York Times* commented in an article entitled "Another of China's Pop Exports: The Chinese Language" that "China is building a warmer and more active social image with the Chinese language and culture." It was also pointed out in *Zaobao* based in Singapore that "the popularization of the Confucius Institute is helpful to the world for learning about China and eliminating the misunderstanding of the outside world regarding China's peaceful rise."[31] *Zaobao* also remarked in an article entitled "China's New-born Soft Strength" that 30 million foreigners

---

[29]Wang Ruzhong, Guan Yongfen. (2014). Confucius Institute Pushing China's Culture to Go Global: A Study of the Current Situation, Problems and Countermeasures. *Study of Ideological and Political Course*, Issue 4, pp. 46–47.

[30]Li Ju. (2008). China's New Form of Multilateral Cultural Diplomacy: The Confucius Institute. *Theoretical Observation*, Issue 2, pp. 6–13.

[31]Wang Yuhe. (2014). An Analysis of China's Soft Power based on Confucius Institutes. *Theoretic Observation*, Issue 9, pp. 58–60.

Table 2.5 The Number of Confucius Institutes, Confucius Classrooms and the Countries Involved

	Number of Countries Involved	Countries with the Confucius Institutes	Number of Confucius Institutes	Countries with Confucius Classrooms	Number of Confucius Classrooms
The Americas	35	18	157	8	544
Europe	45	40	169	28	257
Asia	48	32	110	18	90
Africa	56	32	46	14	23
Oceania	14	3	18	4	86

Source: Hanban's Statistics (2015).

were learning Chinese and it was believed that the number "would grow faster" (Table 2.5).[32]

It is known to all that East Asian countries, including Japan and South Korea, have been deeply influenced by the Chinese culture during the course of history. Therefore, besides teaching traditional Chinese cultural programs, including paper cutting, guessing games, seal cutting, calligraphy, *qin* performance, drawing, tea-tasting, festival activities, and so on, the Confucius Institutes in these countries also carry out in-depth studies of Sinology, making it a characteristic branch of the Sinology research institute in the world. Today, the Confucius Institute is developing fast in Japan. There are elementary teachings such as Chinese language teaching and experiencing China's folk customs and culture; besides, traditional Chinese medicine, Chinese literary classics, a series of courses on Confucianism, studies on Chinese characters, and so on are also taught. For example, the Confucius Institute at Sapporo University, Waseda University, and Hokuriku University are outstanding in their studies on *The Analects*, *Records of the Grand Historian*, and *The History of the Three Kingdoms*; they even stage famous traditional compositions such as the "House of the Flying Daggers," "A Wonderful Night in Spring," and "The

---

[32] Confucius Institute Headquarters. Retrieved from http://conference.chinesecio.com/conference/huigu/10.html.

Butterfly Lovers." South Korea is one of the countries that received education about the Chinese culture the earliest. Besides some basic knowledge about Chinese culture, students from South Korea also study Sinology, Confucianism, and Chinese history. The program of "Carrying forward Chinese culture and improving the friendship between China and South Korea" of the Confucius Institute at Daebul University also proves that South Korea is another successor to Chinese culture; the program of "Learning values from *Records of the Grand Historian*" provided by the Confucius Institute of Chungnam National University also gives us a clearer understanding of the modern significance of the tradition and culture of China.[33]

France, the United Kingdom, Italy, and Russia are European countries with a profound Western culture. They have always been interested in the Chinese culture as it is quite different from theirs. In the Song Dynasty, they sent many missionaries and scholars to China to learn and investigate the Chinese culture, such as the famous Sinologists Matteo Ricci, Michele Ruggieri, and Martino Martini, among others. Marco Polo's visit and the establishment of the first Sinology institute in the West in 1814 showed the interest of the Europeans in China. Hence, it is not only the Chinese language and folkways that are taught in Confucius Institutes set in Europe presently, but there are also Confucius Institutes for Traditional Chinese Medicine and the specialty of sinology, including the Confucius Institute for Traditional Chinese Medicine in London, which is the first Confucius Institute for TCM in the world. The Confucius Institute in the Chinese Culture Center in Paris, France, has programs of studies on ancient Chinese characters and traditional Chinese cuisine and etiquette, and even the themed lecture of the "Philosophy of Confucius and the Spirit of the Chinese"; the Sinological studies at St Petersburg University in Russia have a history of over 150 years, and they have courses such as the study of the ancient phonetics of the Chinese language and characters.[34]

---

[33]Wu Ying. (2009). A Reflection on the Strategy for the Spread of Confucius Institutes for Chinese Culture. *Academic Forum*, Issue 7, pp. 141–145.

[34]Cao Fengxia, Li Biquan. (2014). Thinking about the Popularization and Inheritance of Chinese Culture from the Confucius Institute and the Study on It. *Journal of Changchun University*, Issue 1, pp. 46–49.

Confucius Institutes have also been set up in some African, Southeast Asian, and South American countries, but they do not have as good a number of scholars studying China and Sinology as Japan, South Korea, European, and North American countries. What they care about more is the teaching of the Chinese language. This is closely related to their economy and history. More and more Africans wish to learn about China by learning Chinese, and they are looking for developmental opportunities for the future. They not only learn Chinese, but they also learn some skills for future needs by learning the Chinese language. Statistics show that, as of 2010, 4.4% of the Confucius Institutes in Africa had developed the discipline of the Chinese language (granting a bachelor's degree in the Chinese language), which was officially included as a second language subject in the discipline system of non-Chinese universities; over 30% of the Confucius Institutes and Confucius Classrooms have research programs and practice on the development of the disciplines; over 50% of the Confucius Institutes gave serious consideration to this aspect.[35] With the flourishing of the cultural exchanges between China and Africa, as of January 1, 2015, 46 Confucius Institutes had been set up in 32 countries, and 23 Confucius Classrooms in 14 countries. The cultural and educational exchanges between China and Africa are thus fruitful.

The cultural exchanges between China and the ASEAN community and Central Asian countries have also achieved much. In September 2013, Chinese Premier Li Keqiang pointed out in a speech delivered at the opening ceremony of the 10th China-ASEAN Expo and the China-ASEAN Summit for Commerce and Investment that China and the ASEAN community had jointly created the "ten-year golden" cooperation with each other and would be able to create the new "ten-year diamond" cooperation in the future. He said that both sides should enhance the cultural and people-to-people exchanges, and proposed defining the year of 2014 as the "Year of China-ASEAN

---

[35] Sa Dequan. (2012). Survey and Analysis of the Status Quo of the Development of the Subject of the Chinese Language within the Development of Courses of Study at the Confucius Institutes in Africa. *Selected Papers for the 10th International Chinese Teaching Seminar*, Northern United Publishing & Media (Group) Company Limited, p. 82.

Friendly Communication." In the next three to five years, China will provide 15,000 government scholarships to ASEAN countries; it will invest special funds for regional cooperation in Asia for the purpose of deepening the cultural and people-to-people cooperation. He remarked that both sides should further play an active role as the China-ASEAN Youth Association and the China-ASEAN Think Tank Network and construct the "ten-year diamond."[36] In 2005, China and the ASEAN community signed the *Understanding Memo for China-ASEAN Cultural Cooperation*, started to hold the China-ASEAN Cultural Industry Forum in the China-ASEAN Expo in 2006, and signed the *Nanning Declaration, Understanding the Memo for China-ASEAN Cultural Cooperation*, and *Interactional Plan for the China-ASEAN Cultural Industry*. The signing of these documents has greatly pushed forward the cultural exchanges and cooperation between China and the ASEAN community. During the "ten-year golden" cooperation between China and the ASEAN group, 11 countries have together hosted ten China-ASEAN Expos, and each Expo staged diversified activities for cultural exchanges, thus becoming a great platform for the cultural exchanges between China and the ASEAN community. The Nanning International Folk Song Festival held annually has become a remarkable brand for China-ASEAN cultural exchanges. In the nearly 10 years of its existence, exchanges in and cooperation on education have received considerable attention from both sides, and the scale has been continuously enlarged. The number of ASEAN students coming to study in China increased to 60,000 in 2012 from 10,376 in 2003. In 2012, the number of overseas students from ASEAN countries accounted for 19% of the total number of overseas students in China.

From 2008 to 2015, China and the ASEAN community held eight China-ASEAN Educational Cooperation Weeks, setting up the

---

[36] Li Keqiang. (September 3, 2013). Push the China-ASEAN Long-term Friendly Strategic Partnership for Mutual Benefit and Cooperation up to a New Step: Speech Delivered at the 10th China-ASEAN Expo and China-ASEAN Summit for Commerce and Investment. *People's Daily Online*. Retrieved from http://politics.people.com.cn/n/2013/0904/c1024-22796590.html.

first platform for educational exchanges between China and the ASEAN community. In the first seven weeks of exchanges, there were altogether 80 activities, including roundtable meetings for ministers of education, forums for university presidents, and students' camps; there were 1,050 universities attending the activities in total, involving 4,880 person-times; universities and organizations signed 654 practical cooperation agreements (memos); from 2010 to 2014, the number of overseas students sent by China and the ASEAN countries reached 427,000, including 301,000 overseas students from the ASEAN countries and 126,000 Chinese students who went to study in the ASEAN countries.[37] The two sides held diversified communication activities, such as China-ASEAN university presidents' forums, China-ASEAN university cooperation conferences, China-ASEAN national exhibitions of education, and China-ASEAN youth's art festivals. In 2010, during the 3rd China-ASEAN Education Cooperation Week, China and the ASEAN community kicked off the China-ASEAN Ministers of Education Roundtable Conference, marking a higher level of the educational exchanges and cooperation between the two sides and a deeper exploration.[38] China started to set up Confucius Institutes in ASEAN countries in 2004. In 2008, registered students of Confucius Institutes totaled over 40,000, and the number of people attending the cultural activities held by Confucius Institutes reached 150,000 person-times. In 2012, there were 7.32 million Chinese tourists to the ASEAN countries, having increased by 2.6 times that of 10 years before; thus, China had become the largest source of tourists second only to the EU; there were 5.89 million

---

[37] Yu Shui. (October 9, 2013). China-ASEAN Educational Exchanges and Cooperation Create the "Ten Golden Years". *China Education News Network*. Retrieved from http://www.jyb.cn/world/zwyj/201310/t20131009_554704.html. Chen Yuxiang. (August 6, 2015) Jointly Building the Great Platform for Cultural and People-to-People Communication: An Overview of the 8th China-ASEAN Education Cooperation Week. *China National Radio*. Retrieved from http://www.cnr.cn/guizhou/gzyw/20150806/t20150806_519453089.shtml.

[38] The First Roundtable Conference for Ministers of Education of China and ASEAN Countries Opened in Guiyang. (August 3, 2010). *Eastday*. Retrieved from http://news.eastday.com/c/20100803/u1a5371216.html.

ASEAN tourists who visited China, and ASEAN countries became one of the major sources of tourists for China.[39]

The number of participants in the 8th China-ASEAN Educational Cooperation Week held in August 2015 was 1,400, including over 430 foreign participants. Six significant projects and seven main-body projects, as well as 14 sponsorships carried out in different places and periods, will be conducted sequentially. The participants in this Educational Cooperation Week increased to "10 + 1 + 4" from the previous "10 + 1." Four new guests of honor, namely, Australia, New Zealand, South Korea, and Switzerland, also attended the event.

The people-to-people exchanges between China and Central Asian countries mainly focused on education, science and technology, culture, and healthcare. On August 16, 2007, at the Bishkek Leaders' Summit of the SCO, President Putin of Russia proposed founding "Shanghai Cooperation Organization University"; in the first half year of 2009, the five member states agreed to define five areas of regional studies, ecology, energy studies, IT technology, and nano-technology as the priorities for cooperation, and selected 53 universities for the projects. On October 11, 2012, at the 4th SCO Conference of Ministers of Education, it was adopted that the number of Shanghai Cooperation Organization Universities would increase to 74, including 13 in Kazakhstan, nine in Kyrgyzstan, 20 in China, 21 in Russia, 10 in Tajikistan, and one in Belarus. As of the end of 2015, China had founded 11 Confucius Institutes in Central Asian countries, four in Kazakhstan, three in Kyrgyzstan, two in Tajikistan, and two in Uzbekistan. In the past few years, the Confucius Institute has provided more opportunities for Chinese language learners from Central Asia during the people-to-people exchanges with Central Asian countries, which has changed these peoples' understanding of China, enhanced their mutual understanding, and facilitated the cooperation between China and Central Asia, thus

---

[39] The Information Office of the State Council Held a Press Conference for the 10th Anniversary of the Establishment of the China-ASEAN Strategic Partnership (July 23, 2013). Retrieved from State Council Information Office of China website: http://www.scio.gov.cn/index.htm.

producing a favorable effect among the peoples and governments involved.[40]

On June 22, 2014, at the 38th World Heritage Convention held in Doha, the capital of Qatar, the project of "The Silk Road: The Chang'an-Tianshan Corridor Road Network" jointly filed by China, Kazakhstan, and Kyrgyzstan was listed in the *World Heritage List*. The silk road is a transnational cultural heritage and a cultural route. It travels along 8,700 km, involving 33 historical sites; the total number of areas filed as cultural heritage areas is 42,668.16 hectares, and the buffer area totals 189,963.13 hectares. Of them, 22 archaeological sites and ancient buildings in China, including four in He'nan Province, seven in Shaanxi Province, five in Gansu Province, and six in the Xinjiang Uygur Autonomous Region, with a total heritage area of 29,825.69 hectares and a total buffer area of 176,526.03 hectares. There are eight sites in Kazakhstan and three in Kyrgyzstan. The silk road is the first project that China has jointly filed with other countries as a world heritage. The World Heritage Committee believed that, as a road of integration, communication, and dialogue between the East and the West, the silk road has made significant contributions to the common prosperity of human beings in the past nearly 2,000 years. The section of the silk road filed as a world heritage is outstanding in terms of its traffic and communication system. It was formed in the 2nd century B.C. and flourished from the 6th to the 14th centuries. Used for 16 centuries, the silk road traveled through today's China, Kazakhstan, and Kyrgyzstan. The silk road has witnessed the exchanges in economy, culture, and social development, especially the nomadic and non-nomadic civilizations, across Eurasia from the 2nd century B.C. to the 16th century. It is an outstanding model by which long-distance trade pushes forward the development of large cities and towns and the hydraulic management system supports the traffic and trade; it is directly related to many significant

---

[40]Zhang Quansheng, Guo Weidong. (2014). Cultural and People-to-People Exchanges and Cooperation between China and ASEAN: Taking Confucius Institute as an Example. *Xinjiang Normal University (Philosophy and Social Sciences)*, Issue 4, pp. 64–71.

historical events, such as Zhang Qian's diplomatic mission to the Western regions and reflects the popularization of religions such as Buddhism, Manicheism, and Zoroastrianism and ideas of urban planning in ancient China and Central Asia. The success in the application for including the silk road in the list of world heritage sites is that it is the first silk road project to be included in the *World Heritage List* through joint application. This success imbues the ancient silk road with new vitality, advances the construction of the Silk Road Economic Belt, and manifests the eternal theme of harmonious existence and common prosperity of various countries.

Currently, China has entered the new developmental stage of intensifying reform in all areas and expanding opening-up. Continuing the line of tradition and culture, the Belt and Road Initiative inherits and carries forward the excellent Chinese tradition and culture; it is also a practical action by which each country involved realizes cooperation for win–win results. The Belt and Road Initiative will definitely further push forward the mutual benefits from trade and facilitate the exchanges and integration of diverse civilizations. "Deepening cultural and people-to-people exchanges and advancing mutual learning among diverse civilizations have become an irresistible trend of the era."[41]

---

[41] Liu Yandong. (December 7, 2014). Toward Another 10 Years of the Confucius Institute. *Xinhuanet*. Retrieved from http://www.xinhuanet.com/politics/2014-12/07/c_1113550855.htm.

Chapter

3

A Package Plan for Financial Security

In a global context, it can be seen that the Belt and Road Initiative proposed by China links the longest and most potential economic corridors. It involves various emerging economies and developing countries, benefiting a population of around 4.4 billion, which accounts for 63% of the world's total population, with a total economic turnover of around USD 21 trillion, which accounts for 29% of the world's total economic turnover. Obviously, the Belt and Road Initiative is not only the economic belt with the greatest potential for development in the world, it is also an immense project that requires the longest period and largest fund ever. It is estimated by experts that it will take 30–50 years to complete the Belt and Road Initiative.

There is no doubt that a huge fund is needed for the smooth implementation of the Belt and Road Initiative that features connectivity. It has been proven in reality that, in the existing international financial system and framework, international financial institutions such as the World Bank and the Asian Development Bank (ADB) are unable to meet the developmental demand in the current situation and provide financial support for the construction of the infrastructure with connectivity to the Belt and Road efficiently. To carry out

131

the Belt and Road Initiative more effectively and set up a strategic platform for capital output for investment and financing for the construction of infrastructure for the Belt and Road Initiative, the newly developing countries, with China as the most typical one, and some developed countries are exploring a comprehensive financial cooperation plan. With the establishment of financial institutions such as the BRICS Development Bank, the Shanghai Cooperation Organization (SCO) Development Bank, and the Silk Road Fund, the Belt and Road Initiative has its financial support and the long-lasting drive for sustainable development. With effective cooperation with the standard international financial institutions, these newly established financial institutions will turn the Belt and Road Initiative into a reality.

Undoubtedly, the world's economy and politics are evolving from a single pole to multiple poles, thereby causing significant changes in the international monetary system. Since the global financial crisis in 2008, the international monetary system, led by the US dollar, no longer fits in the multipolarized development of the world. According to the statistics of the International Monetary Fund (IMF), as of the end of June 2014, of the foreign exchange reserves officially recognized globally, the shares of the US dollar, the euro, and the British pound had reduced by 2.5%, 2.5%, and 0.8%, respectively, from what they were before the crisis, while the shares of other currency reserves, mainly from emerging economies, had increased by 5%. The diversified development of the world's economy, politics, and the international monetary system provide great opportunities for the strategy of internationalization of the RMB and a great roadmap for the development of the Belt and Road Initiative.

1. Financial Institutions, Including the Asian Infrastructure Investment Bank (AIIB), Reforming the International Financial Map

On October 2, 2013, Chinese President Xi Jinping met Susilo Bambang Yudhoyono, President of Indonesia, in Djakarta. President Xi proposed for the establishment of the AIIB to boost the building up of connectivity and the process of economic integration and provide financial support for the construction of infrastructures in the developing countries, including the ASEAN countries, in the specific region. In the same month, Chinese Premier Li Keqiang also raised the proposal of establishing the AIIB during his visit to Southeast Asian countries.

On October 24, 2014, the ministers of finance and authorized representatives of the first 21 original members of intention, including China, India, and Singapore, officially signed the *Memo of Establishing the AIIB*, jointly making the decision to establish the AIIB. As a government-run institution for the multilateral development of Asia, the AIIB focuses on supporting the construction of infrastructures. Its objective is to boost the connectivity of the regions in Asia and the process of economic integration and enhance the cooperation between China and other countries and regions in Asia. The headquarters of AIIB is based in Beijing. The statuary capital of the AIIB is USD 100 billion.

As of April 15, 2015, the number of original members of intention of the AIIB was 57, including 37 countries within Asia and 20 outside of Asia. The members include some major Western countries except Japan, the United States, and Canada, and many countries in Eurasia. Its members are from the five continents. Each member completed negotiations and signed the articles of association in the middle of 2015, and completed the formalities for the articles of association to be effective before the AIIB was officially established.

1.1 *The AIIB Coming at the Right Time*

1.1.1 *China's Stronger Economic Power*

China's GDP had a year-on-year increase of 7.4% in 2014, reaching RMB 63.65 trillion; the USD equivalent exceeded 10 trillion for the first time, and the economic aggregate was ranked no. 2 in the world. The total value of the importation and exportation of goods for the whole year was RMB 26.43 trillion, with a year-on-year increase of 2.3%, a trade surplus of RMB 2.35 trillion, and the total value of exports ranked no. 1 in the world, and the total value of imports and exports also ranked no. 1 in the world; for the whole year, the RMB settlement for cross-border trade in aggregate was RMB 6.55 trillion, and the RMB settlement for direct investments in aggregate was RMB 1.05 trillion. The RMB settlements in aggregate for cross-border trade in goods, services, and other regular items; China's outward foreign direct investment (OFDI); and foreign direct investment (FDI) in China were RMB 5.9 trillion, RMB 656.5 billion, RMB 186.6 billion, and RMB 862 billion, respectively (the OFDI was USD 102.9 billion that exceeded USD 100 billion for the first time, thus creating a year-on-year increase of 14.1% and remaining at no. 3 position in the world); the balance of foreign exchange reserves was USD 3.84 trillion. China had become a world's giant for economy, trade, and foreign investments, featuring an economic foundation and comprehensive strength to organize in order to establish the AIIB. Nevertheless, the old international financial system restricted China's capability of serving the ASEAN community, Asia, and even the world in terms of financial resources. By planning the resources in economy, trade, science and technology, and finance in a systematic way and making use of the relative advantages, China is actively participating in regional economic cooperation, and it implements the Free Trade Area (FTA) strategy for dealing with the peripheral countries and regions, with the ASEAN FTA and the China–South Korea FTA in the lead, in order to enhance China's role in regional affairs and urge China to hold more international responsibilities.

1.1.2 *Lack of Funds for Building Infrastructure Facilities in Asia*

The economy of Asia makes up one-third of the world's total, and Asia is the region with the best economic vitality and growth potential in the world. The population of Asia accounts for 60% of the world's total. However, because of limited funds for construction, the construction of infrastructures for railways, highways, bridges, ports, airports, and telecommunication stations is far from enough, which has to some extent restricted the economic development of the region. The investments in internal infrastructures will need USD 8 trillion at least, with an annual average investment of USD 800 billion. Of the

USD 8 trillion, 68% will be used to make new investments in infrastructure, and 32% constitutes the fund for maintaining and repairing the existing infrastructure facilities. On the one hand, the existing multilateral financial institutions are unable to provide such a huge amount of funds, because the ADB and the World Bank together have only USD 223 billion, out of which merely USD 20 billion is provided to Asian countries each year. Therefore, it is impossible for them to meet the financial need. It is rather difficult for private sectors to invest immensely in the infrastructure projects due to factors such as a huge demand for funds, a long period of construction, and an indefinite income flow for infrastructure investments. On the other hand, China has become the third largest country that invests abroad. China's foreign investments had a year-on-year increase of 17.6% in 2012, creating a new record of USD 87.8 billion. Moreover, throughout more than three decades of development and accumulation, China developed a complete industrial chain in the field of equipment manufacturing for infrastructure facilities and is leading in the engineering construction of highways, bridges, tunnels, and railways. It is expected that the industries related to China's construction of infrastructures will go global rapidly. However, it is difficult for the economies in Asia to make use of their own advantages in high-value capital reserves; they are lacking efficient multilateral cooperation mechanisms and investments that will lead to the construction of infrastructures.[1]

1.1.3 *European Countries' Motivation for Joining the AIIB*

The 57 AIIB original members of intention include developed European countries such as the United Kingdom, France, Germany, and Italy. Why does a financial institution led by a developing country attract so many established Western countries?

For the United Kingdom, France, Germany, and Italy, cooperation with China is out of their own practical concern in the first place.

---

[1] Wang Liying. (November 24, 2014). A Guess on the AIIB Roadmap. *People's Daily Online*. Retrieved from http://paper.people.com.cn/gjjrb/html/2014-11/24/content_1501990.htm.

The United Kingdom, which was the first Western developed country to join the AIIB, said "the UK joined the AIIB solely for its own interest." From a different perspective, it is immense opportunities that they will get by joining the AIIB "community."

In terms of economy, there are several important reasons why these European countries favor the AIIB.

The first reason is that Europe has its own investment demand. Although it is difficult for the weariness of the European economy to be alleviated, Europe is not short on money; it is only that different funds need to seek new investment points. Jean-Claude Junker, President of the European Commission who took office in year 2014, had proposed an investment plan of 300 billion Euros to revitalize the economy of Europe. As a mature economy, Europe does not have any new notable economic growth points at present. Faced with a low economic growth rate and a low investment returns rate, these capitals are urgently seeking high-return investment destinations worldwide. As the world's economy is still weak to recover, Asia, the most dynamic and potential region in the world, is an important engine to pull the world's economic growth. Meanwhile, the existing international financial order has been "interrupted"; organizations such as the World Bank, the IMF, and the ADB set high standards and proposed many additional conditions, which cannot meet the huge financial needs. Therefore, it is obvious that those European countries have their practical purposes for joining emerging multilateral developmental mechanisms such as the AIIB and making investments in dynamic regions such as Asia.

The second reason is that, with China's economy gradually becoming more influential in recent years and taking a larger share in the world's economy, the European countries who are important trading partners with China will certainly hope that they may achieve greater results that are beneficial to each other through deepening the trade relationship with China via this platform of the AIIB.

The last reason is that European countries are beginning to realize that a global financial system that is solely led by the United States no longer conforms to the interests of Europe. The economic crisis in recent years has made European countries lose confidence in the

United States, and they have begun to become aware of the importance of building another pivot other than the United States and hence earning Europe a louder say and protecting its own interests. During the debt crisis of Europe, the United States did not purchase European bonds and provide enough aid to European countries; what's worse, several American credit rating institutions kept speaking negatively of the economy of Europe. The performance of the United States makes European countries feel that they were deserted and sold by the United States. The United States carried out the policy of quantitative easing several times after the financial crisis, which was, objectively, a serious blow to the confidence of the euro and undermined the euro's global influence.

From the perspective of geographical importance, according to the analysis by Michel Foucher, a French diplomat and expert on geopolitics, the current international geographic economical structure has changed, and the trend of a world economy that is multicentered and multipolarized is becoming more notable. This requires the international financial order to have its own change accordingly and also demands a corresponding multilateral financial organization, for which the AIIB mechanism is a perfect attempt.

With the step-by-step establishment of the AIIB as proposed by China, several infrastructure projects are being undertaken. The passages traveling through East Asia, Southeast Asia to Central Asia and then to Europe will be linked. China and Europe, the two economies with huge populations at the two ends of Eurasia, will be efficiently connected in an unprecedented way. European countries also expect to be able to dock with the Belt and Road Initiative as proposed by China in this way. It is a logical and rational choice made by Europe to join the AIIB. Mark Boleat, chairman of the London Financial City Government Policy and Resource Commission, remarked that the AIIB will provide more fund for the development of infrastructures in the Asia-Pacific region. The United Kingdom is leading in the areas of infrastructure, advanced engineering technologies, and green financial service technologies, while the Asian economies are growing at a high speed and their needs in these areas are also growing. The United Kingdom's increasing involvement in the cooperation in the abovementioned areas may create new approaches to support the development of the comprehensive strategic relationship between the United Kingdom and its European partners.

For China, the initiator and founder of the AIIB, the participation of France and other European allies that are outside Asia will not only bring a substantial fund to boost the construction of infrastructures in Asia and make the AIIB less stressful in its operational fund, but it will also bring a series of support in terms of talents and intelligence. For example, the experience of Europe in the management policies for complex investment projects, the way of decision-making that conforms to the international standards, and the estimation of the investment return rate of projects, and so on, is very helpful to the newly established AIIB. Of course, this also means higher standards and requirements for the operations of the AIIB. There are extensive common interests and cooperation experience that has been accumulated between China and Europe over the years. The "voice from Europe" will help the AIIB to develop more steadily for a better future, and we believe that China and Europe and the other original members of intention have the intelligence and capability to move in the same direction. It is certain that it is with sincerity and the spirit of consultation that the United Kingdom, France, Germany, and Italy have joined the AIIB.

With the joining of European countries, the AIIB will be naturally rated high at the time of issuing bonds, and a high rating will substantially reduce the cost of finances for the leading projects of the AIIB and help the AIIB to obtain low-interest financing on the international market in the future.

1.1.4 *The Goal of Lean, Clean, and Green Development*

Jin Liqun, a former senior officer of the ADB and the World Bank and chief supervisor of the China Investment Corporation (CIC), a Chinese sovereign wealth fund, was responsible for preparing for the establishment of the AIIB, functioning as secretary general of the interim multilateral secretariat of the AIIB. He talked about the following three goals for the future development of the AIIB: for the organization to be lean, clean, and green. He hoped that the AIIB would be built into an organization with efficiency, flexibility, a simple structure, and convenient operations rather than a purely bureaucratic organization; meanwhile, the AIIB should exclude all possibilities of corruption and avoid the chance of corruption produced by the operations and the organizational structure itself by means of purchasing professional services; the credit policy of the bank would also stick to the principle of green and sustainable development.

The future investments of the AIIB will not only be confined to traditional significant infrastructure projects such as railways, highways, airports, bridges, and hydraulic engineering, but they will also include energy conservation, emission reduction, and agricultural projects; furthermore, the AIIB will not only favor innovative greenfield investment but also brownfield investment (cross-border Merger & Acquisitions) and participate in some existing reconstruction projects with a bright future.

Doris Fischer, a professor with the University of Wuerzburg and an expert on China's issues, pointed out that the Chinese would not take the risk of the failure of the AIIB, but would learn advanced standards and experience from others in implementing environmental protection. "There are many challenges of establishing a brand-new institution like the AIIB from the commercial perspective apart from the political consideration." In addition, Allan Zhang, director of the Consultancy Service Department of Price Waterhouse Coopers, remarked that "It is a critical issue of how to define yourself in the current global economic structure. To a great extent, all doubts and questions come from the little information about its rules. In the nurturing stage, many issues are suspending, such as pattern of commercial operations, management structure, investment policy, and shareholders' financial return; thus, it is normal to have those guesses." In other words, Zhang pointed out that the bank loan had a direct impact on the direction of future economic development; thus, it is an international mainstream trend that the bank should be committed to push forward sustainable development and green growth, and the policy on bank loans needed to reflect such a concept. Therefore, international institutions like the World Bank have clauses on the environment and social policies in evaluating the projects and are satisfying the international guiding principle of the banking industry. In addition, the member states have their own expectations due to their different stages of development. It is not an easy task to coordinate and satisfy the expectations of different member states.[2]

1.1.5 *The Innovative Financial Governance Structure Set up by the AIIB*

China's wish for playing a major role in international affairs is highlighted in the preparation for the establishment of the AIIB. During the past 60 years, the World Bank and the IMF have spread the influence of the United States to remote areas, and the officials of China and those from the West all believed that the AIIB would create an influence of a similar scale. The purpose of founding the AIIB is to provide finance for the infrastructure projects in Asia, while the funds needed in these projects are far beyond the capability of the IMF, the World Bank, and the ADB together. As predicted by China, from now until 2020, the infrastructure projects in Asia will need around USD 730 billion each year. "China will not bully other member states; instead, we will cooperate with them and try our best to reach a consensus on all decisions to be made." Jin Liqun also believed that "China will not show off its position as a majority shareholder." Meanwhile, the Obama administration has not been able to provide more funds to the IMF with the approval of Congress and has suspended the proposal of revising the voting rights policy, which has won a louder voice for China and other emerging economies regarding the decision-making of the IMF.

With regard to the AIIB proposed by China, the President of the World Bank, Jin Yong, said to the public that he supported China in preparing for the AIIB and he had no feeling that the World Bank

---

[2] Shi Yan. (March 20, 2015). Exclusive Decoding of the Three Major Goals of AIIB: Lean, Clean, and Green. *IFeng Finance.* Retrieved from http://finance.ifeng.com/a/20150320/13567369_0.shtml.

would be threatened. Several hours after China announced the launching of the AIIB project, Jin Yong commented that he and his colleagues at the World Bank would "keep close coordination" with Chinese officials. He further added that it is wonderful for China to propose the AIIB project, because developing countries have an "immense demand" for infrastructure investments. The global demand for infrastructure investment loans approaches USD 1.5 trillion, while the multilateral development banks and private investors are only able to provide about USD 205 billion worldwide. "Considering the current shortage in infrastructure investments, the AIIB deserves a warm welcome."

1.2 *The Silk Road Fund*

On November 8, 2014, at the Dialogue on Strengthening the Connectivity Partnership held in Beijing, President Xi Jinping announced that China would invest USD 40 billion in establishing the Silk Road Fund and provide financial support to the projects related to connectivity in the countries along the Belt and Road, including national infrastructure, resource development, industrial cooperation, and financial cooperation. On November 9, 2014, at the APEC CEO Summit, President Xi Jinping delivered the invitation: the Silk Road Fund welcomes investors in and outside of Asia to join, for it is open and allows sub-funds of various types in different industries or different regions. On December 29, 2014, the Silk Road Fund was established in Beijing and officially began its operations. Jointly invested in by China's foreign exchange reserves, the CIC, the China Import & Export Bank, and the China Development Bank, the Silk Road Fund is a medium- and long-term development and investment fund established under the principle of marketization, internationalization, and professionalization in accordance with the *Company Law of the People's Republic of China*, with a focus on seeking investment opportunities and providing corresponding financing services as the Belt and Road develops. The differences between the Silk Road Fund and the AIIB lie in that the AIIB is a regional multilateral development institution in Asia, under whose framework each member state is required to contribute, and the main operation of the AIIB is releasing loans. The Silk Road Fund, somewhat similar to the PE, targets the subjects who have money and the wish to invest and features a larger focus on the proportion of equity investments. The Silk Road Fund aims to invest in the medium- and long-term projects of strategic significance, and the equity investment fund may also match the other financing modes. In the general context of the Belt and Road Initiative, some funds that are able to make medium- and long-term commitments can be used in relevant projects and capability construction related to the Silk Road, including the development of some industries and also the construction of infrastructures, including telecom and roads. The Silk Road Fund will carry forth the idea of commercialized operations, mutual benefit for win–win, and openness and inclusiveness; it will respect the international economic and financial rules and invest in areas such as infrastructure, resource development, industrial cooperation, and financial cooperation through diversified marketization that is equity-dominated in order to boost common development prosperity and realize a reasonable amount of financial income and medium- and long-term sustainable development.[3] It has been suggested by experts that the total Silk Road Fund should reach around USD 400 billion in the future. In addition, it will facilitate the diversification of foreign exchange reserves and also provide more opportunities to relevant enterprises in China and overseas. The infrastructure and resource and energy development in Asia, Africa, and Latin America are very eager to be supported by the capital, personnel, technologies, and management from China, which is quite similar to China's situation in the early years of the reform and opening-up, when China was also yearning for the "outside world." The diversified foreign exchange reserve management and investment will also be helpful in the domestic development in China.

---

[3] Wei Xi. (February 16, 2015). The First-phase Investment of USD 10 Billion in the Silk Road Fund Available, Investment in Foreign Exchange Reserve Accounting for 65%. *Sina Finance*. Retrieved from https://finance.sina.com.cn/china/20150216/145121564818.shtml.

The Silk Road Fund had its first "order intake" in April 2015, that is, the investment in the Karot Hydropower Station, a prioritized project for the China–Pakistan Economic Corridor. The planned capacity of the station is 720 MW, generating 3,213,000 kWh/year. The total investment was valued at around USD 1.65 billion. Construction of the power station is planned to start at the end of the year 2015. The Silk Road Fund will adopt the way of equity plus creditor's rights and the model of "construction-operation-transfer," and be put into operation in 2020.[4] The Silk Road Fund was established with China's financial strength in providing direct support to the Belt and Road Initiative. To choose the corridor energy project as the first project supported by the Silk Road Fund not only fully reflects the concept of common development and prosperity of China and Pakistan, but it also reflects the role of the Belt and Road Initiative in advancing the construction of the corridor. The Three Gorges Corporation will invest in another hydraulic power station on the Jhelum River, that is, the Kohala Hydraulic Power Station with a capacity of 1,100 MW, the construction of which was expected to start in 2016.

1.3 *The BRICS Bank Participating in Global Governance*

Since the financial crisis, the changes in US financial policies have caused a fluctuation in the funds on the international financial market, which has a severe impact on the stability of the monetary value of merging markets. There has been a weak fluctuation in China's currency, but India, Russia, and Brazil all experienced substantial depreciation of their currencies, leading to inflation. Mere dependence on aid from the IMF has been untimely and insufficient. Therefore, in order to evade monetary instability in the next financial crisis, the BRICS countries plan to construct a financial security network. The BRICS may cash some foreign currencies from this "capital pool" for emergencies in case of monetary instability.

---

[4] Zhang Mo. (April 22, 2015). Silk Road Fund Having the First Order-intake, Announcing the Opening of Investments. *People's Daily Online*. Retrieved from http://world.people.com.cn/n/2015/0421/c157278-26879341.html.

On March 28 and 29, 2012, the leaders of the BRICS countries attended the fourth summit in New Delhi, India, jointly signing the *Master Agreement in Extending Credit Facility for the BRICS Bank Cooperation Mechanism for Multilateral Domestic Currencies* and the *Multilateral Confirmed Credit Service Agreement*. According to these agreements, the five banks as the members of the bank cooperation mechanism, that is, the China Development Bank Corp., the State Corporation Bank for Development and Foreign Economic Affairs of Russia, the Brazilian Development Bank, the Exim Bank (of India), and the Development Bank of Southern Africa, will expand the business of standard currency settlement and loans steadily for the purpose of serving the trade among the BRICS and more convenience in investment, and strive for establishing a development bank for the BRICS.

The BRICS Development Bank Agreement was officially signed at the Sixth BRICS Summit held in Fortaleza, Brazil, in 2014. According to the set schedule, the preparatory group for the BRICS Bank will settle in Shanghai around May 2015 and the bank will officially open on July 21, 2015. The establishment and operation of the BRICS Bank is a specific action by which emerging economies, represented by the BRICS, and developing countries push forward the transformation of the international financial system, and it is a new starting point for them to participate in global governance. The launch of the BRICS Bank anticipates, on the one hand, the ending of the monopoly of European countries and the United States over the global financial governance by means of the Bretton Woods System, and on the other hand, the BRICS Bank has no intention of being in opposition to or replacing the existing international financial governing institution, which may be discerned from the "program for sustainable settlement for realizing inclusive growth" released at the BRICS Fortaleza Summit.

As of April 2014, the scale of foreign exchange reserves of the BRICS Bank had exceeded USD 5 trillion, accounting for 75% of the world's total foreign exchange reserve. China's foreign exchange reserve had exceeded USD 4 trillion, ranking no. 1 in the world, and those of Russia and India are also colossal.

According to the agreement, the headquarters of the BRICS Bank will be based in Shanghai, the ratified capital will be USD 100 billion, and the original subscribed contribution of capital will be USD 50 billion, which shall be contributed by the BRICS's original member states, each with an equal voting right. The five-member states will delegate their own ministers of finance or the president of the central bank to perform as the representative director in the Bank, who will be responsible for formulating the specific operational procedures within the bank. The president of the BRICS Bank will have a five-year term of office. The first president comes from India; Brazil and Russia will nominate the Board Chairman and President of the bank, respectively; the Africa Center of the BRICS Bank will be established in Johannesburg, South Africa. The BRICS Bank allows other developing countries to join, but the capital shares held by the original member states may not be less than 55%. The construction of infrastructures is defined as the main operation for the BRICS Bank, with the purpose of making up for the weakness of the IMF and the World Bank, thus providing a new guarantee for the economic development of emerging economies and creating a more diversified world.

Together with the birth of the BRICS Bank is the arrangement of the emergency reserve valued at USD 100 billion for the original capital. This is an attempt made by the BRICS to establish a pattern for the management of independent financial crises. The debt crisis of Latin America in the 1980s and the financial crisis of Southeast Asia in the 1990s had their respective root causes, of course, but they both proved that financial risks were accumulated during the rapid development of emerging markets. Affected by the state's recent economic policy of quantitative easing, the financial market of emerging countries is fluctuating, having seriously affected the restoration and development of the real economy. It is against such a background that the BRICS established the foreign exchange reserve base.

The BRICS Bank cooperates and competes with the IMF and the World Bank, among other international multilateral financial institutions. The existing international multilateral financial institutions focus on the transfusion to developing countries from the perspective of developmental aid, with complicated application procedures, conditions, and requirements. The loan from the World Bank is mainly used in poverty reduction in developing countries, but the long term of application and complicated formalities for the loans and the other high thresholds, as well as incidental conditions such as implementing the policy of liberal democracy in those countries that receive the assistance, required by the World Bank, makes it less welcome. Despite what has been said above, the aid provided by the World Bank is far from enough. It is estimated that international multilateral development banks, including the World Bank, have only satisfied 2%–3% of the global demand for infrastructure investments, while the shortage of funds needed in infrastructure is over USD 1 trillion in developing countries each year.

It is definitely possible for the BRICS Bank to advance with the existing financial system for mutual benefit. The BRICS Bank has expressed its wish to welcome other developing countries to join and also welcome cooperation with developed countries through leveraging equities. This may help to expand the sources of funds and further help to elevate the credibility rating and competitiveness of the countries on the international capital market.[5]

In the Bretton Woods System, the voice of each country is decided by their capability of contribution. The big power that contributes more speaks louder than those that contribute less, and the inequality between the big powers as the lender and the minor countries as the borrower is becoming more obvious. The BRICS countries object to this situation and stressed in their *Fortaleza Declaration* that, despite different levels of capability and development, different countries should enjoy equal rights, opportunities, and participation in global economy, finance, and trade affairs.

In international financial institutions, such as the World Bank and the IMF, it is developed countries that are decision-makers. The point of criticism of the World Bank for a long time was that it is mainly concerned with the need for interest and developmental experience of

---

[5] Ye Yu. (July 14, 2014). The BRICS Development Bank Should Retain Openness. *Eastday*. Retrieved from http://news.eastday.com/eastday/13news/auto/news/world/u7ai2000848_k4.html.

developed countries, advocating the "Washington Consensus" in an inflexible way, and that it ignores the developmental conditions and the needs of developing countries. The main members of the management and the employees of the BRICS Bank will come from the BRICS countries and other developing countries. The change in the structure of human resources will enhance our knowledge about the reality of developing countries, and thus make the services to be provided by the BRICS Bank more specific through optimization of the design.

The preparation and operation of the BRICS Bank will force the reform of international financial institutions such as the IMF. According to the articles of association of the BRICS Bank, its subjects are not limited to the BRICS countries. Any country may apply for aid or financing with the bank. Argentina, Egypt, Nigeria, Kazakhstan, Indonesia, and Turkey are all major emerging economies and are potential members of the BRICS Bank. With joining in of more developing countries, the BRICS Bank will form a huge non-Western financial network and then push the IMF and other international financial institutions to accelerate their reform.[6]

The World Bank and the IMF are both dominated by developed countries in Europe and America. In the World Bank, for example, the BRICS has only 13% voting rights, while the United States alone takes up 15%. In the IMF, the voting rights of the BRICS countries put together does not exceed 11%, while the United States has nearly 17%, and the voting rights held by the United Kingdom and France alone are bigger than any BRICS country. Therefore, the BRICS would be put in a very passive state if they wanted to carry out a large amount of construction of infrastructures through loans. Both the World Bank and the IMF, however, have very harsh terms on releasing loans. They require participation and decide the key points, such as the design of projects, the purchase of materials, and acceptance.

There are mainly four concerns about the IMF's legality and effectiveness globally. The first one is the IMF's governance structure,

---

[6]Fan Yongming, He Ping. (2015). Concept of "Inclusive Competition" and the BRICS Bank. *International Review*, Issue 2, pp. 1–14.

that is, the quota and voting rights in the IMF. There are two very serious issues. The first issue is that the quota and voting rights of emerging countries are seriously disproportioned with their contribution to the world's economy. The BRICS countries are typical examples in this sense, China's situation being the most conspicuous. In contrast, the voting rights of European countries are much higher than their shares in the world's economy. The second issue is that the voice of the poorest countries is too weak in the IMF. This issue is related to the IMF's surveillance function. By surveillance, it means that the IMF is responsible for tracking the macroeconomic operations of its member states and 'providing evaluation reports to the macroeconomic status of the member states regularly under Article IV, which will serve as the evaluation standard for whether to provide loans to the member states or not. The IMF's surveillance function is critical to maintain the stability of the macroeconomy of each country and the quality of the IMF loans. Currently, however, there are two main defects with the IMF's surveillance function: First, it is too much focused on bilateral surveillance (i.e., the surveillance of the macroeconomy of the member states carried out by the IMF staff) and ignores multilateral surveillance (i.e., the surveillance of the world's economy and the global financial market as a whole to spot and respond to global systematic risks in advance); second, the IMF's surveillance has no binding force on the countries that do not borrow from the IMF, especially developed countries, who even impose pressure on the IMF sometimes against the IMF in publishing the macroeconomic surveillance reports that are unfavorable to them. The third point is the IMF's lending system. The major issues with the IMF's loans include the following: First, the size of the loan to be obtained by the member states is quite limited, and the period for the IMF to release a loan is too long; second, the IMF loan has a harsh and rigid conditionality, which usually requires the lending country to implement a tight financial and monetary policy to improve the international income and spending. Such a condition tends to worsen the economic and financial status of a country that is suffering a crisis and to deepen the negative impact of the crisis. This is one of the fundamental reasons for emerging countries and developing countries not to be willing to borrow from the IMF in recent years. The fourth point lies in the utilizable resources. On the one hand, the resources that the IMF can use as loans only value around USD 250 billion, which is not enough to satisfy the financing demand for coping with the global financial crisis; on the other hand, the size of the loan applied with the IMF has become smaller and smaller in recent years and the interest from the loan interest has declined sharply; thus, the IMF itself is faced with an imbalance of budgets.[7]

1.4 *Preparing for the Establishment of the SCO Development Bank*

During his visit to European and Asian countries from December 14 to 20, 2014, Premier Li Keqiang expressed at the 13th Meeting of the Council of the Heads of the Governments of the SCO Member States that China would start the selection of the first projects for the China–Eurasian Economic Cooperation Fund and was willing to set up the bilateral sub-funds with each member to support the implementation of the economic projects within the region. "Meanwhile, in order to play the role of the Silk Road Fund better, we hope that the members of the SCO will push forward the progress of the establishing of the SCO Development Bank through consensus to set up a financing platform featuring long-term stability for Eurasia."

The SCO was established on June 15, 2001. Its member states include China, Russia, Kazakhstan, Kyrgyzstan, Tajikistan, and Uzbekistan, and the observing states include Iran, Pakistan, Afghanistan, Mongolia, and India. The SCO is the first international organization that is named after a city in China. Its six member states cover three-fifth of the area of Eurasia. The Meeting of the Council of the Heads of the Governments of the Member States is held once every year, and it is held regularly only in the member states.

"The Silk Road Economic Belt proposed by China is connected to the developmental strategies of the states involved in the SCO.

---

[7] Zhang Ming. (2010). International Currency System Reform: Background, Reasons, Measures and China's Participation. *International Economic Review*, Issue 2, pp. 114–137.

China is willing to strengthen the deliberation and cooperation with each party and advance the industrial transformation and updating jointly," remarked Li Keqiang. In the *Joint Communiqué*, premiers and prime ministers of the six member states stressed that, according to the *Plan of Implementing the Measures for the "Guidelines for Multilateral Economic and Trade Cooperation among SCO Member States"* and the *List of Measures for the SCO Further Pushing Forward the Project Cooperation 2012–2016*, it is very important to create convenience for practical cooperation in the areas of finance, banking, science and technology, innovation, and energy, including alternative energy and renewable energy, as well as customs, agriculture, traffic, and telecom, and it is expected to establish the financing security mechanism under the SCO framework in order to boost economic growth and expand the economic and trade connections among the member states.

On November 25, 2010, when the 9th Prime Ministers' Meeting of the SCO Member States was held in Dushanbe, the proposal of studying the establishment of the SCO Development Bank was raised and the new ways of joint contribution and common benefit were discussed. There are more than 100 economic cooperation projects under the SCO framework, such as the China–Kazakhstan natural gas pipeline, the Double-West Highway, and the China–Kyrgyzstan and the China–Tajikistan highways. Experts from Kazakhstan said that it was absolutely necessary to establish the SCO Development Bank and the SCO Development Fund for the present, and with a basic common understanding of this point, each country was becoming more pressed to discuss issues such as the contribution to be made by each country and which projects should be given prioritized support, and so on (Table 3.1).[8]

Currently, the SCO is holding an important position in the multipolarized world. The SCO member states involve a total population of around 1.5861 billion people (making up 24% of the world's

[8] Zhou Zhou. (December 17, 2014). China Supports Financing for Economic Projects within the Region and Makes Further Progress in Establishing the SCO Development Bank. *IFeng Finance*. Retrieved from http://finance.ifeng.com/a/20141217/13360819_0.shtml.

Table 3.1 Four Major Capital Pools for the Belt and Road Initiative

	Nature	Investee	Orientation	Original Investment	Schedule
AIIB	Regional multilateral financial development institution	AIIB member states or state of investment intention	Construction of Infrastructures	Statuary capital of USD 100 billion, China subscribed around USD 50 billion and contributed 50%. The equity distribution among the other original members of intention was based on their GDP proportions in the AIIB	Completed negotiations and signing of the articles of association before June 2015; officially founded and put into operation on December 25, 2015
Silk Road Fund	Sovereignty investment fund	Countries and regions along the Belt and Road	Infrastructure, resource development, industrial cooperation, and financial cooperation	Total capital: USD 40 billion. Of the first phase contribution of USD 10 billion, as preliminarily planned, the foreign exchange reserve contributed 65%, the China Import & Export Bank and the CIC both contributed 15%, and the China Development Bank contributed 5%	

(*Continued*)

Table 3.1 *(Continued)*

	Nature	Investee	Orientation	Original Investment	Schedule
BRICS Bank	Regional multilateral financial development institution	Not limited to the five BRICS countries, but extended to all developing countries. BRICS member states have the preemptive right to loans	Construction of infrastructures	Kick-off fund is USD 50 billion, to be shared by the five BRICS countries. It will gradually be increased to USD 100 billion	
SCO Development Bank	Regional multilateral financial development institution	Six member states	For SCO members, demonstrative projects of energy, traffic, and modern information technology		To be established in 2016

total), and it may involve a population of 2.8029 billion (making up 42.5% of the world's total) when including the population of the observing states of 1.3479 billion. Of the SCO member states and observing states, because of the differences in population and speed of economic development, there are some countries that enjoy rich energy resources and production, such as Russia, Iran, Kazakhstan, and Uzbekistan, and also those countries who have less clean energy but feature high energy consumption, such as China and India. Therefore, the SCO has a solid material foundation and sufficient right to voice their opinions — whether it is about the complementary cooperation in energy resources within the SCO or participation of the member states and observing states in solving the issues regarding the global energy market or significant international programs such as the "Millennium Development Plan" of the United Nations and the "United Nations Framework Convention on Climate Change."

1.5 *Preparing to Fund the Asian Financial Cooperation Association (AFCA)*

After taking the lead in establishing the AIIB, China is going to initiate another nongovernmental organization in the financial area of Asia, that is, the AFCA, which was announced by Yang Zaiping, Executive Deputy Director of the China Banking Association at the Asia Cooperation Dialogue: the Cooperation Forum for Jointly Building the Belt and Road and the Asia Conference of Industry and Commerce. This means that China will fill the gap in the area of specialized regional international organizations.

These years have witnessed the prosperous development of Asia as a region, but its financial cooperation has lagged behind and is creating a huge gap between the status quo and the regional demand. This is disproportionate with the financial influence and economic aggregate in the world. Faced with such challenges and opportunities, how will China utilize the advantages of its multilateral financial institutions locally and push forward the financial cooperation for the Belt and Road Initiative? The second part of the Asia Cooperation Dialogue: the Cooperation Forum for Jointly Building the Belt and Road explored this issue.

Yang Zaiping believed that the rapid economic growth of Asia does not mean that Asia will replace the position of Europe and America and become a new sole economic center in the world, nor does it mean that the original economic focus for Europe and America would decline, but it only means that a new economic center has emerged in the world and has added another pole in the world.

Yang Zaiping pointed out that the world's economy has another focus, that is, Asia, and this would not only help in the growth of the world's economy, but it would also benefit the balance of the world's economy. In reality, however, the world's economy has grown in an "imbalanced" way for a long time.

One remarkable representation is the imbalance in international trade. He believed that the imbalance in trade is, to a great extent, attributable to the imbalance in international finance, and the imbalanced finance would further influence the formulation of international rules and cause an imbalance in global governance.

The global governance that facilitates the world's economic and financial balance will not be realized without an non-governmental organizations "Asian voice" or "Asian seat." In such a context, there is a strong need for financial cooperation in Asia. To satisfy such a need in a better way, Asian countries will not only need practice at the governmental level, but they will also need assistance from effective Non-Governmental Organizations (NGO).

To carry out the Belt and Road Initiative properly, the China Banking Association is initiating the establishment of the AFCA.

As a financial NGO in Asia, the association aims to advance the normalization of the financial interconnectivity in Asia, thus boosting a safer and steadier financial development of Asia and serving the economic development of Asia better; it also aims to strengthen the voice and influence of Asian finance in the international financial system and to allow Asia to make a due contribution to global financial governance. thus enabling it to become an important pole in balancing the world's economy and finance and the global economic and financial balance. The AFCA will cooperate with the Silk Road Fund in jointly pushing forward the Belt and Road Initiative, building the nongovernmental financial exchange platform for connectivity in

Asia, and pushing the financial cooperation between China and other Asian countries to a new height.

Currently, the Institute of International Finance (IIF), with its headquarters in Washington, USA, is the only and most influential global association in the financial industry. Its members include all the major commercial banks and financial investment institutions, as well as asset management companies and companies managing pension funds, rating institutions, and insurance companies, in the world, totaling over 400 organizations from over 70 countries and regions. Established in 1983, the original objective of the IIF was to cope with the debt crisis in Latin American countries that was growing in the 1980s. In November 2010, the IIF founded its Asian Representative Office in Beijing with the purpose of enhancing regional cooperation and understanding in Asia.

1.6 *Influence of "the Fund and the Bank"*

Since October 2013, China's proposal of establishing the AIIB and the Silk Road Fund ("the Fund and the Bank" for short) has won extensive international support from both inside and outside the region.

"The Fund and the Bank" has laid the foundation for the successful implementation of the Belt and Road Initiative, accomplishing the effect of regional economic integration. Asia has a large-scale population, capital, and resources, but the development of Asia lacks organization, an efficient multilateral financial organization, in particular, that utilizes the population, capital, and resource advantages efficiently. Once "the Fund and the Bank" are fulfilled, the financial resources inside and outside the region may be gathered and utilized, consolidating the will of the government, industries, and people of the countries along the Belt and Road, enhancing each country's capability for communication, boosting cooperation among industries and coordination among the labor divisions along the value chain, thus allowing the economies at different levels of development to achieve mutual benefit and win–win results through interconnectivity, trade and investment opening-up, and financial and service cooperation. China is actively engaged in organizing "the Fund and the Bank" and advancing the Belt and Road Initiative, encouraging the United States and Russia to accelerate the regional economic organizations led by them.

"The Fund and the Bank" as proposed by China will evoke the effect of international monetary and financial cooperation and innovation. "The Fund and the Bank" per se as a whole is a model for multilateral monetary and financial cooperation and innovation, presenting monetary and financial cooperation among the governments inside and outside the region. The new multilateral financial organization established by joint investments will jointly settle problems and difficulties that each country is faced with, thus boosting the world's economic growth. "The Fund and the Bank" will help each member state to strengthen the monetary and financial coordination among them, push forward cooperation on financial supervision and two-way business cooperation and investments among financial institutions within the region, and it may construct a regional financial security mechanism for preventing monetary and financial risks with concerted efforts. In addition, while the AIIB is winning support from its original members, the United States proposed to cooperate with the AIIB and the World Bank, the IMF expressed its will to enhance cooperation with them, and the ADB also proposed such an appeal; thus, "the Fund and the Bank" has generated extensive cooperation among international financial institutions.

Financial innovation is the source of vitality for "the Fund and the Bank," which will not be confined to the conventional operational models of either the World Bank or the ADB. Instead, they will innovate the developing finance and investment model; adopt open and diversified financing mechanisms; attract global provision of capitals; develop cross-border Internet financing, cross-border trade financing, and financial insurance business; and boost financing and swapping to accelerate the internationalization of RMB.

When the Belt and Road Initiative and preparation for "the Fund and the Bank" were proposed by China in the beginning, they were embodied with the ideas of the culture and values of China. It is not only that the platform of the Belt and Road Initiative is open without any exclusive groups, but also that "the Fund and the Bank" is an open institution, which will win the confidence of the governments, entrepreneurs, and citizens of relevant countries; boost the people-to-people communication; and move together toward the Asian community of destination. They will develop a new line of thought, a new identification, and new choices with China as the center of politics, economy, culture, and values, thus forming a new structure of geopolitics.

The success in establishing "the Fund and the Bank" has not only infused more color into the multilateral financial institutions, but it will also improve the structure of international financial institutions. Although the Silk Road Fund and the AIIB were initiated in the name of jointly building the Belt and Road and were to serve for its development and implementation, their original purpose was to act as complementary institutions rather than the ones that were to replace the existing World Bank or the IMF. However, their actual functions, impact effect, and goals may not be limited to this alone.

In a short period of time, the Belt and Road and "the Fund and the Bank" have become a regional multilateral cooperative organization and a multilateral financial institution, respectively. As they are becoming increasingly mature and influential, the regional economic organization and the financial institution are very likely to be expanded to a global economic organization and a global financial institution. In fact, the newly established multilateral institutions and the existing ones may be complementary to and cooperate with each other, and besides, they would be direct or indirect competitors. There may not necessarily be a threat to the continuance of the existing institutions, but the new ones are going to develop a new international economic order that will coexist with the present ones, thus making the current international economic order more equal and efficient, advancing the organizational reform of the existing international development institutions and the IMF, and changing the structure in which the United States has dominated the international multilateral financial system and global governance for quite a long time.[9]

---

[9] Xia Xianliang. (April 8, 2015). "The Fund and the Bank" Will Evoke Multi-layered Effects. *China Social Sciences Net*. Retrieved from http://www.cssn.cn/skyskl/skyskl_jczx/201504/t20150408_1578680.shtml.

As a nongovernmental regional multilateral development institution in Asia, the AIIB has developed a "community with a common destiny" with peaceful development and cooperation for a win–win situation. Xi Jinping pointed out that "The international community has become a community with a common destiny that is shared by all of us. Faced with the complicated world economic situation and global issues, no country is able to survive or develop completely on its own. Each country is required to cooperate with the others, care about the other countries while pursuing the benefits for one's own country, boost the common development of each country while seeking development of one's own country, build new-type global development partnerships which are more equal and balanced, boost the common interest of human beings, and jointly build a home that is called the earth." The AIIB works energetically to solve the shortage of investment funds in the region of Asia. It is China's action with the idea of "intimacy, sincerity, benefit and inclusiveness," showing China's image as a responsible giant. "China will steadfastly follow the road leading to peaceful development and stick to the strategy of opening-up and cooperation for a win–win situation, and develop friendly cooperation with the other countries around the world on the basis of the five principles of peaceful coexistence. China's peaceful development starts from Asia, relies upon Asia, and will benefit Asia." "As a Chinese saying goes, neighbors wish each other well, just as loved ones do to each other. China will continue to promote friendship and partnerships with its neighbors, consolidate friendly ties and deepen mutually beneficial cooperation with them and ensure that its development will bring even greater benefits to its neighbors." As a world financial institution following the World Bank, the IMF, and the ADB, the AIIB advocates mutual benefit for a win–win situation. It complements and improves the existing international economic order. It is a declaration of action by China for actively participating in the global economic governance system. It reflects China's appeal and conforms to the benefit of the other member states, which has a far-reaching significance in improving the structure of global financial governance and the long-term sustainable development of the world's economy. By taking advantage of the platform of the AIIB, China will further enhance mutual trust in politics with other countries, which is helpful to create an external environment for peaceful development and stability throughout the world.

The AIIB alone will not work. The AIIB, together with the BRICS Bank, the SCO Development Bank, the China–Africa Development Bank, the Silk Road Fund, the China–Africa Development Fund, the China–Africa Forum, the China–Central Asia Cooperation Forum, the China–Arab States Cooperation Forum, the China-ASEAN Forum, and the China–Australia, China–Singapore, China–South Korea, China-ASEAN, China–Chile, and China–Sweden free trade agreements, multilateral trade and investment arrangements, including the regional comprehensive economic partnership, and the financial cooperation and currency swap agreement with peripheral countries, will have a significant proactive influence on advancing the transformation of the world's economic structure.

2. The Investments of the World Bank and the ADB in Asia

2.1 *The Objectives of the World Bank and the ADB and Investments in Asia*

In 1966, the development of the Asian economy and the active participation of the United States and Japan jointly promoted the establishment of the ADB. The ADB is a regional intergovernmental financial development institution dedicated to promoting the economic and social development of developing countries in the Asia-Pacific region. The ADB was founded on November 24, 1966 and is headquartered in Manila, the capital of the Philippines. As of the end of December 2013, the ADB had 67 members, 48 from the Asia-Pacific region and 19 from other regions. After its establishment, the ADB has not only played an important role in the East Asian economy from the 1960s to the 1980s, but it has also assumed an important role in the economic cooperation and social development in the Asia-Pacific region since the beginning of the new century. China joined the ADB on February 17, 1986. In April 1987, China was elected as a board member of the ADB and obtained a separate board seat on the board of directors. On July 1 of the same year, the office of the Chinese board of directors of the ADB was officially established. On June 16, 2000, the representative branch office of the ADB in China was established in Beijing. In August 2003, Jin Liqun became the first vice president of the ADB with Chinese nationality. In August 2008, Zhao Xiaoyu, the deputy president of the China Export–Import Bank, was also appointed as the deputy president of the ADB. At present, China is the third largest shareholder of the ADB.

The objective of establishing the ADB is to help develop its members among countries in the Asia-Pacific region to eliminate poverty and promote economic and social development in the Asia-Pacific region through developmental assistance. The ADB's aid to developing countries mainly takes the following four forms: loans, equity investments, technical assistance, and joint financing guarantees to achieve the ultimate goal of "a poverty-free Asia-Pacific region." The ADB mainly supports its members in the development of infrastructures, energy, environmental protection, educational programs, and healthcare industries through its policy dialogues, loans, guarantees, technical assistance, and grants.

As a regional intergovernmental financial development agency, the ADB is committed to promote the economic and social development of developing countries in the Asian and the Pacific regions. Since 1999, the ADB has placed special emphasis on poverty alleviation as its top agenda. The ADB was founded in 1966 and China joined it during its 20th year of establishment. Japan and the United States are ranked the first together (15.60%) and China is ranked the third (6.44%) according to the shares subscribed by them. Japan and the United States have tied for the first in terms of voting rights (12.78 %). China is also ranked third (5.45%) in this respect.

From the very beginning of the ADB to the end of the 1970s, Japan was a net beneficiary of the ADB's business. In 1977, the proportion of developed countries in the procurement of the ADB was more than 80%, of which the proportion of Japan accounted for almost 40%. Moreover, in 1972, Japan's proportion was as high

A Package Plan for Financial Security 161

as 67%. The high proportion of Japanese procurement also proves the central position of Japan in donations to the ADB. However, as Japan's rate of contribution to the ADB has increased, Japan has gradually become a net price maker. This was mainly due to the fact that Japan's high ratios of contract bids in the late 1960s and the early 1970s caused much dissatisfaction and criticism from other member donors. They strongly demanded that the ADB should strictly implement more international and competitive bidding and publicize the ADB contract in a more widespread manner.[10]

The ADB is a financial institution headed by Japan and the United States and focused on solving the poverty problem in the Asia-Pacific region. Therefore, it can only solve the economic and developmental problems in a limited sense. However, the AIIB is an intergovernmental financial institution headquartered in Beijing that will use the World Bank management system to operate transparently. It is designed to support the construction of infrastructures complementarily. In fact, the AIIB and the ADB are cooperative with and complementary to each other. They compete but also cooperate with each other from time to time. In other words, they are both financial institutions that benefit all the people in Asia.

The existing multilateral financial institutions can only meet a very small portion of the demand of the financial market. The total funding of the ADB is about USD 160 billion and that of the World Bank is USD 223 billion. At present, the two banks can only provide USD 20 billion each as funding for Asian countries annually. Because of the limited funds for construction, the railways, highways, bridges, ports, airports, and communications infrastructures are severely deficient in certain countries. Many projects that could have contributed to improving people's living standards have had to be shelved until a later time, thus making it difficult to improve the living standard of people in those regions as quickly as possible, and the economic development of the regions lags behind. From 2009 to 2013, the ADB provided loans a total of USD 101.7 billion, of which, however, only USD

---

[10]Liu Xinghong. (2013). Study on the Power Distribution among the ADB Members. *Southeast Journal*, Issue 1.

9.284 billion and USD 10.186 billion in the form of loans were released in 2012 and 2013, respectively. It is impossible to completely fill the funding gaps among countries if we rely solely on the funding from the ADB. In addition, the funds of the ADB were dispersed widely. In 2013, for example, the funds of the ADB were mainly invested in industries such as energy, transportation, communications, finance, and so on, whereas the investments in infrastructures accounted for only 33.62%. Instead, the investments of the AIIB are mainly in the area of infrastructure, with clear objectives and without any overlapping with the ADB, from which we can see clearly its complementary role to the economic growth of Asian countries.

Since China joined the ADB in 1986, the two sides have cooperated extensively on economic development, poverty elimination, and environmental protection. The number of cooperation projects grew originally from few to more than 90 in 2013. Since 1994, China has become the largest annual borrower from the ADB. All the ADB loans to China are hard loans with an annual interest rate of approximately 6.5%–6.9% and with the loan period of 15–25 years.

By 2013, China had become the second largest borrowing country, the largest granter of technical assistance, and the third largest shareholder to the ADB in the world. The projects implemented by China's use of the ADB loans included major projects such as the Beijing–Kowloon Railway, the harness of the Suzhou River in Shanghai, and environmental protection in Beijing. With the investment loans borrowed from the ADB, China has built 3,000 km of expressways and 5,515 km of railways, and has improved roads that connect the poor countries for a total length of 4,500 km, and so on. With the implementation of the strategic development of the western part of China, China's joining the World Trade Organization (WTO), and the changes in the ADB policy, China's cooperation with the ADB has begun to show new trends. To help China cope better with the challenges of development, the ADB's business strategy is now focusing on improving administration systems, strengthening environmental protection and natural resource management, and promoting economic growth so as to reduce poverty in the inland provinces of China.

The majority of the ADB's loan programs to China target the inland provinces, especially the western part of China. These programs include expressway development in southern Sichuan, western Yunnan, Shanxi, Ningxia, Guangxi, and Hunan provinces; the railway from Hubei to Chongqing and that from Zhongwei to Taiyuan; the city road development in Xi'an, the clean energy projects in Gansu Province, the high-voltage circuit in northwestern China, and so on.

The World Bank Group is generally called the World Bank. It comprises five member institutions, namely the International Bank for Reconstruction and Development (IBRD), the International Development Association (IDA), the International Finance Corporation, the Multilateral Investment Guarantee Agency, and the International Center for the Settlement of Investment Disputes. It was founded in 1944 and began to operate in June 1946. The "World Bank" in the narrow sense refers only to the IBRD and the IDA. According to the convention, the top leader of the World Bank Group will be an American for a term of five years. As an international institution, the World Bank's original mission was to help the reconstruction of countries destroyed in the Second World War. The main task was to finance those countries to overcome poverty. The Institutions under the World Bank Group play unique roles in alleviating poverty and improving people's living standards. In 2012, the World Bank provided loans or assistance of approximately USD 30 billion for the development of transitional countries.

In the past 30 years, China has received approximately USD 55 billion in loans from the World Bank's subdivisions such as the IBRD and the IDA. It includes 350 construction projects covering transportation, agriculture, energy, urban construction, the environment, industry, education, healthcare, and so on. These World Bank loans have not only made important contributions to the economic and social development of China in the construction of infrastructures, but they also disseminated many advanced concepts, knowledge, systems, methods, and experiences related to economic and social development to China. The nonmaterial effects it has exerted on China even exceed the direct economic benefits of the project itself.

2.2 *The ADB Increases Its Infrastructure Investment in Asia*

"In view of the huge infrastructure needs in Asia, we can understand the initial purposes of establishing the AIIB," commented by Takehiko Nakao, president of the ADB, on the AIIB. In Asia, where the economy continues to grow, there will be a demand for USD 800 billion each year, which cannot be satisfied solely by the ADB. If infrastructure development slows down, it will have a negative impact on economic growth, and there will still be a long way to go to eradicate poverty. The China-led AIIB is increasingly strengthening its cohesion. In this circumstance, the ADB will have to undergo reforms to become an "active bank." It will be important for them to think over the key issues, such as providing various kinds of projects that are expected to improve its profitability and how to attract private funds.

The General Assembly of the ADB was held in Azerbaijan, from May 2 to 6, 2015. Its president Takehiko Nakao indicated at the meeting that they would increase the annual capacity of financing by 1.5 times more than they did before, which is approximately USD 20 billion/year (approximately RMB 124.002 billion). This initiative is called a "historic reform."

It has been reported that since the beginning of 2016, ADB has shortened the time for the supervision of financial projects to 15 months, that is, a decrease by 6 months, compared with 21 months in 2012. In addition, it will also increase the ratio of its financing in education and healthcare. The amount of financing has also increased by 50% since 2017, and the reform of the "quality and quantity" of financing projects has also been strengthened. Nakao pointed out that with the expansion of capital demand in Asia, the current situation of the ADB has been difficult; thus in the future, it will not abandon the capital increase. However, the fact is that ADB has not increased its capital since 2009. According to the estimation of the ADB, between 2010 and 2020, an average investment of at least USD 8 trillion in domestic infrastructure, which means USD 800 billion/year, will be needed if Asian countries need to maintain their current development of economic growth. The existing multilateral international financial institutions obviously cannot provide such huge amounts of money. Despite the numerous criticisms, the reform of the international financial institutions dominated by the United States and Japan still has not made any substantial progress. The current funding provided by the ADB and the World Bank to Asian countries is definitely insufficient. However, if they aim to increase the capital, the proportion of investment from developing countries such as China will become the focus of attention. According to the ratio of investments of ADB (by the end of 2014), Japan was the largest investor with a rate of 15.7%, followed by 15.6% by the United States, while China and India were only 6.5% and 6.4%, respectively. If the proportion of capital investment from developing countries increases greatly, it will undermine the dominant position of Japan and the United States in the ADB.[11]

Japan's Finance Minister, Aso Taro, stated at the ADB annual meeting in 2015 that the Japanese government would work with Japanese companies to increase investments in the construction of infrastructures in Asia, advocating that this approach aims to promote the benign development of infrastructures in Asia. He further said that these projects are "friendly to the environment and local communities" and will "contribute a lot to Asia's high-quality economic growth."

"The Asian Development Bank will take advantage of its long-term experience and expertise in the Asian region to cooperate with the AIIB on the financing of infrastructures across Asia," said Takehiko Nakao.

On May 21, 2015, Japan announced an investment plan of approximately USD 110 billion for the development of infrastructure in Asia over the next five years.

Compared with the scale of the investment from Japan in infrastructure in the past five years, the amount of this plan has increased by 30%, among which half of the funds have come from national organizations such as the Japan International Cooperation Agency and the Japan International Cooperation Bank. The new plan is intended

---

[11] Wang Lilan. (May 7, 2015). ADB Reforms Forced by the AIIB for Investment Market Share. *Global Times*. Retrieved from https://world.huanqiu.com/article/9CaKrnJKIJo.

to show that Japan is committed to build "high-quality infrastructures" in Asia through the development of human resources and assistance for technology transfer while "differing much from the investments of the AIIB." The Japanese government looks forward to initiate this plan to attract private investment in order to meet a large amount of capital that is needed for the construction of infrastructures in Asia. Niu Zhongjun, an associate professor at the Foreign Affairs Department of China Foreign Affairs University, believes that this plan of Japan demonstrates clearly the purposes of seizing the opportunity of taking the lead in the market in the construction of Asian infrastructures and weakening the influence of the AIIB. It is also a measure taken by the Abe government to cope with the pressure of public opinion within Japan. This plan "essentially belongs to Japan's foreign economic policy. It has no such impact on the Belt and Road Initiative and the AIIB as overemphasized by some media coverage. The over-interpretation of this plan is not necessary. Also, we do not need to regard it as a national strategy (opposed to the AIIB)," A part of the Japanese investment plan will be provided to the targeted countries in the form of official development assistance (ODA). Japan's ODA started quite early among the Western countries, and it has relatively matured through practice during many years in Southeast Asia and other regions. Niu Zhongjun believes that the development of the AIIB also requires exchanges and cooperation with other agencies, including the ADB. "There was not a lot of investments in infrastructures from the ADB before. We hope that both parties will initiate cooperative construction and achieve complementary cooperation from the shared perspective of regional development."[12]

3. The Internationalization of the RMB Paving the Way for the Silk Road Development

In 2014, the Silk Road Fund with a capital of about USD 40 billion was established, and the AIIB was also established in 2015. China is

---

[12] Japan's USD 110 Billion Investment in Asian Infrastructure Accused of Being Infuriated with the AIIB. (May 23, 2015). *China Internet Information Center.* Retrieved from http://news.china.com.cn/2015-05/23/content_35640320.htm.

carrying out a multilayered strategic layout with the world's largest foreign exchange reserve of USD 4 trillion in order to ensure win–win cooperation and the smooth implementation of the Belt and Road Initiative. However, what cannot be overlooked on the more competitive and fierce international financial market is that a sound system of competition is necessary if we want to strengthen the overall quality and quantity of infrastructure in Asia, Africa, and Europe in order to tap the potential of Asia's economy as the center of the world's financial growth.[13] It is also worth noting, in this process, that the internationalization of the RMB is not only necessary but also urgent.

3.1 *The Steady Growth in Foreign Investment Helps the Internationalization of the RMB*

In 1997, the report of the 15th National Congress of the Communist Party of China put forward the idea of "encouraging foreign investments that can leverage China's cutting-edge advantages." In the 1997 Southeast Asian financial crisis, China insisted on the non-devaluation of the RMB, actively implemented foreign economic assistance to other countries, and made positive contributions to the maintenance of the macroeconomic and domestic political stability among the Southeast Asian countries. This political achievement was acknowledged by Southeast Asian and neighboring countries and laid a solid foundation for the establishment of the China-ASEAN FTA in 2002 and the establishment of the China-ROK FTA in 2014. In 2001, China successfully joined the WTO, which has expanded China's opening-up and boosted its economy continuously. By 2004, China's foreign investments had increased rapidly, with a total OFDI of USD 5.33 billion. By the end of 2004, China's accumulated OFDI amounted to USD 44.9 billion. According to the 2004 World Investment Report released by the UNCTAD, the global FDI flow (outflow) was USD 612.2 billion in 2003, and the stock was USD 8,196.9 billion. With this year as the base period, China's OFDI in 2004 was equivalent to 0.9% and 0.55% of the

---

[13] Japanese Media: China Used Foreign Exchange Reserves for a Multi-layered Strategic Layout. (February 21, 2015). *Sina Finance.* https://news.sina.cn/gn/2015-02-21/detail-iavxeafs1241780.d.html

total global OFDI flow (outflow) and stock, respectively.[14] On July 16, 2004, the State Council adopted the *Decision on the Reform of the Investment System* to distinguish the two categories of projects, namely the projects "approved by the investment authority of the State Council" and those "approved by the competent investment authority of the local government," and subdivided the approval of application and filing systems based on the industry and amount difference. The Chinese government since then has introduced a series of financial policies to encourage foreign investments. Its main investors include the China Development Bank, the China Export–Import Bank, and the China Export Credit Insurance Corporation as well as various types of funds established by China in recent years, such as the Sino-Swiss Cooperation Foundation (1998), the China-ASEAN Small-Medium Enterprise Investment Fund (2003), the China–Belgium Direct Equity Investment Fund (2004), the China-Africa Development Fund (2007), the SCO Fund, the AIIB Fund, and so on. In 2014, the State Council issued the *Catalogue of Investment Projects Approved by the Government*, which greatly reduced the categories of projects compared with previous ones.

Since 2010, China has become the world's fifth largest capital exporter, ranking first among developing countries and surpassing Japan, the United Kingdom, and other traditional economic powers, with an annual investment scale of USD 60 billion. In 2013 and 2014, China's foreign investments continued to exceed USD 100 billion. In January 2006, according to the purchasing power parity measurements of *The Economist*, a reputed finance journal in the United Kingdom, the emerging economies accounted for approximately 50% of the global output in 2005 for the first time. In October 2012, the IMF Deputy President, Zhu Min, pointed out in his speech at the China Society of World Economics that the emerging economies and low-income countries accounted for more than 50% of the world's total amount in 2012, which indicates a huge change in the historical structure of the world economic powers. Moreover, it is probable that the proportion of emerging economies and developing countries in global trade will continue to rise in the future. In the

---

[14]Yao Yujie. (September 29, 2004). The statistics of the Ministry of Commerce in UNCTAD's 2004 World Investment Report. Retrieved from http://www.cas.org.cn/xwdt/zhxx/8127.htm.

coming years, the contribution of emerging economies to global economic growth will reach about two-thirds.[15]

3.2 *The Reality and Possibility of the Internationalization of the RMB*

The program of the internationalization of the RMB is the mid- and long-term task that was adopted by the Chinese government in advancing the capacity of the RMB against the background of economic and financial globalization and remarkable economic strength. It includes a number of reforms such as RMB convertibility, opening capital account, exchange rate reform, construction of an offshore financial market, and so on. The internationalization of the RMB will help to enhance its position in the international currency system, and ultimately achieve an effective transformation and a long-term and stable growth of the Chinese economy. Specifically, the connotations of the internationalization of the RMB can be understood from the following aspects: (1) For the free convertibility of the RMB, we can promote the free exchange of capital account items and lead to the convenience of using RMB; (2) With regard to the opening of a capital account, we can promote the opening of financial markets to the outside world, increase the wide usage of the RMB, and harness the circulation channels of the RMB; (3) In terms of exchange rate reform, the mechanism of the RMB exchange rate will be improved to maintain the stability of the RMB currency; and (4) With regard to the construction of an offshore financial market, the function of Hong Kong's offshore financial center will be improved, the construction of Shanghai offshore financial center will be promoted, the RMB financial trading market will be strengthened, and the regional development of the RMB will be enhanced accordingly.[16]

---

[15] Zhu Min. (October 18, 2012). "The Changing World", a speech delivered at the lecture presentation of the China Society of World Economics in 2012. Retrieved from http://money.163.com/special/imfzhuminyanjiang/.

[16] Ba Shusong, Guo Yunzhao. (2008). *Study on the Development of Offshore Financial Markets — International Trends and China's Paths.* Beijing, China: Peking University Press, p. 31.

After the subprime mortgage crisis in 2008, the US government adopted a quantitative easing monetary policy to rescue its financial system, putting China at risk of a passive supply of currency and the loss of foreign exchange reserves because of the depreciation of the US dollar. In this context, the Chinese government has actively promoted the internationalization of the RMB, hoping to increase the independence of its domesticated monetary policy, reduce its dependence on the US dollar, and compensate some of its foreign exchange reserves loss through the internationalization of the RMB. For example, at the level of the international currency system, Zhou Xiaochuan, president of the People's Bank of China, called for the creation of a super-sovereign reserve currency. At the regional level, the Chinese government has actively promoted the negotiation and creation of currency swap agreements; at the national level, the Chinese government has actively promoted the construction of RMB settlement in cross-border trade and in offshore financial market of RMB.

In the current situation of the pattern of the world's economic and financial operations and the status quo of China's economic development, there are preliminary conditions for promoting the internationalization of the RMB: (1) The internationalization of a certain currency is accompanied by an increase in the economic strength of the country in which the currency is used. At present, China's current economic aggregate has ranked second in the world, together with being the world's largest exporter and second largest importer. Therefore, the position of the RMB in the international currency system has been secured and there is still room for its improvement; (2) From the perspective of the current international situation, the quantitative easing monetary policy adopted by the United States to solve its domestic economic recession resulted finally in the devaluation of the US dollar. The fluctuation of commodity prices brought increasingly high costs to other countries. The defects in the European unified monetary system led to the intensification of the sovereign debt crisis, rendering the international currency exchange rate much more unstable. The fluctuation of the major reserve currencies led to a significant impact on the global financial market. Therefore, the internationalization of the RMB and the improvement of its role within the currency system will not only increase the national economy of China, but it will also be conducive to the improvement of the stalemate of the international monetary system; and (3) The strengthening of economic and trade cooperation in Asia will facilitate the frequency of using the RMB in this region and therefore will improve its potential influence. According to China's import and export statistical data, at the end of 2012, China's exports to and imports from Asia accounted for approximately 40% and 30% of its total exports and imports respectively, which became a good impetus for promoting the use of the RMB in the region.[17] According to the statistics of the Ministry of Commerce of the People's Republic of China, China's overseas direct investments in 2014 increased by 14% compared with the previous year, with an amount of RMB 632 billion. From January to April 2015, it also increased significantly by 36% year-on-year to RMB 214.3 billion. Although no specific amount of direct investment was published for each country, the direct investments in the EU have increased by 487% year-on-year. On the contrary, investments in Australia, which quenched enthusiasm in resource exploitation, have dropped by 65% year-on-year, and investments in Japan have also decreased by 14%.[18]

Significant progress has been made in the RMB settlement in cross-border trade. From July 2009 to August 2011, the People's Bank of China and related departments focused on a series of policy initiatives that facilitate cross-border trade settlement and the investment of the RMB, such as the establishment and promotion of a pilot program for the RMB settlement in cross-border trade, thereby allowing three types of institutions to invest in the domestic interbank bond market and implementing the OFDI and FDI of the RMB.

---

[17] Liu Hui, Ba Shusong. (2014). Analysis of the Conditions of the Internationalization of the RMB: Historical Opportunities and Realistic Choices. *Journal of Beijing University of Aeronautics and Astronautics* (Social Sciences), Issue 2, pp. 66–73.
[18] China's Foreign Investment and Economic Cooperation from January to April of 2015. (May 18, 2015). Retrieved from http://news.hexun.com/2015-05-18/175888802.html.

According to the data of the People's Bank of China, since the pilot program of RMB settlement in cross-border trade started in 2009, the amount of RMB settlement in cross-border trade has risen sharply from RMB 506.1 billion in 2010 to RMB 4.63 trillion in 2013. According to the data released by the Society for Worldwide Interbank Financial Telecommunication (SWIFT) in February 2014, the RMB was ranked eighth among the global settlement currencies, following the US dollar, the euro, the British pound, the Japanese yen, the Australian dollar, the Canadian dollar, and the Swiss franc. In October 2010, however, the RMB ranked only 35th among the global settlement currencies. In terms of transactions on the global foreign exchange market, the RMB has leaped to the top ten most actively traded currencies, and its trading position has risen from the 17th in the world in 2010 to the 9th (according to the Bank of International Settlements [BIS]). However, in terms of the proportion of foreign exchange reserves, the proportion of the RMB is still less than 1%, which is not shown in the statistics (as the IMF only takes into account the currencies whose international reserves exceed 1%). At present, China has signed a bilateral swap agreement with Russia for RMB 150 billion or RUB 815 billion, and a bilateral swap agreement of RMB 190 billion or BRL 60 billion with Brazil. With the establishment and development of the business activities of the BRICS Bank, the economic ties among the BRICS countries have become increasingly close. It will also sign RMB swap agreements with other BRICS countries in order to increase the RMB shares in the international reserves of those countries. The enhanced position of the RMB reserves in the BRICS countries will further increase the position of the RMB in the international reserve on the world's financial market.

According to the "Offshore RMB Index (ORI)" launched by the Bank of China, the offshore RMB market has achieved rapid development. Offshore RMB deposits have exceeded RMB 2 trillion, accounting for 1.34% of the total offshore market currencies; in addition, the RMB-denominated bonds and equity investments have developed rapidly on the offshore market, such as the dim sum bond initiated by Hong Kong (with more than RMB 270 billion in 2013), the lion city bond initiated by Singapore, the treasure island bond introduced in Taiwan, and various RMB-denominated bonds issued in London and Luxembourg. On the one hand, the RMB-denominated stocks have been listed on the Hong Kong financial market. However, on the other hand, the offshore RMB loan balance is only approximately RMB 400 billion, which is indeed a very limited total amount.

At present, Hong Kong, London, Singapore, and Taipei have grown into the four most important offshore financial centers in the world. Among them, Hong Kong has the largest share of global RMB offshore trading by virtue of its unique advantages. The Chinese government also intends to make the Hong Kong Special Administrative Region the world's most important RMB offshore center. By the end of February 2014, the scale of RMB deposits in Hong Kong had grown rapidly, reaching a total amount of RMB 920.3 billion.[19]

Since the pilot program of RMB settlement in cross-border trade started in 2009, the internationalization of the RMB has made positive progress. However, compared with the major international currencies such as the US dollar and the euro, there is still a long way to go for the internationalization of the RMB, which is seen clearly in the following aspects:

From the perspective of a trade pricing currency, the internationalization of the RMB has not advanced to a much higher level. In 2013, approximately 5.3% of China's import and export trading was denominated in RMBs. Considering that bilateral trade outside of China is often priced less in RMBs, the current share of RMBs as a denominated currency among the international trading currencies is approximately 0.6%, whereas the proportions of the US dollar and the euro as international trading currencies are as high as 48.1% and 28.9%, respectively.

From the currency of foreign exchange transactions, the use of the RMB in the global foreign exchange market is less frequent than that of other currencies. In April 2013, the amount of RMBs in the total

---

[19] Nie Zhao, Li Ming. (2014). The Internationalization of the RMB: Development, Current Situation and Implementing Methods. *International Economic Cooperation*, Issue 11, pp. 89–95.

foreign exchange transactions accounted for only 2.2%, ranking 9th among all the currencies in the world, which was equivalent to only one-fortieth of the transactions in US dollars, one-fifteenth of those in euros, one-tenth of those in the trading amount in Japanese yens, and one-fifth of the total amount of transactions in British pounds.

From the perspective of international payment currencies, there is still a huge gap to fill between the RMB and major settlement currencies in the world. According to statistics from the SWIFT, in July 2014, the share of RMBs among the currencies used for global payment occupied 1.57%, which was only one-twenty-seventh of that using the US dollar, one-twentieth of that using the euro, and one-sixth of that using the British pound.

From the perspective of an international reserve currency, RMB is used less by foreign exchange stock exchanges. At the end of June 2013, according to the foreign exchange reserves recognized officially by the global market, the US dollar accounted for 60.6%, the euro 24.2%, the British pound 3.9%, the Japanese yen 4.0%, the Canadian dollar 2.0%, the Australian dollar 1.9%, and the Swiss franc 0.3%, whereas the other currencies, including the RMB, accounted for only 3.1%. At present, China has signed a bilateral swap agreement with Russia for RMB 150 billion or RUB 815 billion, and a bilateral swap agreement of RMB 190 billion or BRL 60 billion with Brazil. With the establishment and development of the business activities of the BRICS Bank, the economic ties between the BRICS countries have become increasingly close. China will also sign RMB swap agreements with other BRICS countries in order to increase the RMB shares in the international reserves of the BRICS countries. The enhanced position of the RMB reserves in the BRICS countries will further increase the position of the RMB in the international reserve on the world's financial market.

The reasons for the relatively low level of the internationalization of the RMB currently are as follows: First, despite the fact that China's overall national strength ranks among the top ones in the world, there is still room to further strengthen our overall national power. In terms of economic quality, financial structure, and per capita economic indicators, China still has a huge gap compared with those of the developed countries. Currently, China is still at a low rung on the ladder of the system of the international industrial division of labor; thus the competitive advantages of our national enterprises on the international market is quite weak, resulting in our limited right to formulate trade rules. In addition, the economic growth of China mainly depends on its being investment-driven and factor-driven rather than innovation-driven, which requires further transformation. The lack of capacity for scientific and technological innovation also restricts the improvement of our economic capacity. Second, there is still a long way for China to go before the RMB is fully and freely convertible on the world market. China has achieved the convertibility of most items under the RMB, but there are still certain restrictions and barriers on noncitizen cross-border security investments, monetary market trading, and cross-border financial derivatives trading, thus making it difficult to formulate a smooth mechanism for cross-border circulation of the RMB. Third, the interest rate and exchange rate of the RMB need to be raised further. The marketization of interest rates and the relatively free-floating exchange rate are the common features of the international currencies such as the US dollar, the euro, the Japanese yen, and so on. On the one hand, China's money market interest rate, bond market interest rate, foreign currency deposit, and loan interest rate have become gradually market-oriented, and the RMB loan interest rate control has been fully liberalized to the leverage of the market. However, the current RMB deposit interest rate is still subject to cap management. On the other hand, many current account projects have already achieved the settlement and sale of foreign exchange, but there are still certain restrictions on the settlement and sale of capital accounts, making the foreign exchange market just reflect much more about the situation of the current account of the sale and purchase of foreign exchange while neglecting the latter capital accounts; this easily causes an imbalance in supply and demand on the foreign exchange market. Fourth, the financial market in China is still underdeveloped and with low-level internationalization. At present, the development of China's financial market cannot meet the objective demands of the internationalization of the RMB. China's financial market is not yet open completely to the outside world, and the proportion of the Chinese financial ratio in the international transactions is relatively low; this means that transactions on China's domestic financial market do not have a strong influence on the world market, and fewer noncitizens have participated in the transactions on the domestic financial market. All the abovementioned factors are not conducive to the construction of a system of bilateral circulation of the RMB on the international financial market.[20]

3.3 *The RMB Will Change and Revise the Map of the World's Currencies*

Although the share of RMB within the global market is only 2.17%, it is already the fifth most frequently used currency as a payment currency. According to the principles of the economic theory, importing USD 100 billion worth of goods can create 20 million jobs for the exporting countries. Being the world's largest trading nation, China's annual volume of trade is almost equal to USD 5 trillion. For example, even taking the basic imports of USD 2 trillion for goods every year into account, it is almost equivalent to providing 400 million jobs for the relevant countries. Since the implementation of RMB settlement in cross-border trade in China, it was only RMB 3.58 billion in 2009; however, the value reached RMB 4.8 trillion in the first three quarters of 2014. In 2014, the RMB even became the second largest cross-border payment currency in China, which accounts for approximately 25% of all cross-border revenues and expenditures of the local and foreign currency, and exceeds 15% of the settlement rate of trade in goods in imports and exports. It can be said that after 6 years' implementation of the RMB settlement in cross-border trading, it has laid a relatively solid foundation for the internationalization of the RMB.

According to relevant forecasts, China's volume of trade will reach USD 8 trillion in the next 5 years. China is bound to become the most powerful engine of economic growth in the world. Operating business activities with China means seeking development and any discrimination against the RMB will definitely lose opportunities.

---

[20]Wang Jingwu. (2014). Promoting the Internationalization of the RMB Together with the 21st-Century Marine Silk Road. *Southern Finance*, Issue 11, pp. 4–6.

The Society for Worldwide Interbank Financial Telecommunication (SWIFT) based in Belgium is the most authoritative organization of the international banking industry. Ninety percent of the world's banks are using the data from SWIFT, which makes its reports the most influential over the other relevant ones in the world. The latest report of SWIFT revealed that the RMB has jumped to the fifth largest currency in the world, and the payment amount has increased by 107% within one year. This rapid increase is astonishing. The use of the RMB for liquidation has become the consensus of many countries. The Beijing Government has established RMB offshore centers in Hong Kong, London, New York, and other places, allowing the RMB network system to grow maturely, which is also the best evidence of the internationalization of the RMB. With an increasing number of countries doing several businesses with China, it is very hopeful that the RMB will become a member of the "basket of currencies with special drawing rights (SDR)" in the near future.

China currently owns USD 4 trillion of foreign exchange reserves, ranking first in the world. Now, the RMB has solidly and steadily become the ninth largest foreign exchange currency and the seventh largest reserve currency in the world, gradually surpassing the euro to become the world's second largest trade investment currency. China has already implemented cross-border RMB payments with more than 170 countries and signed bilateral currency swap agreements with 28 countries with a total amount of RMB 3 trillion. More than 30 countries have announced the inclusion of the RMB in their reserve currencies. "The internationalization of the RMB" is becoming the consensus of the world's financial industry. With the further increase in Chinese companies and capitals entering the world market, the use of the RMB to export funds will greatly reduce exchange rate risks and increase the competitiveness of Chinese companies in the international market. At the end of 2014, the People's Bank of China signed bilateral currency swap agreements with monetary authorities or overseas banks of 26 countries such as Belarus, Indonesia, Argentina, Brazil, the United Kingdom, and the European Central Bank, amounting to the equivalent of RMB 2.9 trillion. On October 15, 2014, the British government issued RMB 5.8 billion in its sovereign-denominated

RMB bonds, becoming the first Western country to use the RMB as a foreign exchange reserve. Subsequently, Australia announced that its government agencies will also issue offshore RMB bonds, and some central banks or monetary authorities of Australia have also indicated that they intend to include the RMB in their foreign exchange reserve currency. The relevant data show that the RMB has already become the world's seventh largest reserve currency.

In January 2015, the growth rate of the RMB as a global payment currency was as high as 30.6%, whereas the growth rate of other payment currencies during the same period was only 4.8%, which thoroughly puzzled and shocked some Western countries. The area in which the RMB is used as the currency of payment is mainly Hong Kong, which accounts for approximately 73%. Furthermore, we have already explored new paths for further development, attracting countries such as the United Kingdom, Singapore, and the United States to use the RMB for payment and causing a rapid increase in the regions where the RMB is used.

The powerful leap of the RMB has increased the choices and opportunities in the international financial and business circles and has also rapidly boosted China's foreign trade. Experts predict that the inclusion of the RMB as part of the IMF's "basket of currencies with special drawing rights" is just around the corner. Currently, the currencies with SDR include the US dollar, the British pound, the euro, and the Japanese yen. The RMB has become the fifth most frequently used currency in the world, slightly behind the US dollar, the euro, the British pound, and the Japanese yen. This strong momentum proves that China is not only a trading power, but that the RMB's influence in the currency system is also increasing. Spanish media have pointed out that, with the concerted efforts of China and the United Kingdom, London will be an RMB offshore bond issuance center and will become the golden key for Chinese commercial banks to set up their branches within the territory of the United Kingdom. The British media had boldly predicted that the RMB will leap to a higher status within 3 years on the international money market and in less than 10 years, it will surpass the US dollar as the most important reserve currency, so that those who refuse to accept this trendy fact will pay high economic and political costs. The British media warned that a strong RMB means that China has the ability to face an increasingly fierce currency war and will eventually rechart the map of world currencies. They believe that in the near future, regardless of whether it is international trade, exchange markets, or the fund market, none of them will be free of the RMB. SWIFT officials pointed out that the rapid development of the RMB and its "very significant" increase indicate that there will be greater changes in the world's currency market. The data from the People's Bank of China show that the trade, investment, and other financial projects that were paid in RMBs accounted for 20% of all Chinese international trade payments in 2014. The executive of the Royal Bank of Scotland Group believes that the financial crisis that erupted in the United States and Europe demonstrates that the world currency market demands a more stable reserve currency. The rapid growth of RMB transactions is now making up for this status. At present, 166 foreign institutions have been allowed to enter the interbank bond market, and 108 overseas institutions have obtained the qualification of an RMB Qualified Foreign Investor (RQFII).

3.4 *The Rationality for the RMB Joining the SDR*

The SDR is the accounting unit created by the IMF in 1969 to record the reserves of the supplementary Official Member States. Its value is determined by a basket of currencies. Currently, the SDR basket consists of the US dollar, the euro, the Japanese yen, and the British pound. The composition of the currency basket of SDR reflects the changes in the roles of different national currencies in the global trade and financial system.

On December 1, 2015, the IMF officially announced that it had decided to include the RMB in the SDR currency basket after regular voting. This decision was made be effective from October 1, 2016. The Central Bank of all the IMF member states will automatically be exposed to the RMB through holding their own SDRs. The dream that the RMB can stand on an equal footing with the US dollar and the euro is now no longer out of China's reach.

Zhao Yang, the chief economist of the program "Nomura China," believes that although China's long-term economic growth will gradually slow down to a medium-high growth rate, its growth rate is much higher than the major economies in the world. This means that even though there is an obvious difference in the productivity and the growth rate of labor productivity between China and the developed countries, the growth rate of labor productivity is definitely and always a key factor that supports the stability of the value of the RMB. The entry of the RMB into the currency basket has a strategic and landmark significance. It can promote the cross-border use of the RMB in the future and represents the unique features of the SDR. The GDP represented by the currency basket has continued to decline rapidly since 2000 (decreased to 40% by 2012). If the RMB can join the currency basket, the GDP represented by the basket currencies will have a significant increase and will also greatly slow down its rate of decline. Arvind Subramanian, an Indian economist, pointed out in 2014 that seven out of 10 countries' currencies in East Asia have established a closer currency relationship with the RMB than with the US dollar. Once the RMB has been appreciated by 1%, the currencies of these seven countries will also be appreciated by 0.55%, whereas when the dollar is appreciated by 1%, the currency of those seven countries will only be appreciated by 0.34% (Table 3.2).[21]

What criteria must the RMB meet in order to enter the SDR currency basket? In fact, there are currently two major standards. One is the standard of "major exporters," and the other is the standard of "free use." According to the 2010 evaluation, the RMB has already met the "major exporters" standard, but there is still a gap to be filled with the "free-use" standard. Historically speaking, when the Japanese yen entered the SDR in 1981, it was not completely open then. It was only in 1983 that the Japanese yen was fully involved in and open on the market. In 2014, the RMB clearing bank was set up in Frankfurt.

---

[21] Zhou Ailin. (March 20, 2015). RMB Joining the SDR Wins the Support of Germany and Has the Potential to Be on an Equal Footing With the US Dollar. *Panorama Network*. Retrieved from http://www.p5w.net/news/xwpl/201503/t20150320_988399.htm

Table 3.2   The GDP Share and the IMF Share of Some Countries in 2011

	Global GDP Share in 2011 (%)	IMF Share (%)	Share Difference (%)
The United States	21.668	17.670	3.998
Japan	8.426	6.556	1.870
Germany	5.135	6.110	−0.975
China	10.477	3.996	6.481
Brazil	3.579	1.783	1.796
India	2.406	2.442	−0.036

Note: The data retrieved from the IMF database.

Frankfurt is expected to compete with London and become Europe's main offshore RMB financial market. China's offshore RMB market is blooming everywhere, which plays a positive role in promoting RMB's accession to SDR.

As of the end of 2011, China's share of the global economy had reached 10.477%, exceeding 10%, though it was still less than 4% of the IMF share. In the IMF, China's voting rights and its economic power are seriously mismatched. It should also be noted that among the BRICS countries, China, Brazil, and India, the world's three most important developing countries, have a total share of 8.221% in the IMF share, less than half of that of the United States. This situation is obviously unreasonable. It is high time to carry out the reform to a certain degree.

At present, the People's Bank of China has signed currency swap agreements with 28 countries or regions, with a total amount of RMB 3.1 trillion. The growth of the RMB in international use and transactions is also very fast. The SWIFT, the international currency clearing system, announced that the RMB has now become one of the top five payment currencies in the world. In the past two years, the use of the RMB in the world has increased by a three-digit rate every year, which means that the growth rate exceeds 100%. The use of the RMB exceeded that of the Australian and Canadian dollars last year. In terms of international transactions, the RMB now follows only the US dollar, the euro, the British pound, and the Japanese yen.

This development has led some people to believe that China will strive to make RMB as one of the reserve currencies with SDR used internally by the IMF. Previously, the rejection of the RMB to join the SDR was because it cannot be converted freely.

John McCormick, the Chief Executive of the Royal Bank of Scotland in the Asia-Pacific region, wrote recently in the *European Monetary Journal* that people's recognition of the RMB as one of the major international currencies is now strengthened. "Based on what we currently see in the G7, we believe that China has a great opportunity to add its RMB to the IMF reserve currency basket, which will indeed improve the position of the RMB on the international stage."

Michael Pettis, a professor of finance at Peking University and a researcher at the Carnegie Endowment for International Peace, said that the trading volume on the money market is a much more important factor in measuring the strengths and popularity of a certain currency. Although China is the world's largest nation in trading goods, the quantitative number and volume of transactions of RMB on the foreign exchange market are relatively very small, even less than the transaction of the peso from Mexico. Pettis said, "At present, settlements with the RMB in trade have undergone a rapid growth, but many of the settlement activities based on the RMB are merely cosmetic measures. These activities pretend to be trading business."

In 2007, China established an RMB-denominated "dim sum bond" in the market in order to start the process of the internationalization of the RMB. It also encourages the developing countries in Africa and some Asian neighbors such as Bangladesh, Pakistan, and Burma to use the RMB to settle their trade in goods instead of some traditional settlements. Traditionally, China has its currency pegged to the US dollar to calculate the exchange rate while providing low-interest loans to support such transactions.

China with its international experience realized that the process of currency internationalization does not happen overnight. Specifically, if we want to achieve it, we need to make the RMB the third largest currency in the world, second only to the US dollar and the euro, in international settlements and payments. It also needs to have more than 5% of the SDRs and account for approximately 10% of the total world reserve currency, with an RMB internationalization index of more than 15%. However, this ultimate goal may take two to three decades or even a longer period of time to achieve. The internationalization of the RMB will surely encounter an extremely long and uneven rough road. When the United States became the first economic power, it took more than half a century for the United States to achieve the standardization of the US dollar, replacing the former British pound.

China's Belt and Road Initiative was based on the reestablishment of the rights acclaimed among Eurasian countries in the new era and which, in return, has laid the solid foundation for reestablishment in Eurasia. At present, the advancement of high-speed bullet railways and the heavy-load railway technologies in China will certainly accelerate the return of acclaiming its land rights. The economic development of any region cannot be separated from the construction of some important infrastructures such as the railways, bridges, highways, and airports. The AIIB can clearly meet the requirements of Asian countries. However, more importantly, the AIIB also plays a very important role in driving the new economic engine and in promoting the Belt and Road Initiative in all Southeast Asian countries. Once the construction of infrastructures in Southeast Asia has become the heated topic in people's minds, the status of the AIIB in Asia and even in the world will be further enhanced.

3.5 Combining the Internationalization of the RMB with the Construction of the Belt and Road Initiative

The ultimate goal of the internationalization of the RMB is to realize the circulation of the RMB abroad and to play a monetary function such as the value scale, a means of circulation, a means of payment, and a means of storage throughout the world. The Belt and Road Initiative passes through Asia, Africa, and Europe. It provides major communication hubs for both land and maritime transportation in the world; it is also an important channel for China to have political, economic, and cultural exchanges and cooperation with the outside world, and it is the focus of China's economic diplomacy strategy in the new era. Therefore, to promote the internationalization of the RMB, we must focus on countries and regions along the Belt and Road Initiative in the right direction. On the basis of what we have achieved in the previous period regarding the significant advances in the regionalization and use of the RMB in our neighborhoods, we must follow the principle of gradual, orderly, and holistic progress; strengthen our currency cooperation with countries along the route; expand the cross-border use of the RMB; and realize the globalization and internationalization of the RMB through the radiation effects of countries along the route.

Accelerate the process of industrial transformation and upgrading, and strengthen the economic foundation of the internationalization of the RMB. With the innovation of new information technology, new energy, and new materials, China will support in issuing policies and increase its investment in the pioneering and internationally emerging industries that are using technological innovations. It will accelerate the development of increasing the technological element of our economic entity to create new competitive advantages. The innovation approach of integrating finance with science, technology, and industry will also be considered, thus providing a platform for multitiered production and financing activities and issuing structural monetary policies such as targeted rate cuts, targeted cuts, and small- and medium-sized loans to guide the flow of financial resources to strategic emerging industries and to improve the financial environment for our economic entities to create more and good profits.

The Belt and Road Initiative is considered as an opportunity to promote the use of the RMB for settlement and pricing in trading actions between China and the countries along the route. China and the countries in Southeast Asia and the Middle East have deficits in their annual imports and exports. International trade is generally a buyer's market, and importers are usually active in choosing a currency for trade settlements and pricing. It is vital for China to expand trade with countries along the route and use the RMB for settlement and pricing. Relying on the status of China as a major importer of international bulk commodities, consultations with relevant countries along the route will be strengthened and the settlement and pricing of the RMB in the import trade of iron ore, agricultural products, and other bulk commodities will be promoted. Furthermore, domestic banks and commercial banks will be guided to provide financing for traders in countries along the route and to use credit leverage to promote the cross-border trade settlement and pricing of the RMB. The Belt and Road Initiative through regional economic cooperation will not only help China out of the predicaments of constraints in foreign trade imposed by the traditional European and American markets, but it will also expand the overall market within the Silk Road Economic Zone and achieve smooth trading via the Maritime Silk Road. More importantly, the economic advantages of the central Asian countries and China are greatly complementary to each other. Central Asian countries can provide abundant and cheap oil and natural gas resources to China; thus the problematic demand of an insufficient external market to achieve win–win cooperation can be solved. The final multiplier effect in foreign trading has important implications for the sustainable development of the Chinese economy. The expansion of the trading market can enable RMB settlement to reduce transaction costs, improve transaction efficiency, and further promote the regionalization of RMB settlement and provide the RMB a leading role in regional trading.

Promote cross-border RMB financing investment in countries along the route and expand the cross-border capital flow channel for RMB. Domestic institutions and enterprises are encouraged to issue RMB-denominated stocks, bonds, and other financial products in offshore centers such as Singapore, London, Kuala Lumpur, and Dubai. The overseas funds from a lower cost of the RMB will be used for major domestic construction of infrastructures and the development of emerging industries, which provide support for domestic economic restructuring and industrial restructuring and upgrading. Further expansion of the opening of the interbank bond market to countries along the route; allowing more overseas central banks, commercial banks, insurance companies, security companies, and fund management companies to invest in the interbank bond market; and supporting the entry of foreign institutions such as multinational banks and corporations that issue RMB bonds in the interbank bond market are also important steps to implement. In addition, we encourage domestic enterprises to conduct cross-border direct investment in the RMB in countries along the route, encourage the domestic banks to provide RMB loans for major bilateral and multilateral cooperation projects, and use overseas branches of those banks to provide follow-up financial services for Chinese enterprises that "go global." With increasing financial institutions "going global," the RMB's "going global" into the world market is inevitable. China needs to promote the countries along the route to issue sovereign-denominated bonds denominated in RMB, raise overseas RMB funds for its official foreign exchange reserves, and improve the status of the RMB as an international reserve currency.

Support the construction of RMB offshore centers in countries along the route in order to promote the interaction between the RMB onshore market and the offshore market. On the one hand, China must support the countries along the route in expanding their market size of RMB offshore centers. We will support the RMB offshore centers in issuing and innovating their trading mechanisms of RMB bonds, stocks, and other financial instruments, and establishing offshore financial market trading platforms for RMB bonds, stocks, futures, and gold. We need to guide the local Chinese-funded financial institutions to actively design and develop new RMB products in order to facilitate the enrichment of offshore RMB financial products, improve the services, and make the transactions more active and effective. On the other hand, it is necessary to promote the interactive development of the offshore RMB market and the offshore RMB market in the countries along the route. Gradually, we will expand the business scope of RQFII, promote the development of RQFII business, guide Chinese-funded financial institutions to develop shared domestic and overseas RMB financial products, and promote the orderly and controllable two-way connectivity of the onshore and offshore markets of the RMB.

Strengthen cooperation with the countries along the route to promote the cross-border settlement in RMBs in the area of financial infrastructure. We will accelerate the construction of the RMB cross-border payment system, strive to establish cross-border RMB clearing arrangements with more countries along the route to increase the efficiency and security of cross-border RMB clearing and transactions, and reduce the cost of the RMB in cross-border transactions.[22]

Improve the position of the RMB in the neighboring countries by means of strengthening the communication ties in culture and people exchanges. Interregional trade and international trade contain tangible goods and intangible services, but what is more important is the cross-cultural communication, understanding, and tolerance among various nations and their people. Against the background of the Belt and Road Initiative, China promises to provide 20,000 training centers for interconnection and intercommunication to neighboring countries in the next five years, which will improve people's understanding of China's politics, economy, culture, and education in other countries. At the same time, with the enhancement of China's overall national strength and the improvement of people's living standards, China's tourism trade has now shown a deficit. On the one hand, we strive to develop China's tourism industry. On the other hand, the development of overseas tourism in China and the various foreign-related exchanges will allow people of China and people from all other countries to become more connected with each other, thereby enabling all the people in the world to become more integrated and trustworthy toward one another and consolidating the position of the RMB on the world market after the final realization of the internationalization of the RMB.[23]

The internationalization of the RMB is not only a national currency strategy aiming at the position of the RMB in the international currency system, but it is also the best manifestation of the political,

---

[22] Wang Jingwu. (2014). Advancing the Internationalization of RMB Based on the Construction of the 21st-century Maritime Silk Road. *Southern Finance*, Issue 11, pp. 4–6.

[23] Huang Weiping, Huang Jian. (2015) How to Advance the RMB Internationalization under the Belt and Road Initiative. *Academic Frontier*, Issue 3, pp. 30–39.

economic, and diplomatic strengths of our country. The enlargement of China's economic scale and its economic development requires the internationalization of the RMB. Fortunately, the Belt and Road Initiative is the major and important strategy proposed by China when confronted with the new political and economic structures in the world. This strategy aims at win–win cooperation, which will lead to the new and sustainable development of the economy, both in China and throughout the world.

New Ideas in the Period of Economic Transformation

Through the rapid growth after implementing the policy of the reform and opening-up for more than 30 years, China has become the second largest economy in the world. Although the Chinese economy has maintained an ultra-high speed of growth for a long time, it has accumulated many issues in terms of coordination and balance. Specifically, there are two solutions to the issues. First, the manner of growth has to change from export-oriented and investment-driven to demand-oriented and innovation-driven. Second, the pace of growth needs to be changed from an ultra-high growth rate (8.5%–11.5%) to a medium-high growth rate (6.5%–8.5%). Economic growth will depart from the high growth rate of about 10% in the past 30 years and will depart from the traditional mode of extensive growth that was unbalanced, uncoordinated, and unsustainable. In May 2014, when President Xi Jinping inspected Henan, he pointed out that "China's development is still in an important period of strategic opportunities. We must strengthen our confidence, proceed from the current phase of China's economic development, adapt to the new normal, and maintain a strategically normal attitude." In November, Xi Jinping elaborated on the "new normal" for the first time at the APEC CEO Summit. In Xi Jinping's view, the new normal has several principal features as follows: speed — "change from high-speed growth to medium-high speed growth," structure — "continuous optimization and upgrading of the economic structure," and motivation — "change from factors-driven, investment-driven to innovation-driven." On December 5, the Political Bureau of the CPC Central Committee mentioned the "new normal" for the first time. In its communiqué, there are three references to the new normal: "China has entered the new normal of economic development. It has good economic resilience, has sufficient potential, and has plenty of room for maneuvers." "The tendency towards change that has emerged against the background of the new normal of economic development has given rise to many difficulties and challenges facing economic and social development." "We will actively adapt to the new normal of economic development and keep the economy running in a reasonable range."

After China's economy entering the new normal and expanding new space for regional development, the Chinese government has coordinately implemented the policy of "Four Major Sectors" and "Three Major Supporting Zones." The former refers to the Great Western Development of China, the revitalization of Northeastern China, the rise of central China, and the pioneering development of the eastern region, and the latter refers to the Belt and Road Initiative, the Yangtze River Economic Belt, and the coordinated development of Beijing, Tianjin, and Hebei. It is worth noting that the Belt and Road Initiative is an important focal point for China's westward break-through, and it has provided new impetus for the prosperity and development of countries, regions, and Eurasian economies along the route.

1. China's Economy Entering the New Normal of Transformation and Upgrading

At the opening ceremony of the APEC CEO Summit in November 2014, President Xi Jinping pointed out that "The new normal of

China's economy has emerged with several principal features. First, economic growth has changed from high-speed growth to medium-high speed growth. Second, the economic structure has been constantly optimized and upgraded as the tertiary industry and consumer demand have gradually become the mainstay, the gap between urban and rural areas has gradually narrowed, the proportion of residents' income has risen, and the results of development have benefited a wider portion of the public. The third is the shift from being factors-driven and investment-driven to being innovation-driven."

The Central Economic Work Conference held from December 9 to 11, 2014, elaborated on the nine major features of the new normal as follows:

From the perspective of consumer demand, in the past, China's consumption had a distinct model of a wave of imitation, and now it has basically been replaced by the personalized and diversified type of consumption that is becoming the mainstream. In addition, the importance of ensuring product quality and safety as well as activating demand through innovation has increased significantly. Standard consumer policies must be adopted to unlock consumer potential so that consumption continues to play a fundamental role in promoting economic development.

From the perspective of investment demand, after more than 30 years of high-intensity and large-scale development and construction, the traditional industries are relatively saturated, but there are a large number of investment opportunities in infrastructure interconnectivity and in new technologies, new products, new formats, and new business models, which put forward new requirements for the innovation of investment and financing. We must improve our abilities to grasp the direction of investment and eliminate investment barriers so that investment can continue to play a key role in economic development.

In terms of exports and international balance of payment, the international market expanded rapidly before the international financial crisis, and exports were an important driving force for the rapid development of China's economy. At present, however, the total global demand is weak, and China's comparative advantages of low costs have also changed. At the same time, the competitive advantages of China's exports still exist. High-level imports and large-scale out-flows are occurring simultaneously. We must step up the cultivation of new comparative advantages so that exports can continue to play a supporting role in economic development.

From the perspective of production capacity and industrial organization, the past supply shortages were a major problem affecting China's economy for a long time. Currently, the supply capacity of traditional industry largely exceeds the demand. Therefore, the industrial structure must be optimized and upgraded; however, corporate mergers and reorganizations and a relative concentration of production are inevitable. The role of the emerging industries, the service industry, and small and micro enterprises will become more prominent. Furthermore, miniaturization, intellectualization, and professionalization will become new features of industrial organizations.

In terms of the relative advantages of production factors, the low labor cost in the past was the biggest advantage. The introduction of technology and management can quickly make that labor force into productive forces. Currently, the aging population is growing and the surplus labor force in agriculture is decreasing; thus, the driving force based on the scale of the factors is weakening. As a result, economic growth will rely more on the quality of human capital and technological advancement, and innovation must become the new engine that drives development.

From the angle of the characteristics of market competition, in the past, the market mainly focused on quantity expansion and price competition. Currently, it is gradually shifting to attach significance to quality-based and differentiated competition. Unifying the national market and increasing the efficiency of resource allocation are endogenous requirements for economic development. Therefore, we must intensify the implementation of the reform and opening-up and accelerate the establishment of a unified, transparent, orderly, and standardized market environment.

From the perspective of constraints on resources and on the environment, the space for energy resources and an ecological environment in the past was relatively large. Currently, the environmental supporting capacity has reached or is approaching its upper limit;

thus, we must comply with people's expectations of a favorable eco-logical environment and promote a new way of development that is green, low-carbon, and includes recycling.

In terms of the accumulation and resolution of economic risks, various kinds of hidden risks will gradually become increasingly apparent, and they will be increasingly controllable with the slowdown in economic growth. However, resolving various risks that feature high leverage and bubbles will continue for some time. We must treat both the symptoms and "the root" causes, act appropriately according to the situation, and establish and improve the institutional mechanisms for resolving various risks.

Judging from the resource allocation and macro-control meth-ods, the marginal effects of policies of comprehensive stimulus have diminished significantly. Therefore, it is necessary to comprehensively resolve the excess production capacity and to explore the direction of future industrial development through the exploitation of market mechanisms. It is also necessary to fully grasp the new changes in the total supply and demand, and carry out scientific macro-control.

These economic phenomena show that, because of more than 30 years of reform and opening-up, China is currently standing on a new historical starting point. It is currently an economic giant and has already been an influential economic giant. However, it is not yet a truly global economic power. It can only rely on reform and innova-tion to solve a series of prominent contradictions and issues with its development in order to achieve the leap from an economic giant to an economic power.

1.1 *The Main Features of the "New Normal" in China's Economy*

First, economic growth has slowed down, displaying fewer obvious structural features.[1] Positive factors such as the demographic dividend, cheap labor under a dual economy, development of

---

[1] Zhang Ping. (2015). The "New Normal" of China's Economy and Deceleration Governance: Economic Prospects for 2015. *Modern Economic Research*, Issue 1, pp. 5–9.

industrialization, learning-by-doing effect in technological advancement, and the demand caused by global prosperity have gradually come to an end, and the structural factors of acceleration have become factors of deceleration. Over the past 30 years of the implementation of the reform and opening-up, the average annual growth rate of China's economy has maintained an ultra-high and high growth rate close to 10%. In 2008, it slowed down due to the international financial crisis, and it further decreased to 7.7% in 2012 and 2013, 7.4% in 2014, and 6.9% in 2015. Judging from international experiences, after World War II, some countries such as Japan, South Korea, and Germany, whose economies developed rapidly, were revitalized through industrialization and experienced a widespread economic growth slowdown after sustained high-speed growth in the 1960s and the 1970s. Judging from the domestic situation, after more than 30 years of high-intensity and large-scale development and construction in China, the constraints from energy, resources, and the environment have become increasingly obvious. The rapid economic growth featuring an over-reliance on factors-driven and investment-driven growth is difficult to sustain, and thus, economic development is facing the pressure of transformation and upgrading.

Second, economic structural adjustment is moving toward a broader area. The significance of economic restructuring is first and foremost regarding how to revitalize domestic demand, that is, to stimulate China's economy through domestic demand. The second is how to increase the proportion of consumer demand in domestic demand, the important content of which is to adjust the income distribution. The third is to continuously improve the efficiency of the service industry and manufacturing industries. Finally, the new urbanization and spatial structure adjustments will enhance China's development from a spatial perspective. For a long time, China's industrial developmental methods have been extensive, and industries with high investment, high consumption, and low output have occupied a large proportion of all industries. The industrial structure is mainly at the medium and low end of the global value chain. Apart from its relatively low comparative interests, there are many issues such as scientific and technological innovation incapability, insufficient integration of technology and industry, weak industrial competitiveness, and that the core technologies depended on others. Over the past 30 years, the economy of shirts, slippers, and toys has been exhausted, and that of the steel, cement, and glass economy has reached its peak. The statistical data of 2013 show that the added value of China's tertiary industry accounted for 46.1% of the gross domestic product (GDP), surpassing that of the secondary industry for the first time. In 2014, this proportion exceeded 50%. At the same time, the role of emerging industries, service industries, and small and micro enterprises has become more prominent, and miniaturization, intelligence, specialization, and personalization have gradually become new features of industrial organizations, which are all signs of structural optimization. Under the economic new normal, it is necessary to further promote the development of industries such as strategic emerging industries and advanced manufacturing industries, give priority to the development of productive and livelihood service industries, and gradually decrease the risk of overcapacity in order to improve the status of Chinese industries in the global value chain.

Third, the supply of high-cost elements has become a new normal. The contributors to China's economic growth should be the improvement of total factor productivity and human capital, and only market-oriented reforms can effectively promote labor productivity and technological progress. Faced with the new wave of technological innovation and industrial revolution in the world, the willingness of Chinese enterprises to actively transform and strengthen the ability for innovation has been significantly strengthened, and the driving force of economic growth is gradually becoming the new normal of innovation-driven growth. In 2013, the level of total factor productivity in China was nearly three times that of 1978. In an overall analysis, this is the result of a combination of factors, such as institutional reform, technological progress, and structural optimization. Moreover, some new technologies, new products, new formats, and new business models will undoubtedly become new impetus and growth points for economic development.

Fourth, the market-based allocation of resources has become a new normal for comprehensively intensifying reforms. The *Decision* of the Third Plenary Session of the 18th CPC Central Committee put forward the concept of "making the market play a decisive role in the allocation of resources and giving better play to the role of the government." The Fourth Plenary Session of the 18th CPC Central Committee proposed that "the socialist market economy is essentially an economy ruled by law," indicating that the party's understanding of the laws of a market economy has reached a new height. Excessive reliance on the pattern of resource allocation by the government in the traditional catch-up process must give way to that by the market, including factor price adjustments, state-owned enterprise reforms, interest rate and exchange rate market reforms, government administrative reform, institutional classification reform, rural land reforms, urban household registration system reforms, taxation and fiscal system reforms, and many other aspects, all of which will be the most important part of China's current stage of promoting efficient development and transformation. By means of transforming functions, simplifying administration, decentralizing power, reducing taxes and profits, encouraging entrepreneurship, and supporting innovation, China will accelerate the construction of a unified, transparent, and orderly market environment, and allow the decision-making authority for allocation of resources to the market, and use market-oriented methods to solve various types of risks with high leverage and foaming.

Fifth, the developmental mode has transformed from the growth of scale and speed to that of quality and efficiency. This is the basic requirement of the economic new normal. Over the past 30 years of reform and opening-up, China's economic development has grown by leaps and bounds and has made remarkable achievements that have attracted the world's attention. However, issues such as unbalanced, uncoordinated, and unsustainable development caused by paying too much attention to scale and speed are also prominent. The extensive growth of "overexploiting natural resources" is extremely common as Black GDP and bloody GDP have been worrying China for many years. Besides, market competition mainly depends on quantity expansion and disorderly price competition, and the environmental carrying capacity has reached or is approaching its upper limit.

Moreover, the relationship between investment and consumption does not match, the development of urban and rural areas is not coordinated, the total employment pressure and structural contradictions coexist, the issue of income distribution is prominent, and so on. Tacking all these issues require that the mode of economic development must be changed and an upgraded version of China's economy must be built as China's consumer demand shifts from an imitative and self-propelled pattern to an individualized and diversified one, and also its exports are changing from simple, low-cost, and rapid expansion to attaching the same importance to high-level imports and large-scale exports, and the relative advantages of production factors are changing from traditional demographic dividends to the quality of human capital and the advantages of technological advancement.[2]

From the theoretical perspective of economic growth, China's "new normal" should be understood as a form of the transitional period, that is, an adjustment from the stage of high growth promoted by industrialization to the phase of balanced growth, and the direction of that transition is from structural catching-up to a highly efficient and balanced phase of growth: (1) The transition is from the dual economic structure to the combination of modern sectors. (2) The market economy system has been initially established, and the market has played a decisive role in the allocation of resources. However, the reform of state-owned enterprises, public institutions, regulatory agencies, and government administrative reforms still have a long way to go. (3) The biggest issue in current growth is that the contribution rate of total factor productivity has not increased enough. Therefore, it is necessary to ensure the decisive role of technological progress and human capital in the process of transformation of the production mode.

1.2 *Challenges and Opportunities under the New Normal of China's Economy*

At present, China is faced with two major challenges and opportunities.

---

[2] Zhang Zhanbin. (2015). Trend Features and Policy Orientation of the New Normal of China's Economy. *Journal of National School of Administration*, Issue 1, pp. 15–20.

First, developed countries, led by the United States, have actively promoted Trans-Pacific Partnership and Transatlantic Trade and Investment Partnership, and the six countries with the Federal Reserve System ("Fed") as the center have implemented currency swaps, bringing new challenges to China's deep integration into the global economy and the division of labor in industry. Second, the world is brewing new technological revolutions and industrial changes. These changes often have disruptive or even devastating effects on traditional industries and may directly damage the existing industrial system. Certainly, this is both a challenge and an opportunity for the Chinese economy under the new normal.

Against the background of the above new normal, the Chinese economy can still continue to support China's peaceful rise.[3] In 2014, the world's steel production was less than 1.6 billion tons, in which China produced 800 million tons; in 2014, the world's cement output was 4 billion tons, in which China produced 2.42 billion tons; in the same year, the world's coal production was about 7 billion tons, in which China produced 3.7 billion tons. In addition to iron and steel raw materials, the major producers of cement and coal production that rely on rock extraction and downhole mining are located in China. China possesses almost all the elements that require for production under today's technological conditions, and it can maintain sustainable development on the scale that affects the world. Although the physical strength of China's population has shown a turning point, the intellectual dividend of China's population is again of unlimited supply. Therefore, the second condition for China's growth is that the super-large size of its population provides both world-class physical strength and intelligence of human resources that are needed for the rise of China. China's megacities are rapidly developing, and city belts are rapidly emerging. After the appearance of the two Deltas and the Bohai Rim urban agglomerations, the Chengdu–Chongqing City Group, the Guanzhong–Tianshui City Group, the Shenyang–Changchun–Harbin

---

[3] Cao Heping, Li Wei, Tang Lisha. (March 13, 2015). The New Normal of China's Economy and the Rise of China. *People's Daily*. Retrieved from http://world.people.com.cn/n/2015/0313/c188725-26689698.html.

City Group, and the Changsha–Zhuzhou–Xiangtan City Group have also emerged, all of which are world-class and rely on the connection of a city-function complex formed by industry-supported production and consumer population. In terms of civilization inclusiveness, China has not only surpassed Japan, which is seeking to establish a single and pure Yamato nation, or the European countries with a strong sense of local elites, but it has also surpassed a multiethnic country with a short history and integrated culture such as the United States. Only if a country is culturally tolerant, can its brilliance of intelligence bloom comprehensively. Today, China's comprehensively intensifying reforms are overall reforms and innovations that are nearly impossible for any country or any party in history to achieve. It is also the internal institutional arrangements that enable China to accept new technologies, new economies, new intelligence, and new ideas faster than any other parties in the world. So, any country in the world does not have the above-mentioned conditions from historical perspectives if taking a century as a unit. This is an important reason why China can continue to rise.

2. Integration of High-Speed Railways, Equipment Manufacturing, and International and Regional Economic Cooperation into the Belt and Road Initiative

On January 28, 2015, Premier Li Keqiang of the State Council held the executive meeting of the State Council to deploy and accelerate the implementation of the "going global" policy of China-made equipment such as railways, nuclear power, and building material production lines.

2.1 *High-Speed Railways Go Abroad*

In 2014, Chinese companies signed a total value of USD 24.7 billion in foreign contracts in the area of railways. The China Railway Construction Corporation (CRCC) and Nigeria signed a contract of USD 11.97 billion for the construction of a railway, which is the largest value in a single contract signed by Chinese companies. In 2014,

Table 4.1   Performance Comparison of China's Four Major Railway Companies in 2014 (Unit: USD 100 Million)

	Revenue/Growth Rate	Net Profit/ Growth Rate	Amount of Newly Signed Overseas Contracts
China CSR (China Southern car)	1,197.24 (20.48%)	58.15 (27.61%)	29.94
China CNR (China North Locomotive)	1,042.9 (7.3%)	54.9 (33.0%)	37.6
China Railway Group Limited	6,125.59 (9.3%)	103.59 (10.51%)	N/A
CRCC	5,919.58 (0.88%)	113.43 (9.65%)	200.94

Source: Annual reports of the corporations for 2014.

Chinese enterprises participated in 348 overseas railway construction projects and exported locomotives and vehicles of a value of USD 3.74 billion.

On March 30, China's four major railway equipment and construction companies all disclosed their 2014 annual reports that their profits had all reached a record high, their total operating income had exceeded RMB 1.4 trillion, and overseas business, in particular, had also achieved significant growth (see Table 4.1).

The total value of overseas contracts signed by the CSR and the CNR exceeded USD 6 billion, an increase of over 60% year-on-year. Among them, the exportation of the Boston Subway project obtained by the CNR was the first time that China's railway transportation equipment had landed in the United States. In 2014, the CNR achieved steady growth in its domestic railway transportation business; meanwhile, its overseas business grew rapidly. The annual value of export contracts was USD 2.994 billion, an increase of 73% from the previous year.

CNR's diesel locomotives entered the European Union market for the first time; the contract of exporting 232 diesel locomotives signed with South Africa is China's largest single deal of this type; the 160 km quasi-high-speed electric multiple unit (EMU) exported to

Malaysia was the first high-speed railway export project in China; and the contract of 284 subway vehicles was signed with the United States, marking the first time that these vehicles had entered the US market and that Chinese railway transportation equipment companies had participated in the US transnational investment/operations. While increasing product exports, China actively promoted the "going global" of technologies, standards, and services. Its overseas business patterns have been expanding as CNR has invested in the acquisition of the Australia Pacific Railway Engineering Co., Ltd., and invested in the newly established CNR Pioneer (India) Electric Company, the CNR (USA) Corporation, and the CNR Vehicle (South Africa) Corporation. In May 2014, CNR's H-shares were successfully listed on the Hong Kong Stock Exchange, further promoting the globalization of resource allocation.

In 2014, the CSR had "deeply cultivated" and "exploited" the overseas markets, and had completed the signing of 35 locomotive and vehicle projects and the exportation of a number of railway components and new industrial products, realizing a total of USD 3.76 billion in new export orders and reaching a historical high. Among them, vehicle export contracts accounted for more than 90% of the total number of contracts, including electric locomotives, diesel locomotives, electric EMUs, internal-combustion EMUs, metro light rails, passenger cars, and trucks for 38 countries or regions, including Macedonia, South Africa, Turkey, India, Singapore, Australia, and Argentina. In the South African market, CSR received orders for more than USD 2 billion in electric locomotives in the same year and that became the largest order for the exportation of high-end railway transportation equipment in China; in the Singapore market, the Metro T251 project achieved a breakthrough in the exportation of CSR's unmanned metro vehicles; on the Macedonia market, the six EMU procurement contracts enabled China's EMU vehicle products to successfully enter the European market for the first time.

On December 30, 2014, the two major railway equipment manufacturing companies, CNR and CSR, merged into the China Railway Stock Corp. (CRRC). This will not only strongly accelerate the transition from "Made in China" to "Created in China" in China's railway industry, but it will also efficiently promote the industrial upgrading of China's high-end equipment industry and push ahead with China's move from a "manufacturing giant" to a "manufacturing power." Thus, it conforms to the general trend of economic globalization and market integration and is also in line with the Belt and Road Initiative and China's industrial policy of optimizing industrial layout and developing high-end equipment manufacturing. The merged CRRC will not only become the world's largest supplier of high-speed railway technology, but it will also consolidate the CRRC's position as the world's largest rail transportation equipment manufacturer. In particular, the merged entity companies will benefit from a greater scale, higher operational efficiency, higher R&D efficiency, lower procurement costs, and a unified global strategy, and will achieve greater international competitiveness. At present, electric, diesel locomotives, and railway equipment produced by more than 30 factories of the two major groups (i.e., CNR and CSR) account for 80% of the Chinese market and are exported to more than 80 countries. In 2014, their share in the world market was 10%. In fact, they had already been the world's leading railway equipment manufacturer with many more sales before the merger — far ahead of Siemens, Alstom, Bombardier, and Japanese companies.

According to the Information Telegraphic Agency of Russia-Telegraph Agency of the Soviet Union (ITAR-TASS), on April 30, 2015, the winner of the Moscow–Kazan high-speed railway project was the Russian–Chinese joint consortium. The consortium was led by the Moscow National Transport Engineering Survey and Design Institute, with Nizhny Novgorod Metro Design Co., Ltd., and the China Railway Eryuan Engineering Group Co., Ltd. as the members. The successful bidder is responsible for the completion of the engineering survey, land survey, the drawing-up of the plans, and document design for the construction of the high-speed railway in the Moscow–Kazan section in 2015–2016. The value of the contract is 20 billion rubles (about RMB 2.433 billion). The total cost of the Moscow–Kazan high-speed railway is 1.068 trillion roubles. In the future, the Moscow–Kazan railway will become part of the Moscow–Beijing high-speed railway line and the New Silk Road project. The total length of the Moscow–Kazan high-speed railway line is about 770 km, and the maximum speed designed is 400 km/h.[4]

On June 3, 2015, the Deutsche Bahn AG (DB) will purchase trains and parts for the first time from Chinese locomotive equipment manufacturers, and the purchased products will be used on the Asian–European freight lines from China to Germany. In addition, in the autumn of 2015, DB will also set up a procurement office in Beijing. The cooperation between Chinese locomotive equipment manufacturers and German companies can be seen as a combination of great powers under the influence of the Belt and Road Initiative. DB was founded in 1835 and began its nationalization in 1920. In 2014, the German passenger railways and light railways transported more than 2.6 billion passengers, a year-on-year increase of 2.1%; the volume of cargo transportation was 365 million tons, and about 40% of the company's freight traffic came from transnational transportation. Its Director, Heike Hanahart, said, "In the next three to five years, Asia, especially China, will be able to meet the demand for trains and accessories purchased by DB." According to media reports before, its profitability of freight logistics in China was promising. In 2014, there were more than 300 freight trains between China and Germany and nearly 30,000 containers (15,000 in 2013) were shipped. The DB officials also stated publicly that the company had increased the number of trains from China to Germany at the end of 2015 from three in a week to four. Trains from Germany to China can be increased from one or two shifts to three or four shifts per week. It is hoped that by the end of 2015, trains from Hamburg, Germany to Shanghai, China will have increased from one shift every other week to one per week. At present, the potential partners of DB include CRRC, Taiyuan Heavy Industry, and Huawei.[5]

---

[4] Russian Media: Sino-Russian Consortium Wins Bid for the Moscow–Kazan High-speed Railway. (May 2, 2015). *Eastmoney*. Retrieved from http://finance.eastmoney.com/news/1344,20150502502768120.html.

[5] Wang You. (June 4, 2015). Deutsche Bahn AG (DB) Purchases Chinese Trains and Parts for Use in Asia–Europe Railways. *Sina Finance*. Retrieved from http://finance.sina.com.cn/chanjing/cyxw/20150607/023922367368.shtml.

On September 17, 2015, China's Central Finance Office revealed at the China–US Economic Cooperation Conference that China and the United States will form a joint-venture company to build and operate the US West Express Line, with a total length of 370 km. The estimated total investment was USD 12.7 billion. The project linked Las Vegas to Los Angeles, which was China's first high-speed railway project built in the United States. It was estimated that the total investment will be USD 12.7 billion, and the project was scheduled to start in September 2016.[6]

On September 19, 2015, at the China-ASEAN Expo, Thailand's Deputy Prime Minister Tanasa stated that "Thailand and China are negotiating and collaborating on a project of an 840 km railway line … In the future, this railway will become an important channel for Thai intermediaries and material transportation. At present, Thailand and China are working closely together to ensure that the railway project is implemented as soon as possible, and the project is expected to be launched within this year." According to the previous design plan, the railway line built by China and Thailand is designed in a herringbone pattern, which runs from Thailand's Nong Khai City, the capital of Nongkhai Province, and heads south. It passes through Udon Thani, Khon Kaen Province, and Nakhon Ratchasima Province and branches into the southeastern and southwestern parts in Krabi County, Saraburi Province in central Thailand. The former will go to the important logistics port in Map Ta Phut County of Rayong Province. The latter will end in the capital Bangkok. The total length of the Nong Khai-Kaeng Khoi-Map Ta Phut line is more than 700 km, and the Kaeng Khoi-Bangkok line is more than 130 km.[7]

On September 23, 2015, it was learned from the China Railway Corporation that the India High-speed Railway Company had

---

[6] Fan Yunbo. (September 17, 2015). China Is to Start Construction of the High-Speed Railway in the USA in September Next Year. *Xinhuanet*. Retrieved from http://www.xinhuanet.com/world/2015-09/17/c_1116594216.htm

[7] Sino-Thai Joint-track Railway Will Be Launched within the Year and Deputy Prime Minister of Thailand Called Himself a Fan of China's. (September 20, 2015). *People's Daily Online*. Retrieved from http://world.people.com.cn/n/2015/0920/c157278-27608818.html.

formally issued a letter of award to the consortium of local Indian companies led by the Third Railway Survey and Design Institute Group Co., Ltd., an enterprise affiliated to the China Railway Corporation. The consortium undertakes the feasibility study of the high-speed railway from New Delhi to Mumbai. It is known that the Delhi–Mumbai high-speed railway connects New Delhi, the capital city of India, and Mumbai, the economic center of India, with a total length of about 1,200 km. In December 2014, the India High-speed Railway Company had issued a global public tender for the feasibility study of three high-speed railways from New Delhi to Mumbai, Mumbai to Chennai, and New Delhi to Calcutta. A total of 12 well-known consulting companies from China, the United States, Germany, France, Italy, Spain, and Belgium participated in the bid. The Chinese–Indian consortium winning the bid for the high-speed railway from New Delhi to Mumbai in India fully reflects the recognition of China's high-speed rail technology by the international community and the international high-speed railway market as well as the strength of China's railway construction. This is another result of the "going global" of the Chinese railways. After winning the bid, the Chinese–Indian consortium will arrange for experts on high-speed railways in the near future to initiate the project's feasibility study.[8]

Since 2005, China has begun the large-scale introduction and independent development of high-speed railway technology. It has absorbed technologies from Alstom, Siemens, Bombardier Canada, and Kawasaki, and has independently developed high-speed trains with a speed of over 350 km/h, showing China's high-tech strength and economic strength. China's technological superiority and production capacity in the area of high-speed railways are leading in the world, and the number of patents applied has exceeded 2,000. Among all the high-speed railway technology patent applications in the world, those from China have accounted for 70%, followed by Japan, the United States, and European countries, which accounted

---

[8] China Railway Corporation Wins Bid for Indian High-speed Railway Project with a Total Length of Approximately 1,200 km. (September 20, 2015). *China News Service.* Retrieved from http://www.chinanews.com/cj/2015/09-23/7540786.shtml.

for 13%, 8%, and 7%, respectively. In addition, the reason why China's high-speed railway is competitive internationally is mainly because of its perfect combination of high technology and practicality. It is characterized by high speed, stable operations, and a relatively low cost. In July 2014, the World Bank office in China pointed out in a report on the construction cost of a high-speed railway in China that the weighted average unit cost of high-speed railways in China is 129 million yuan/km for a project with a speed of 350 km/h and 87 million yuan/km for a speed of 250 km/h, which is far lower than the international cost of more than 300 million yuan/km. Therefore, China has not only the technological capability but also the economic strength to repair high-speed railways abroad. At present, the high-speed railway between Lanzhou and Urumchi in China is in use. The high-speed railway network linking China's western part and Central Asian countries is under construction and will eventually be linked to the European railway network. Once completed, the speed of passenger transportation will be up to 300 km/h, and the speed of freight will be up to 200 km/h. The railway will connect Urumqi, China and Kazakhstan, Uzbekistan, Turkmenistan, and other countries in Central Asia together. In addition, China is also negotiating with Iran and Pakistan on the laying of high-speed railway lines.[9]

2.2 *Railway Network Connecting the Regions of Eurasia*

The vision and action of the Belt and Road Initiative proposed that "The countries along the route should strengthen the connection between infrastructure planning and the technical standard system, and jointly promote the construction of international backbone channels." This injected a strong driving force into the *Intergovernmental Agreement on the Trans-Asian Railway Network* that was signed 10 years ago, and a number of international railway construction projects are continuously being accelerated.

---

[9] Huang Weiping. (2015). The New Silk Road Economic Belt and the New Development of Sino-European Economic and Trade Patterns-Also on the Strategic Value of Trans-Asia-Europe High-speed Railway. *China Business and Market*, Issue 1, pp. 84–90.

At present, Baofeng Tunnel, the controlling project of the Kunming–Yuxi Railway, is under construction. This 7-km-long tunnel, which is located in China, is the intersection of the two international railway lines between China and Laos and China and Vietnam. In the future, trains departing from Yunnan will have direct access to the Trans-Asian Railway.

The Trans-Asian Railway of Southeast Asian section consists of three lines: East, Central, and West lines. They all start from Kunming, China, pass through Vietnam, Cambodia, Laos, Myanmar, and other countries and reach the terminal in Singapore after passing through Kuala Lumpur and meeting up in Bangkok, Thailand. Among them, the Yuxi to Hekou and Kunming to Dali sections in China are in use currently; the Kunming to Yuxi and Dali to Ruili sections are under construction; and the Yuxi–Mohan section connecting China and Laos and China and Thailand railways will begin within the year. Kunming, which has long been at the tip of the railway network, is becoming a new hub of the Belt and Road Initiative.

According to Wang Gengjie, deputy chief engineer of the Kunming Railway Bureau, the railway line starts from Kunming, going north (to Xi'an), it can connect to the Silk Road Economic Belt, and going south, it can connect to the Pacific Ocean and the Indian Ocean; then, it can connect to the 21st-century Maritime Silk Road, going east, it can connect to the Yangtze River Economic Belt, and going west, it can pass through the China–Myanmar–India international channel and can connect up with the Bangladesh–China–India–Myanmar Economic Corridor. Moreover, overseas railway construction is also stepping up. In the 8th Five-Year Plan that Laos began to implement this year, the construction of transportation infrastructure is an important strategy. The project that ranks first is the China–Laos Railway at the Port of Boten and Vientiane, and Indonesia's investment in infrastructure development in 2015 has been increased to a record high of USD 24.4 billion; after the Sino-Thai Railway, signed at the end of 2014, has been completed and opened to traffic, Bangkok will become an important site for the 21st-century Maritime Silk Road. In accordance with the plan of the *Intergovernmental Agreement on the Trans-Asian Railway Network*, a four-line railway network connecting Eurasia has already been formed as follows: the northern channel that connects the Korean Peninsula, Russia, China, Mongolia, Kazakhstan, and other countries to Europe; the southern channel connects southern China, Myanmar, India, Iran, Turkey, and so on; the north–south channel links Russia, Central Asia, and the Persian Gulf; and the China-ASEAN channel links China, the ASEAN countries, and the Indo-China Peninsula. The four lines will connect 28 countries and regions, with a total mileage of more than 80,000 km.

Asia and the peripheral areas: To serve the Belt and Road Initiative, China plans to build a high-speed railway running through Southeast Asia and having direct access to Malaysia and Singapore, and to construct a high-speed railway linking Central Asia and Europe for the Silk Road Economic Belt. China and Thailand have reached an agreement on railway cooperation; the Laos Railway has only been "close to the door"; an inter-governmental cooperation document signed with India determines the areas of cooperation and action plans for the construction of the Sino-Indian railway; the China–Pakistan Economic Corridor and the Bangladesh–China–India–Myanmar Economic Corridor are under planning, and the interconnected railway corridors are expected to take shape.

Africa: The "iron and steel dragon" built by China is connecting many countries from West Africa to East Africa. In 2014, the Benguela Railway across the entire territory of Angola was completed; the railway connecting Nigeria to the capital Abuja and to Kaduna was completed, and a contract has been signed for the coastal railway; the railway connecting Ethiopia and Djibouti is under construction.

Europe: The second phase of a high-speed railway line between Ankara and Istanbul, the first 250 km/h high-speed railway in Turkey, that Chinese companies participated in was successfully open to traffic; the China–Russia high-speed railway cooperation has reached preliminary consensus and has signed cooperation documents; railway cooperation projects between China and Eastern Europe, and between China, Kyrgyzstan, and Uzbekistan, should be actively promoted.

The Americas: China, Brazil, and Peru have established a joint working group for the "Two Oceans Railway"; a consortium, led by the China Railway Corporation, is negotiating with the US party about the US West Express Line.

At present, the most important competitiveness of China's high-speed railway is mainly in the aspects of vehicle manufacturing, contact wire network, traction power supply systems, and train operation control systems. Among them, contact wire network and the traction power supply systems are localized by the Baoji Baodeli Electric Co., Ltd. after assimilating the German and Italian technologies. The aluminum alloy body is manufactured by the Shandong Jungle Aluminum Corporation using the world's first 10,000-ton hydraulic double-action aluminum extrusion machine designed by the Xi'an Heavy Machinery Research Institute; and as the principal technology of the high-speed railway, the China Railway Signal & Communication Corp assimilated the experience of Siemens and Hitachi and successfully developed a CTCS-3 level train control system with independent intellectual property rights. In addition, the 250/350 km high-speed bogie was mastered by China alone, and China has its own intellectual property rights of the ballastless track slab in the high-speed railway infrastructure.

In the construction of the Silk Road Economic Belt, the first is the logistics that spans Asia and Europe, and many domestic cities have opened freight trains to Europe and Central Asia. Before 2013, there was only the Chongqing–Xinjiang–Europe train. At present, there are three major passages and many trains, such as the Chengdu–Xinjiang–Europe, Zhengzhou–Europe, and Yiwu–Xinjiang–Europe routes. Most of the trains pass through the western passage of Alashankou in Xinjiang to Kazakhstan and then reach Europe.

2.3 *Overseas Reengineering of Equipment Manufacturing*

The data released by the China International Contractors Association show that in 2014, China's foreign contracted engineering business completed a turnover of USD 142.11 billion, a total of RMB 800 billion, a year-on-year increase of 3.8%; the value of new contracts reached USD 191.76 billion, about RMB 1.2 trillion, an increase of 11.7% year-on-year. While consolidating the traditional Asian and African markets, companies have successively signed important projects in North America, Latin America, and Europe. For example, the China State Construction Engineering Corporation won the bid for the US Pulaski viaduct project, and the China Gezhouba (Group) Corporation won the bid for the Argentina hydropower project. In addition, Kenya's Mombasa–Nairobi Railway undertaken by China Road & Bridge Corporation adopts Chinese technology standards, taking a key step in "China standards going global." In the process of overseas development, China's contracted engineering companies also realized the importance of offshore investments. Through investments, mergers, and acquisitions, they began the transformation and upgrading of their businesses. In 2014, China State Construction Engineering Corporation completed the first single overseas M&A transaction and acquired PLAZA, a well-known US contractor. The China Communications Construction Company Ltd. obtained the right to operate the important ports in South Asia through joint mergers and acquisitions. With the rapid growth of China's foreign investments, it will also drive the implementation of infrastructure projects such as energy and real estate.[10]

According to the British Broadcasting Corporation website quoting from the *Financial Times* of the United Kingdom on June 4, the person-in-charge of engineering of China Harbor Engineering Co., Ltd. (CHEC) said that the project marks a strategic decision to enter the United Kingdom infrastructure and construction market. He also said that this is the cornerstone project of the company's business development strategy in the United Kingdom and throughout Europe. The Swansea Tidal Power Plant has raised 200 million pounds, but it is still waiting for the government to agree to allocate funds for electricity to them. As a part of the agreement, CHEC has established a subsidiary in the United Kingdom to find more infrastructure investment opportunities in the United Kingdom over the next 10 years. CHEC is a subsidiary of China Communications Construction Company Ltd. and is a state-owned enterprise. At the same time, CHEC has also signed a memorandum with the Swansea Tidal Power Plant to expand more relevant projects in Asia, especially along China's more than 18,000 km coastline. It is believed that the

---

[10] Jiang Wei. (January 29, 2015). The Number of Foreign Contracted Projects Increased by 11.7% Last Year, the Peripheral Region Will Be the Focus of the Belt and Road Initiative. *Hexun*. Retrieved from http://news.hexun.com/2015-01-29/172851962.html.

project's planning permission will be approved this month and will begin in 2016. In addition, Chinese developers have also invested heavily in the real estate industry in the United Kingdom, including a GBP 650 million business district project near Manchester Airport.

"After the infrastructure of the Belt and Road Initiative is completed, there are many industries in China that can 'go global' as a whole, and it is entirely possible to recreate a Chinese manufacturing industry abroad. Therefore, at some stage in the future, the GDP will be a geographical concept, and its growth rate may slow down. However, on the other hand, the growth rate of the gross national product (GNP) will accelerate in the future," said Fan Jianping, chief economist of the State Information Center. "Through the exportation of funds and technology, it will in turn drive the exportation of equipment and commodities." Fan Jianping predicts that in the future, China can imitate the construction of Singapore's existing industrial park in Suzhou and build an industrial park in China's Belt and Road Initiative-related countries in order to drive manufacturing exports. In the future, once China's manufacturing industry goes abroad, it will free up space for industrial upgrading for domestic manufacturing. "Otherwise, everyone is now in a deadlock in the case of excess capacity, and from followers to leaders, they engage in the Free Trade Area of the Asia-Pacific (FTAAP) and develop hardware and software together, which will open up a new path for peace and development in the world."[11]

2.4 *Broad Prospects for Energy Cooperation*

As of 10:55 p.m., November 13, 2014 Beijing time, when the China-Central Asia natural gas pipeline was put into operation, it has cumulatively delivered 100 billion m^3 of natural gas from Central Asia and delivered 70 million tons of crude oil.

In 1997, PetroChina acquired the Aktobe project in Kazakhstan. This is widely considered to be the first step in the "going global" of Chinese oil companies. Seventeen years later, China has now become

---

[11] Wang Yue, Fan Jianping. (January 9, 2015). The Belt and Road Will Help China's Manufacturing Industry Reconstruct Overseas. *Chinairn*. Retrieved from http://www.chinairn.com/news/20150109/095415302.shtml.

an important player in energy cooperation on the Silk Road Economic Belt. In 2013, the related countries in the Silk Road Economic Belt produced a total of approximately 1.1 billion tons of crude oil, which exceeded 1/4 of the world's total production. The total production of natural gas was 1,074.4 billion m³, accounting for approximately 1/3 of the world's total production. The increase in oil and gas production and the increase in the share of the world market show that the energy industry along the New Silk Road has made considerable progress. At the same time, the vigorous development of the energy industry echoes the overall development of the national economy. The countries related to the Silk Road Economic Belt have been developing rapidly in the past 10 years. Apart from being affected by the international financial crisis in 2009, all the countries have maintained a relatively high economic growth rate that exceeds the world's average.

For more than 10 years, Chinese companies have participated extensively in the energy cooperation of countries in the Silk Road Economic Belt. At present, PetroChina has formed a complete oil industry chain integrating exploration and development, pipeline transportation, oil refining, chemical industries, and product sales in Central Asia. It has built a strategic channel of new energy in the northwest of China. In the next step, PetroChina will highlight Central Asia in the construction of the five major overseas oil and gas cooperation zones in Central Asia, Africa, the Middle East, the Americas, and the Asia-Pacific.

Statistics show that, in 2013, the major energy-producing countries in the Silk Road Economic Belt exported 58.67 million tons of crude oil to China, which exceeded 1/4 of China's total imports and 274 trillion m³ of natural gas, exceeding half of the total volume of imports of China's natural gas. The proportion of China's oil and gas exported to relevant exporting countries is also increasing. In addition, the construction of the Central Asia Natural Gas Pipeline D to China, the China–Kazakhstan Natural Gas Pipeline Phase II, and the China–Russia Natural Gas Pipeline have begun their construction, which will further enhance China's natural gas trade with these countries.

Oil and gas pipelines linking China with Russia and Central Asian countries have been completed recently, which has greatly increased the volume of energy trade between China and related countries. Among them, the total transportation capacity of crude oil pipelines has reached 35 million tons/year. Because it has reached an expansion agreement with Russia, it is expected that the total transportation capacity of the China–Kazakhstan and the China–Russia crude oil pipelines will increase to 50 million tons/year from 2018 onward. After Line D of the Central Asia natural gas pipeline is completed, the total transportation capacity will reach 85 billion m³/year.

"At the end of 2015, PetroChina will have achieved a capacity of 50 million tons of oil and gas production in Central Asia; by the end of 2020, Central Asia will have the capacity to deliver resources equivalent to 90 million tons of oil and gas to China each year," said Cao Yaming, general manager of Trans-Asia Gas Pipeline Company Limited.z[12]

The following are the pipeline operations of PetroChina's oil and natural gas from 2012 to 2014 (Table 4.2).

It is worth noting that this is the first time that China has had the opportunity to participate in the formulation of international energy finance game rules established by the Belt and Road Initiative. For

Table 4.2 Domestic and Overseas Operating Mileages (in km) of the PetroChina Pipeline (2012–2014)

	2012	2013	2014
Domestic operating mileages of oil and gas pipelines	66,801	72,878	79,054
Crude oil pipeline mileage	16,369	17,640	18,132
Natural gas pipeline mileage	40,995	45,704	50,836
Refined oil pipeline mileage	9,437	9,534	10,086
Overseas operating mileages of oil and gas pipelines	10,494	13,257	15,218
Crude oil pipeline mileage	6,672	6,671	7,653
Natural gas pipeline mileage	3,822	6,586	7,565

Source: Annual report of the China National Petroleum Corporation 2014.

---

[12] Qi Hui. (November 15, 2014). PetroChina: New Opportunities for the Development of Energy "New Silk Road". Retrieved from http://www.cnmc.com.cn/detail.jsp?article_id=6059&column_no=010301.

China, its domestic capital can help the development of foreign energy industries. Besides, domestic energy and financial markets can also try to gradually open up to large-scale energy companies in friendly countries, especially to large state-owned energy companies. Based on that, China can also build an energy and financial settlement system with the RMB as one of the major currencies. Furthermore, China can also compile indices of energy production, trade, and logistics and develop related derivative transactions. All the abovementioned benefits are positively significant for promoting the internationalization of the RMB and for improving China's energy pricing power and discourse power. The futures market, options market, and settlement system all center on obtaining energy pricing rights, which is also the most important part of energy finance. Currently, the mass energy futures trading volume of China ranks first in the world, but the country has no pricing power on the international market, which leads to the higher risk in change costs and exchange rates and makes China suffer losses because of price fluctuations on the international energy market.[13]

Energy cooperation among China, Russia, and Central Asian countries is an important part of the Belt and Road Initiative. At present, there are numerous opportunities for development. After the Belt and Road Initiative was proposed, China, Russia, and related Central Asian countries further intensified their energy cooperation and strengthened the energy links among countries in the region, forming a new pattern of regional energy cooperation.

2.5 *Further International Regional Cooperation*

With the introduction of Vision and Proposed Actions for the Belt and Road Initiative, the international subregional cooperation around China will also meet further development, which mainly includes the following economic cooperation between China and other countries.

---

[13] Zhao Ya. (June 16, 2015). The Belt and Road Initiative Contains Opportunities for the Construction of China's Energy Finance Market. Retrieved from https://www.in-en.com/article/html/energy-2234186.shtml.

The China–Mongolia–Russia Economic Belt: This Belt basically connects Japan and South Korea in the east and connects Europe through Russia in the west with the help of the traffic and energy channel through the Bohai Bay Area, Northeastern China, Russia, Mongolia, and other countries. The area mainly includes the Changjitu Development and Opening Pilot Area in Jilin Province.

The New Eurasian Land Bridge Economic Belt: This Belt connects Kazakhstan and some countries in Central Asia, Western Asia, Central Europe, and Eastern Europe through Xinjiang Province in the west based on the old Eurasian Continental Bridge.

The China-Southern Asia-Western Asia Economic Belt: This Belt connects Pakistan, India, Myanmar, Thailand, Laos, Cambodia, Malaysia, Vietnam, Singapore, and other countries through Yunnan Province and Guangxi Province and connects Pakistan, Afghanistan, Iran, Turkey, and other countries through the southern line of the Eurasian Continental Bridge.

The Maritime Strategic Fortress: This area mainly includes the coastal countries or regions of the Pacific Ocean and Indian Ocean connected by the Changjitu Development and Opening Pilot Area and ports in Bohai Bay, the Yangtze River Delta, the Western Taiwan Straits, the Pearl River Delta, North Bay, and other districts.

In the next decade, China's exports to the Belt and Road region are expected to increase to 1/3 and the total investments to the Belt and Road Initiative are expected to reach USD 1.6 trillion. In the 13th China Enterprises' Going Global Strategy Implementation Forum Overseas Project News Conference, Liu Jinsong, Deputy Director of the Department of International Economics of the Ministry of Foreign Affairs, said that China's investments in more than 60 countries around the Belt and Road region accounted for about 17% of China's total foreign investments, while the amount of investments that China absorbed from these countries were only equivalent to approximately 7% of the total foreign investments absorbed by China, showing that China, along with the Belt and Road countries and regions, has a great potential for growth in investments so that these countries are worthy of further cooperation with and investment by Chinese enterprises.

In November 2014, Premier Li Keqiang visited Kazakhstan, signing a USD 14 billion document between China and Kazakhstan. Again, in March 2015, China and Kazakhstan signed 33 production capacity documents, involving a total amount of USD 23.6 billion. In addition, China has deepened its cooperation with other countries in Central Asia.

In April 2015, President Xi Jinping visited Pakistan, helping China and Pakistan by investing a total of USD 28 billion in infrastructure projects out of the total investments of USD 46 billion, including the transformation of Pakistan's railways and the construction of power plants. According to reports by Pakistani media, the two sides signed 51 agreements, including the following projects: a financing project that is worth USD 4.3 billion signed with the Industrial and Commercial Bank of China; an agreement on a 900 MW PV power plant signed with ZTE Corporation that holds 23.26% share of ZTE Energy; a cooperation agreement on a coalfield, coal and electricity integration project signed with Shanghai Electric, and so on. There were at least 15 Chinese companies participating in the signing of cooperation agreements and memos.

President Xi then visited Indonesia and helped the two sides signing the Indonesian high-speed rail project that is worth USD 6 billion. Furthermore, China will provide it with a loan of USD 50 billion, involving railways, electricity, and metallurgy, according to Indonesia.

On September 13, 2015, Lu Wei, Director of the China National Internet Information Office, said at the China-ASEAN Information Harbor Forum that China would promote the establishment of the China-ASEAN Information Harbor Construction Fund. With the help of the Asian Infrastructure Investment Bank and the Silk Road Fund, as well as the increasing number of investments in information infrastructure, China will build a China-ASEAN Information Harbor portal to break information barriers and share information services with ASEAN countries on economics and finance, education and scientific research, medical and healthcare, disaster warning, and other issues so that the construction of information harbors will benefit the people of all these countries. At present, with the joint efforts of all parties, the information harbor construction project has become an important part of the Belt and Road Initiative. A number of key projects facing the ASEAN community and based in Guangxi have been successively landed. Besides, China has accelerated the construction of four cross-border land cables and submarine cables and has launched the China-ASEAN Information Harbor Base, the China-ASEAN E-commerce Industrial Park, and other projects. All the abovementioned projects lead to and stimulate the comprehensive exchanges between China and ASEAN countries and arouse the heat of cooperation among Internet-based enterprises. Based on the abovementioned factors, a large number of technology transfer and innovation cooperation projects have been successfully signed so that the network of cultural exchanges has become closer.[14]

3. China's Regional Economic Development Linking the Belt and Road Initiative

Regional policy has always been one of the vital measures that China has applied to promote coordinated and comprehensive development in all areas. The establishment of the economic zone has always been an important issue of China in the history of social development because of the vast territory of the country.

From the division of the seven economic zones and the top ten economic zones proposed in the 1950s and the 1960s to the division of the three major economic zones of the east, central, and west during the period of the 7th Five-Year Plan, China's economic development has entered a new round of growth. During the period, the overall strategy for the coordinated development of four sections — the eastern, central, western, and northeastern sections — was gradually established. Since the beginning of the 21st century, strategies for developing the western area, rejuvenating the old industrial base in

---

[14] Lu Wei. (September 13, 2015). Rely on the Asian Infrastructure Investment Bank to Establish the China-ASEAN Information Harbor Construction Fund. *Haiwainet*. Retrieved from http://m.haiwainet.cn/middle/456935/2015/0922/content_29188424_1.html.

the northeast, and promoting the rise of the central part have been implemented one after another. Together with the coastal areas, they have constituted the pattern for regional development. With the redistribution of resource elements and the continuous innovation of an institutional system, the four major sections have a strong sense of competition, resulting in a rise in the position of the central and western parts in the national development chessboard so that the trend of a widening developmental gap among the eastern, central, and western regions has been alleviated.

3.1 *Comprehensive Survey of Regional Economic Development*

The characteristics of China's economic zone settings are generally typical of the multilayer circle structure. At the macro-level, there are the four East, Central, West, and Northeast sections. At the meso-level, there are interprovincial economic zone settings such as the Central Plains Economic Zone, the Yangtze River Delta Economic Belt, the Pearl River Delta Economic Belt, the Beijing–Tianjin–Hebei Economic Belt, the Economic Zone along the Yangtze River, the Economic Belt along the Edge, and so on. Micro-level economic zone settings are often limited within a province to a large extent, such as the Shenzhen Special Economic Zone, the Pudong New Area, and the Binhai New Area. Surely, provincial-level economic zone settings are also considered at the micro level. For example, He'nan is a major grain-producing area and Shanxi is a pilot area for the comprehensive utilization of resources. For a certain period of time, the economic zones at the macro level will remain stable, while the meso-level and micro-level economic zone settings will continue to emerge, providing different opportunities for development for the rational allocation of resources and market-oriented zoning experiments.

Since the reform and opening-up, the form of development of China's regional setup at the micro level has been the establishment of special economic zones and various types of economic development zones. The basic idea is still to form a large-scale regional growth pole and follow the gradient law to promote the gradual development of other regions. (1) The development and open area during the initial period of reform and opening-up was concentrated in the coastal and border areas, and also in the areas along the rivers (mainly the Yangtze River) and the form is to establish special economic zones and various types of economic development zones, including two types of development zones at the national level and the local level. The development zones were set up first in coastal cities and then inland. To date, more than 130 national development zones have been set up. In 1984, a multiform and multilevel development pattern was gradually formulated nationwide according to the order of "special economic zones–open coastal cities–coastal economic open areas–open riverside and inland cities–open border cities." Special economic functional zones such as special economic zones, national-level economic and technological development zones, bonded zones, high-tech industrial development zones, and export processing zones became the engines of economic development within certain regions. The increase in the size of the special economic zones and the establishment of new special economic zones and development zones have become a new trend in China's regional economic development, which "not only reflects the life-cycle theory of special economic zones, but it also mirrors the need for coordinated development of the regional economy in China."[15] (2) After more than 20 years of development, the originally designed single function of the economic development zones could not cope with the increasing demand for social management and services in around 2005. To meet the need for overall reform, the country made appropriate adjustments to regional economic development models, and thus, comprehensive integrated reform pilot zones have emerged. On June 21, 2005, the Pudong New Area, as the first comprehensive reform pilot area, was approved in China. To date, there are 14 national new districts, such as the Binhai New Area, the Shenzhen Special Economic Zone, the Tianfu New Area, the Xixian New Area,

---

[15] Wang Jiating. (2007). An Analysis of the Mechanism of Spatial Diffusion in the Institutional Innovation of the National Comprehensive Reform Testing Zone, *Nanjing Social Sciences*, Issue 7, pp. 39–44.

and the Liangjiang New Area. (3) Since June 2007, China has successively approved nine thematic comprehensive reform pilot zones in Chengdu, Chongqing, Wuhan City Circle, Changsha–Zhuzhou–Xiangtan City Group, Shenyang, Shanxi, Yiwu, Hainan, and Zhoushan. (4) At the end of the 11th Five-Year Plan, there was an upsurge of attempts to raise local regional plans to national strategies among local governments. In 2009 and 2010, a total of 24 regional plans were upgraded to national development strategies.

After 2008, the pattern of China's regional economic development began to be further refined. It evolved from the "four major sections" to "six core economic circles (belts)" that include the Capital Economic Circle, the Bohai Rim Economic Circle, the East China Sea Economic Circle, the South China Sea Economic Circle, the Upper and middle-stream Yangtze River Economic Belt, and the Middle-stream Yellow River Economic Belt. Based on the coastal and riverside areas, this spatial pattern covers the entire coastal area from the northeast to the southwest, including North China, North and South China, the central and some western and northeastern parts. The main pattern of the eastern coastal area can be described as "three major areas and five small economic belts." "Three major areas" refer to the Bohai Rim, the Yangtze River Delta, and the Pearl River Delta. The "five small economic belts" are the Liaoning Coastal Economic Belt, the Shandong Yellow River Delta Ecological Economic Zone, the Jiangsu Coastal Economic Zone, the Western Taiwan Straits Economic Zone, and the Guangxi Beihai Economic Zone. The principal economic belts of the inland areas are based on the Yangtze River Basin and the Yellow River Basin. The economic belt in the middle and upper reaches of the Yangtze River is focused on the Wuhan City Circle, the Changsha–Zhuzhou–Xiangtan City Group, the Chengdu–Chongqing area, and the Nanchang–Jiujiang area, while the Middle-stream Yellow River Economic Belt is formed based on the Central Plains, the Guanzhong Area, and the National Energy Base. Therefore, four sections have built up regional cooperation in the pan-region and formed a multilevel economic system integrating the economic circle, the coastal economic belt, and the national comprehensive reform pilot area to connect regions and promote common development. At present, the Yangtze River Delta urban agglomerations, the Beijing–Tianjin urban agglomerations, and the Pearl River Delta urban agglomerations have become the three major urban agglomerations that have guided regional economic development. In addition, the city groups of Shandong Peninsula, the middle and southern part of Liaoning, the Central Plains, the middle reaches of the Yangtze River, the Western Taiwan Straits, Sichuan–Chongqing, and Guanzhong–Tianshui were also formed one after another. Affected by the two major effects of "polarization" and "diffusion" in the city circle, the region has met the optimization of resource allocation within the area, resulting in strong economic synergy and cohesion. In the rise of the Central China strategy, the regional economic development of the Changsha–Zhuzhou–Xiangtan City Group, the Wuhan City Circle, and the Anhui–Jiangsu City Belt are driven by urban agglomerations. Different economic circles and city belts intersect vertically and horizontally to form a network pattern.

3.2 The Development Plan of the Large-Scale Transportation Industry Provides the Regional Economy with Momentum for Sustainable Development

In October 2007, the State Council Executive Meeting reviewed and basically approved the *Long-Term Development Plan for the Comprehensive Transportation Network*. For the first time, the plan put forward the concept of a "comprehensive transportation channel," and proposed 10 comprehensive transportation lanes of "five verticals and five horizontals" and four international regional transportation corridors after optimization and selection based on the principle of "Develop in the most appropriate way" in order to develop land transportation on the plains, water transportation on rivers, and air transportation in the spacious area. According to the location, function, role of the comprehensive transportation hub, the number of connected transportation lines, the service scope for attracting and radiating, and the passenger and freight volume and growth potential, the transportation system can be divided into a national comprehensive transportation hub, a regional comprehensive transportation hub, and a local comprehensive transportation hub. The plan proposes 42 national comprehensive transportation hubs (node cities).

The *Long-Term Development Plan for a Comprehensive Transportation Network* is of great practical significance and long-term benefits to realize China's strategy for sustainable development, narrowing the gap among regions, and achieving coordinated development of all modes of transportation. From the analysis of the geographical features of China's economy, east–west and north–south transportation will continue to exist for a long time. Transportation, as a basic industry, plays a strong leading role in economic development. The comprehensive medium- and long-term plan of the transportation network will consider the characteristics of China's resource allocation, industrial layout, urban distribution, and population distribution, especially the possible future layout of economic division and that of the economic center in China. The transportation network focuses on the formation of a number of state-level transportation corridors that will transport things between the north and the south. Furthermore, it will guide and promote the balanced development of the country and provide basic conditions for narrowing the gap among regions in China.

It is estimated that after the implementation of the *Medium- and long-term Railway Network Plan*, which was approved by the State Council Executive Meeting at the beginning of 2004, the total amount of investments in railway construction will exceed RMB 5 trillion by 2020, and the railway mileage will reach more than 120,000 km. Currently, China has the following high-speed railways: the Beijing–Tianjin Intercity Railway, the Nanchang–Jiujiang Intercity Railway, the Shijiazhuang–Taiyuan Passenger-only Railway, the Changchun–Jilin Intercity Railway, the Qingdao–Ji'nan Passenger-only Railway, the Shanghai–Nanjing High-speed Railway, the Wuhan–Guangzhou Passenger-only Railway, the Zhengzhou–Xi'an High-speed Railway, the Wenzhou–Fuzhou Railway, the Wuhan–Yichang High-speed Railway, the Fuzhou–Xiamen Railway, the Chengdu–Dujiangyan High-speed Railway, the Shanghai–Hangzhou High-speed Railway, the Shanghai–Nanjing Intercity Railway, the

Guangzhou–Zhuhai Intercity Railway, the Hainan East Ring Railway, and the Beijing–Shanghai High-speed Railway. In China, nearly 1,200 EMU trains are operated each day and the operating mileage is over 9,358 km. China has become the country with the longest operating mileage and fastest operating speed in the world. It is expected that by 2020, the total mileage of high-speed rail will have reached more than 16,000 km. At that time, it will take 8 hours at the most to travel from Beijing to any other provincial capital city. According to estimates by experts, China's highway network has a long-term scale of 5.965 million km, including 150,000 km of a national highway network, 265,000 km of ordinary national highways, 550,000 km of provincial roads, and 5 million km of rural roads. The length of the railway network is approximately 190,000 km, approximately including 40,000 km of passenger-only railways and 150,000 km of ordinary railways.

Taken other relevant factors into consideration, the main line of the highway is planned according to the national trunk highway network (abbreviated as the national highway network, including the capital radiation lines, the north–south vertical lines, and the east–west horizontal lines). The main lines include 12 national trunk roads that are basically comprised high-grade highways, with a total length of about 35,000 km, known as the "five vertical and seven horizontal trunk national highways" that run from east to west across the border. They run through the Capital, municipalities, and capital cities of provinces (autonomous regions), connecting all of the megacities with a population of over 1 million and 93% of the metropolises with a population of more than 500,000. In addition, over 200 cities are connected together, and the population covered is around 600 million, accounting for approximately 50% of the total population of the country.

In accordance with the characteristics of the distribution of China's productivity and the T-shape distribution of water resources, China will focus on the construction of major sea transportation in developed areas of the southeastern coast and inland waterways of major navigable rivers. The overall national plans for the main channel of water transportation is to develop five main waterways known as

224 Belt and Road Initiative: Interregional Cooperation Between Asia and Europe

the "two verticals and three horizontals." The "two verticals" are the main channel from the north to the south of the coast and the main channel of the Huaihe River and the Beijing–Hangzhou Canal. The "three horizontals" are the main channel of the Yangtze River and its primary tributaries, the main channel of the Xijiang River and its primary tributaries, and the main channel of the Songhua River in Heilongjiang Province. The main inland river comprises four-grade navigation channels through which even a 1,000-ton fleet can sail, with a total of 20 rivers and a total length of 15,000 km in addition to the main north–south coastal channel. The channels connect 17 provincial capitals and central cities, 24 open cities, and five special economic zones.

Since 2010, China has basically completed the construction of a highly efficient southern–northern maritime transportation channel compatible with foreign trade transportation and maritime transportation. In terms of inland navigation, China will focus on the construction of the Yangtze River Line and its vital tributaries, further developing the Pearl River and the Beijing–Hangzhou Canal and initially forming the main channel of "one vertical and three horizontals," including the main channel of 20 major inland waterways with a total length of approximately 15,000 km, making it a shipping system for the economic development of industrial belts along the Yangtze River.

The plan of the national hub port is to develop 43 main hubs, including 20 coastal ports, 23 inland river ports, covering 14 open cities along the coast, four special economic zones, the provincial capital of the Hainan Special Economic Zone, and all of the provincial capitals on the main waterways and 66% of the large- and medium-sized cities. At the same time, the plan of the national highway hub station is to develop 45 passenger and cargo hub stations that cover 30 provincial capitals, 80.6% of the megacities with a population of over 1 million, and 73.3% of the cities with an industrial output value of over RMB 10 billion.

Over the past 30 years of reform and opening-up, civil aviation has grown at an average annual rate of 17.6%, which is far higher than other modes of transportation. China has built the second largest air transportation system in the world after the United States. In the next decade, it will remain the golden period for the rapid development of civil aviation. During the period of the 12th Five-Year Plan, China plans to build more than 70 new airports and rebuild (expand) 101 airports, and the total industrial investment will exceed RMB 1.5 trillion. It is expected that in 2020 and 2030, passenger traffic in China will reach 700 million person-times and 1.5 billion person-times, respectively.

3.3 *Transportation Infrastructure Supports the Belt and Road Initiative*

In 2013, during his visit to Central Asia and Southeast Asian countries, President Xi Jinping put forward the constructive initiatives of jointly building the Silk Road Economic Belt and the 21st-century Maritime Silk Road (collectively, "the Belt and Road Initiative"), which received great attention and positive response from the international community. The Belt and Road Initiative will provide new impetus for the economic development of China and the world. It connects the two ends of the Eurasian Continent, namely the developed European economic circle and the most dynamic East Asian economic circle, it promotes the integration of the Eurasian market by driving the development of Central Asia, Western Asia, Southern Asia, and Southeastern Asia, and also leads the development of Africa and other regions.

The implementation of the projects of cooperation and the promotional measures of the Belt and Road Initiative will inevitably create a broad radiation effect on the countries along the route, narrow the regional developmental gap, and accelerate the process of regional integration. There are more than 60 countries in the Belt and Road domain, with a population of about 4.4 billion people, accounting for 63% of the world's population. The project focuses on the construction of transportation infrastructure as the priority area of cooperation, in line with the actual needs of Asia and Europe, especially in Asia, as the infrastructure in many countries and regions is in urgent need of upgrading. Strengthening investments in the construction of infrastructures can not only create new economic growth points, driving forward the economic development of the countries in the region, but it can also promote investments and consumption, create demand and employment, and lay a solid foundation for the future development of the countries in the region. According to the multiplier effect of the construction of infrastructures, 30,000–80,000 jobs will be created for every USD 1 billion invested in that construction, and the GDP will increase by USD 2.5 billion. The mission of jointly carrying out the Belt and Road Initiative is to promote the development of 2/3 of the global population. Having seen the cumulative growth of China's trade with the Belt and Road region from 2003 to 2013, China's growth in the region was significantly higher than the average growth rate of its foreign trade. China's cumulative importations increased 3.7 times, and its global exports increased fourfold, while in the Belt and Road region, that number clearly exceeded. The cumulative increase in imports was 4.8 times and the cumulative increase in exports was 7.2 times. According to the data from the World Bank, the average annual growth rate of global trade and cross-border direct investment was 7.8% and 9.7%, respectively, from 1990 to 2013, while the average annual growth rate of global trade and cross-border direct investment of 65 countries related to the Belt and Road Initiative during the same period reached 13.1% and 16.5%, respectively; especially from 2010 to 2013, the average annual growth rate of foreign trade and foreign net inflows from the Silk Road reached 13.9% and 6.2%, respectively, after the international financial crisis, that is, 4.6% and 3.4% points higher than the average global growth rate. Hence, the initiative has played a significant role in stimulating the recovery of global trade investments. From 1990 to 2013, the average annual growth rate of the overall GDP of the Silk Road region reached 5.1%, which is equivalent to twice the global average growth rate during the same period. Even during the period from 2010 to 2013 when the international financial crisis affected the recovery of the global economy, the average annual growth rate of the Silk Road region still managed to reach 4.7%, which was 2.3% points higher than the average global growth rate. It is estimated that in the next five years, China's cumulative imports will exceed the scale of

USD 10 trillion, and if about half of the money comes from the countries involved in the Belt and Road Initiative, it will provide more than USD 5 trillion in export opportunities for this region.

Throughout the period of over 30 years of the reform and opening-up, the construction of infrastructures in China's border areas has been greatly improved, especially in related fields such as transportation infrastructure, power communication infrastructure, water infrastructure, and education and health infrastructure, providing effective support for advancing international subregional economic cooperation. With the continuous development of China's overall strategy for regional development and the strategy of priority development zones, border areas receive more support and assistance from the country, especially in terms of the construction of infrastructures, which will benefit the border areas, promoting better and rapid development for themselves. To date, China has taken important steps toward international subregional cooperation, forming a pattern of subregional cooperation with Southeast Asia, Southern Asia, Central Asia, and Northeastern Asia. Since the first direct international freight train from Chongqing to Duisburg operated in October 2011, the railway line from the Chinese mainland to Europe has become increasingly busy. After China carried out the Belt and Road Initiative, provinces have spared no expense in subsidizing the establishment of China–EU train lines so that the China Railway Corporation had to make adjustments to the train schedules in the second half of 2014, which increased the number of operating routes from 8 to 19. The New Silk Road across the Eurasian Continental Bridge is becoming increasingly crowded. At present, China has officially opened eight China–Europe trains through three major international passages in the east, central, and west to reach Europe. The western passage exits through Alashankou (Khorgos), the middle passage exits through Erenhot, and the eastern passage passes through Manzhouli (the Suifen River). Among all cities connected to China–Europe trains, Chongqing, Zhengzhou, Chengdu, Hefei, Wuhan, and Changsha are all located in the central and western regions except Yiwu and Suzhou. According to the statistics of the China Railway Corporation, it had opened 308 China–Europe trains and sent 26,070 twenty-foot equivalent units

(TEUs) of containers in 2014, which increased by 285% of what it was in the same period of the previous year, namely having 228 lines, promoting the development of economic and trade exchanges among countries along the China–Europe border. After joining the WTO, China's shipping industry has accelerated its entry into the international shipping market and promoted its development. During the 10 years from 1999 to 2008, China's growth in trade accounted for 30% of the total growth in maritime trade. There are up to several thousand international and coastal waterway routes in China and more than 2,000 international container liner routes. Moreover, the country's port cargo throughput has ranked first in the world for six consecutive years.[16] In 2010, China became the world's second largest economy, the largest exporter of trade, and the third largest shipping country. Its port throughput and container handling capacity ranked first in the world for several years in a row. Currently, China has developed into a world port country, a shipping power, and a container shipping powerhouse, which exemplifies the shift of the world's trading center to East Asia as a shipping base.

The Asian Infrastructure Investment Bank and the Silk Road Fund have become the financial platforms for the successful implementation of the Belt and Road Initiative. Asia has huge population, capitals, and resources, but Asian development lacks organizations to effectively use these elements, and it especially lacks effective multilateral financial organizations. However, the two financial institutions will pool and use financial resources both inside and outside the region to gather the will of governments, industries, and people along the Belt and Road to strengthen their cooperation, improve the level of open exchange among countries, promote industrial cooperation and the division of labor in the value chain so that different developmental-level economies can benefit from win–win results through interconnectivity, trade and investment opening-up, and financial and service cooperation. According to the statistics from the Asian

---

[16] Great Changes in Chinese Shipping Logistics for 60 Years. (September 15, 2009). *People's Daily Online.* Retrieved from http://world.people.com.cn/n/2014/0221/c1002-24422237.html.

Development Bank, Asia needs at least RMB 8 trillion to invest in infrastructure from 2010 to 2020.

The Belt and Road Initiative is currently ongoing in many countries along the route. The Kunming–Yuxi Railway of the Trans-Asian Railway China Section that connects China–Laos and China–Vietnam Railways is under construction, and the Yuxi-Mohan Section that connects China–Laos and China–Thailand Railways will be started within year 2016. According to the plan of *Intergovernmental Agreement on the Trans-Asian Railway Network*, a four-lane railway network connecting Eurasia has been formed, which includes the northern channel that connects the Korean Peninsula, Russia, China, Mongolia, Kazakhstan, and other countries to Europe; the southern channel connecting southern China, Myanmar, India, Iran, Turkey, and other countries; the north–south channel connecting Russia, Central Asia, and the Persian Gulf; the China-ASEAN channel connecting China, ASEAN countries, and the Indo–China Peninsula. The four lines will connect 28 countries and regions, with a total mileage of more than 80,000 km. In April 2015, China and Pakistan initiated a total of USD 28 billion in infrastructure projects out of the total investment worth USD 46 billion, including the transformation of Pakistan's railways and the construction of power plants. In May 2015, President Xi Jinping attended the 60th anniversary of the Bandung Conference and the third summit of Asian and African leaders. During that period of time, China and Indonesia signed a high-speed railway project in Indonesia that is worth USD 6 billion, and China will provide it with a loan of USD 50 billion, involving railways, electricity, and metallurgy, according to Indonesia. In November 2014, Premier Li Keqiang visited Kazakhstan and the two sides signed a USD 14 billion document. In March 2015, China and Kazakhstan signed 33 production documents, involving a total amount of USD 23.6 billion. China has also deepened its cooperation with other countries in Central Asia. CRCC China–Africa Construction Co., Ltd. signed construction orders in April 2015 with a total amount of nearly USD 5.5 billion. A commercial contract for the Ogun State Intercity Railway Project in Nigeria was signed, with a total contract value of USD 3.506 billion. China also helped on the largest housing project in Zimbabwe's history — a hero housing project worths USD 1.93 billion. Based on the abovementioned achievements, the CRCC China-Africa Construction Co., Ltd. has become Africa's largest railway traffic contractor. In May 2015, a Russian–Chinese joint consortium became the successful bidder and signed a contract of 20 billion rubles for the Moscow–Kazan high-speed railway project that costs 1.068 trillion rubles in total. In the future, the Moscow–Kazan high-speed railway will probably become part of the Moscow–Beijing high-speed railway line and the New Silk Road project. In addition, the Singapore–Malaysia high-speed railway under construction that will connect Kuala Lumpur and Singapore, with a total length of around 350 km and an engineering investment of USD 12–15 billion, is also a hot project in the current national competition. On May 9, 2015, President Xi Jinping, who attended the military parade for the 70th anniversary of Russia's victory in WW II, and signed 32 large China–Russia trade contracts with Russia for a total value of USD 25 billion, including an infrastructure loan valued billions of dollars for Russia. Among the contracts, there is a loan of 300 billion roubles (about USD 6 billion) for the construction of a high-speed railway. This will enable the Silk Road Economic Belt to better interface with the Eurasian Economic Union.

It is worth noting that the most influential cooperation mechanisms in Central Asia at present are the "Integrated Study of the Silk Road — Dialogue Road" project initiated by UNESCO in 1988, the Silk Road Diplomacy of Japan, the New Silk Road Plan of the United States, the North–South Corridor Plan, and so on. All these mechanisms face many challenges in their development. However, the Belt and Road Initiative that focuses on the construction of infrastructures is expected to open up a new path because of the experience of successful domestic regional development and transportation infrastructure.

3.4 *Thirty One Provinces, Municipalities, and Autonomous Regions Docking with the Belt and Road Initiative*

The Belt and Road Initiative at the state level has been approved, which includes a number of elements, such as infrastructure, trade, and industrial transfer. A reform roadmap has been released, which takes the free trade area (FTA) as a trade bridgehead and the Belt and Road Initiative as the capital traction. With the help of 31 provinces, municipalities, and autonomous regions, the Belt and Road Initiative stimulates internal vitality.

According to the plan, the most important area of the Belt and Road Initiative includes 16 provinces. The Silk Road Economic Belt mainly covers southwestern China, including Xinjiang, Qinghai, Gansu, Shaanxi, and Ningxia provinces and northwestern China, including Chongqing, Sichuan, Guangxi and Yunnan provinces and autonomous regions, as well as Inner Mongolia that has been newly included. On the other hand, the 21st-century Maritime Silk Road includes Jiangsu, Zhejiang, Fujian, Guangdong, Hainan, five eastern coastal provinces, and Shandong Province that has been newly included.

Jiangxi Province will be connected with China–EU international railway lines. It will expand the sea-railway combined transportation to Ningbo, Xiamen, and Shenzhen and organize the implementation of the special plan for Belt and Road cultural exchanges and cooperation.

Liaoning will implement a new round of opening-up to the outside world, actively integrating into the Belt and Road Initiative and accelerating the construction of the China–Mongolia–Russia Economic Corridor led by cross-border logistics that takes Dalian, Yingkou, Jinzhou, and Dandong Ports as its important node cities. At the same time, it will actively integrate the Liaoning–Manzhouli–Europe and the Liaoning–Mongolia–Europe comprehensive transportation corridors and promote the construction of the Arctic northeastern waterway. According to the plan, Shenyang, Dalian, Dandong, Jinzhou, and Yingkou will be taken as important node cities to actively participate in the construction of the China–Mongolia–Russia Economic Corridor.

The Tibet Autonomous Region will speed up the construction of a major South Asian channel, linking up with the Belt and Road and the Bangladesh–China–India–Myanmar Economic Corridor and promoting the development of the economic cooperation zone in the Himalayas.

Henan has seized the major opportunities brought by the Belt and Road Initiative and is fully integrating into the initiative to enhance the radiative capability of Zhengzhou and Luoyang as major node cities.

Rizhao was identified by Shandong Province as the major node city in the Belt and Road Initiative and it will exert its efforts in ports, industries, and urban infrastructures to improve its ability to comprehensively carry on the Belt and Road Initiative.

Chongqing will plan a group of major infrastructure projects to realize the positioning of "national megacities" to connect the Belt and Road Initiative and the Yangtze River Economic Belt.

Hebei is taking advantage of the Belt and Road Initiative to speed up the opening of its own industries and explicitly proposes to encourage enterprises with excess production capacity and comparative advantages in photovoltaic, steel, glass, cement, and other areas to build a number of production bases abroad, driving equipment, technology, capital, and labor exportation.

Xinjiang's Position: Xinjiang will rely on its geographical advantages to deepen exchanges and cooperation with neighboring countries and regions, forming an important transportation hub and a center of trade logistics and cultural science and technology on the Silk Road Economic Belt, and creating an important area of the Silk Road Economic Belt. The main node cities are Urumqi and Kashgar. In its government work report released on January 20, 2015, Xinjiang proposed that it must promote the construction of the most important area of the Silk Road Economic Belt in the same year, speed up the implementation of the nodal areas of the Silk Road Economic Belt, implement opinions and action plans, and accelerate the construction of the five major centers. In accordance with the Northern, Central, and Southern channel construction plans, it will effectively grasp the construction and reserve of major infrastructure projects. It is reported that Urumqi will apply for the Asia–Europe Economic and Trade Cooperation Experimental Zone in 2015. The Kashgar Comprehensive Bonded Zone received national approval on January 8, 2015. The Khorgos Economic Development Zone will be listed as an important industrial park.

Qinghai's Position: Qinghai is building a strategic corridor, an important fulcrum, and a cultural exchange center for the Silk Road Economic Belt, making the Belt the main district open to the west of Qinghai Province and a new growth pole for promoting the economic development of the province. The node cities are Xining, Haidong, and Golmud. Qinghai's government work report for 2015 proposed to build a modern transportation network that effectively links aviation, railways, and highways among the countries along the Silk Road and neighboring provinces and regions, strengthen cooperation with the coastal regions, and build a bonded logistics center in Caojiabao. Following the opening of the Xining Caojiabao International Airport in December 2014, and the opening of three new routes, namely the Xining–Bangkok, the Xining–Seoul, and the Xining–Taipei routes, 41 projects, such as the International Mall, the Bonded Warehouse, and the Xunhua Muslim Industrial Park, are being implemented.

Gansu's Position: Gansu is the golden city of the Silk Road Economic Belt, an important gateway to the west of China and a strategic base for subregional cooperation. The important node cities are Lanzhou, Baiyin, Jiuquan, Jiayuguan, and Dunhuang. In May 2014, the *General Plan for the Construction of the Gansu Section of the Silk Road Economic Belt* was formally issued. It is proposed to build the Silk Road Economic Belt in the Gansu Golden Section and to construct three strategic platforms including the Lanzhou New District, the Dunhuang International Cultural Tourism City, and the China Silk Road Expo. It focuses on advancing the six major projects of road connectivity, economic and trade technology exchanges, industrial cooperation, economic growth, people-to-people exchanges and cooperation, and the construction of strategic platforms. Among them, there is one strategy to strengthen trade and economic cooperation with countries along the Silk Road, including resource development, equipment manufacturing, new energy, the processing of special agricultural products, and other industries.

Shaanxi's Position: Efforts will be made to build an important fulcrum for the Silk Road Economic Belt and form an important hub for China to open to the west. The important node city is Xi'an.

Next, it will speed up the construction of a new starting point for the Silk Road Economic Belt and strengthen cooperation with countries in Central Asia and Australia in resource exploration and development. It will actively apply for the construction of the FTA of the Silk Road Economic Belt and build the National Aviation City Experimental Area. It will also promote the provincial resource trading center to settle in the energy finance and trade center and encourage various energy companies to actively participate in the construction of the Xixian New Area, it will support the construction of a three-dimensional integrated transportation system in the Xixian New Area and start the construction of subway extension lines, giving priority to carrying on the Central and provincial major industrial projects in the Xixian New Area.

Ningxia's Position: Based on the Belt and Road Initiative, it will further build a strategic fulcrum for the Silk Road Economic Belt. In 2015, the Ningxia Government Work Report proposed that taking the Ningxia Inland Open Economic Experimental Zone as a platform, it should make good use of the "Golden Brand" of the China–Arab States Expo to implement four action plans and accelerate the construction of land, online, and aerial Silk Roads. The first of the four action plans is to implement the open access expansion plan. A group of railway and highway projects will be opened to build the Yinchuan Hedong International Airport into a portal airport for Arab countries.

Inner Mongolia's Position: At the two sessions in Inner Mongolia on January 26, 2015, Bartel, Chairman of the Government of the Inner Mongolia Autonomous Region, clearly stated that Inner Mongolia was included in the construction of the Silk Road Economic Belt and that important steps were being taken to open the bridgehead to the north. Inner Mongolia will compile and promote the implementation plan for the development of the Silk Road Economic Belt, and strive to incorporate the major issues and projects of Inner Mongolia into the national top-level design. In 2015, Inner Mongolia will also speed up the national key development and the opening of experimental zones in Manzhouli and Erenhot and the China–Russia–Mongolia cooperation pilot zone in Hulunbeir, organize the China–Mongolia Expo, increase the strength of port construction, and promote connectivity with Russia–Mongolia infrastructures.

Chongqing's Position: In December 2014, the Chongqing Municipal Party Committee and the Municipal Government formally issued the *Implementation of the National Belt and Road Initiative and the Implementation Opinions for the Construction of the Yangtze River Economic Belt*, and proposed that Chongqing be built as the western hub of the Yangtze River Economic Belt. Next, it would accelerate the construction of a comprehensive transportation hub in the upper reaches of the Yangtze River and create an open upland inland area. In 2015, the Chongqing government work report further pointed out that the economic and trade exchanges with countries along the Belt and Road Initiative, international friendship cities, Hong Kong, Macao, and Taiwan should be strengthened to promote cooperation with the provinces and cities along the Yangtze River Economic Belt, and pragmatically promote the integration of the Chengdu–Chongqing Economic Zone. It should actively organize the cargoes in the surrounding areas for the Chongqing–Xinjiang–Europe train, promote the official operation of the international postal trains, and increase the number of Chongqing–Xinjiang–Europe train trips and container traffic.

Sichuan's Position: The province is to be built into an important transportation hub and an economic hinterland in China's move to implement the Belt and Road Initiative. The Sichuan Provincial Business Work Conference held on January 15, 2015 proposed the implementation of the Belt and Road Initiative and the "251 Three-Year Plan of Action." That is to say, along the Belt and Road, 20 countries that have comparative advantages in industry and trade will be selected to implement key development projects and in-depth development projects. Among the 20 key countries, 50 major projects for two-way investment will be selected to implement vital tracking and strong promotion. Among nearly 10,000 foreign trade companies within the province, 100 key enterprises with good trade and investment bases along the Belt and Road will be selected to implement key guidance and form demonstrations.

Yunnan's Position: Yunnan has positioned itself as a strategic pivot for the Belt and Road Initiative to connect the gateway hubs of Southern Asian and Southeastern Asian countries. As early as 2014, the planning of the Yunnan Section of the Silk Road Economic Belt was proposed to the National Development and Reform Commission, and it is expected to be introduced in the near future. According to the plan, Yunnan Province will use the Border Gold Reform Pilot Zone as one of the key points in the development of the Silk Road Economic Belt and attract financial institutions such as banks and securities in Southeast Asian and South Asian countries to settle in Yunnan to fully enhance cross-border financial services. The 2015 Yunnan Government Work Report pointed out that the construction of infrastructures such as integrated transportation, power, information, and warehousing and logistics in Yunnan will be accelerated.

Guangxi's Position: Guangxi is an important gateway for the effective convergence of the Belt and Road Initiative, and a new strategic fulcrum of the Southwest Opening and Development Strategy. Construction in Guangxi mainly focuses on the Beibu Gulf. The province will speed up the application for the establishment of the Beibu Gulf Free Trade Pilot Zone and is expected to become the third batch of approved FTAs. In 2015, the Guangxi Government Work Report pointed out that the upgrading of the development of the Beibu Gulf Economic Zone will focus on 256 key projects such as infrastructure, industrial upgrading, and port logistics.

The construction of the Silk Road Economic Belt has made many western and central provinces to become hubs of the international logistics channel, and they are basically peripheral cities in the current international logistics channel, which is mainly based on ocean shipping. The transition from a peripheral position to that of a node will bring more logistics and a larger flow of people, capital, and industry to the central and western regions. At the same time, because of their important position in the Silk Road Economic Belt, they will become pillars in economic policy, rather than supportive targets, which will give them more space and opportunities for development under the current policies. At present, China's regional economic development is uneven, and the level of development in the eastern region is far higher than that in the central and western regions and the northeastern region. Accordingly, this pattern has a considerable correlation with coastal openness. The opening-up of the coastal areas has given emphasis to the eastern region logistics channel and core areas by policies, thus accumulating capital and labor. The Silk Road Economic Belt will promote the opening of inland areas and create a situation in which coastal openness and inland openness go hand in hand. This will help the regions to develop more evenly. It is not foreign trade that plays a decisive role in the process of balanced development. During this process, foreign trade plays only an inspiring role. It is the flow of domestic capital and labor that are of greater importance. Therefore, the scale of inland open trade will not be as large as that of the coastal area, but the process of rebalancing the regional economy will be greatly accelerated under the stimulation of domestic capital and labor.

World Harmony and the China Dream: A Dream of Great Harmony

Glancing over the rise and fall of world powers along the course of the past 500 years of history, we can see that different developmental models have dominated the world in different historical periods. The fact that Portugal, Spain, and the Netherlands were able to become great powers in the world in the very beginning depended on their maritime supremacy over other countries. The strength of these maritime powers laid a solid foundation for them in establishing a large number of colonies around the world. The reason why the United Kingdom was able to rule one-quarter of the world's population before World War I (WWI) was that the industrial revolution provided Britain the substantial materials support to conquer the world, and a powerful navy was undoubtedly an important foundation for Britain to achieve global hegemony at that time. Due to the special geography and more specific developmental history, there have been no wars that occurred on the mainland of the United States since the 20th century. Moreover, the United States has developed itself through WWI, strengthened its power throughout WWII, and gradually formed the image of a powerful world power up until today. The financial crisis that broke out in the United States in 2008 and then spread around the world has not only undermined the world's economy, but it has also challenged the capitalist developmental model featuring neoliberalism. By contrast, with the reform and opening-up over the past 30 years, China's international status and influence have been improving day by day, playing a pivotal role in world peace and its development. The developmental path of socialism with Chinese characteristics has achieved eye-catching achievements in the world. In addition, China has put forward the developmental concept of "Amity, Sincerity, Mutual Benefit, and Inclusiveness," and presented the Belt and Road Initiative that focuses on the global community with a common destiny and is gradually winning consensus among different people. Therefore, the developmental model and experience of China have begun to influence the world.

1. The British and American Developmental Models and the Change in the Structure of the World's Economic Center

In the course of the development of modernization, human society has successively witnessed the emergence of a series of great powers, such as Portugal, Spain, the Netherlands, Britain, France, Germany, Japan, Russia, and the United States; among them, the British and American developmental models are comparatively outstanding and representative.

Since Portugal became an independent kingdom in 1143, it has grown rapidly. In the 15th and 16th centuries, it established a large number of colonies in Africa, Asia, and the Americas and consequently became a maritime power. In the struggle against foreign aggression, Spain won the victory of the "Recovery Movement" in 1492. In October of the same year, along with Columbus' discovery of the West Indies, Spain gradually became a powerful nation on the sea and then established a large number of colonies in Europe, the Americas, Africa, and Asia. In the course of the history of worldwide modernization, the United Kingdom was as ambitious as Spain.

In 1588, the British navy defeated the Spanish force which was once called "The Invincible Armada"'; thus Spain fell out of power and was finally utterly defeated. The Netherlands was the world's second largest colonial country, following Spain. Since the 18th century, the Dutch colonial system encountered many challenges from the United Kingdom, and due to its incompetence, the Netherlands gradually fell from its original power status as a colonial power. After it defeated the Spanish "Invincible Armada" in 1588, Britain gradually replaced Spain as an emerging maritime hegemony and began its colonial expansion overseas. Through Britain's successive years of wars with the Netherlands and France, it finally defeated its powerful rivals and took possession of many colonies that formerly belonged to the Netherlands and France, finally establishing its dominance at sea.

1.1 *Two Industrial Revolutions Boost the Rise of the Power of Britain and of the United States*

The rise of the United Kingdom is because of its seizing of the opportunity of the Industrial Revolution. The industrial revolution that first originated in Britain and then spread to major European countries and to the United States had epoch-making significance and exerted an unprecedented and profound influence on the development of our society. It laid a solid material foundation for the new capitalist system, prompting the European and American countries to achieve industrialization and change from agricultural countries to industrial countries one after another. It provided a historical opportunity for the United Kingdom to utilize its cutting-edge advantage of industrialization and established its status as the "world's factory." In the era of industrial capital, the British industrial revolution was the source of the globalization of capital in the following years, which certainly and profoundly influenced the historical process. The Industrial Revolution began in the United Kingdom in the 1760s and around the 1830s, the Western countries gradually entered the stage of large-scale industrialization. According to the statistics, during the 50 years before 1918, the world's economy grew by 2.1% year-on-year, which was two times the average growth rate of the first half of the whole

19th century. Calculated according to the constant price, from 1800 to 1900, the world's economy grew at an average annual rate of 1.54%.[1] Economic development had enabled the West to become increasingly dominant in global politics. Countries that stood in the capital centers and controlled more world trade and resources enjoyed a larger share of the worldwide growth of wealth.

From the middle of the 18th century to the beginning of the 20th century, the United Kingdom was undoubtedly a marine overlord. This hegemonic position was seized from the Netherlands. In the heyday of the rise of the Netherlands, the merchant tonnage of the Netherlands accounted for three-quarters of the total European merchant ship tonnage, which enabled it to monopolize the maritime trade between the East and the West, and therefore, it accumulated enormous wealth. In order to break the maritime trade monopoly of the Netherlands, the United Kingdom issued the "Shipping Regulations" in 1651, which stipulated that only ships owned or manufactured by the United Kingdom or its various colonies could transport goods from the British colonies. Products manufactured in other countries had to go through the British mainland and could not be shipped directly to the colonies. What Britain was challenging here was not the freedom of the marine trade as an abstract principle, but the monopoly of Dutch merchants on the free sea. This kind of challenge had brought Britain several prolonged wars. Britain had to fight with the Netherlands and France, because the latter also ambitiously aimed at maritime dominance. In the end, the Netherlands, the size of a city–state, was defeated by the country-sized United Kingdom. In the battles with France, Britain's geography of an isolated island proved to be an insurmountable congenital advantage. It could finance other land-based allies against the land hegemony of France. Then, it could freely monopolize overseas. In the seven-years' war between the United Kingdom and France from 1756 to 1763, the United Kingdom completely defeated France and established the new maritime empire with the maritime hegemony at sea. Before long,

---

[1] Zhang Yuefa, Liu Yangjie. (1999). *Nation State and World Economy: 1500–1900*. Beijing, China: Current Affairs Press, p. 365.

Britain began its industrial revolution. By the middle of the 19th century, Britain had become the world's factory. After achieving military dominance, its economy also became the global leader. By the middle of the 19th century, the United Kingdom had established a unilateral free trade policy. Whether or not other countries had implemented free trade with the United Kingdom, the United Kingdom could have free trade with them. The commercial capital and financial capital of the United Kingdom had also been quietly transformed and gradually merged with its industrial capital. The landlord class could no longer monopolize politics. The unbounded and liquidity principle of capital had finally defeated the bounded and fixed principle of the land. The cosmopolitan transformation of Britain at an institutional level had also been completed by then. As a result of the Industrial Revolution, Britain imported raw materials and food from other countries and exported finished products to them. Free trade was able to reduce the cost of manufactured goods, which made it possible for Britain to be more competitive on the international market. This led to the accumulation of huge wealth in Britain so that it became the international financial center. As a maritime hegemon and an international financial center, Britain also had the ability to manipulate the financial and trading rules of the entire globe.

In the two hundred years since the founding of the United States of America, the economic strength of the United States has been on the rise, and in the late 19th century and the early 20th century, it laid the foundation of global economic hegemony for America, which was further consolidated and strengthened by two WWs. In the late 19th century, the second industrial revolution took place, with power, internal combustion, and chemical industries as the dominant factors. The United Kingdom had no growth in these areas, and gradually, it lost its leading position in manufacturing to the United States and Germany. The United States accelerated its process of industrialization so that its rapid economic development not only quickly surpassed that of the United Kingdom, but it also made America the world's largest industrial nation by the end of the 19th century, and it underwent with even greater acceleration subsequently. For example, in 1910, the industrial output of the United States was almost two times the size of that of Germany, which ranked second in the world. Britain ranked third in the world. The United States then had a population of 100 million. The power of the United States was ranked first at that time, and it had huge productivity in the agricultural industry and the military industry. In terms of education and science and technology, the Lincoln government stipulated that the government could use public space to establish schools and universities and set up the public university system and vocational education system, in order to meet the needs of the rapid development of the social economy in the American society. At the same time, the United States, which had started from being the European "science and technology colony" at the very beginning, became a big and powerful country in education and technology in the early 20th century. At the end of the 19th century, the United States launched a progressive movement aimed to fight corruption, promote political, economic, and social justice as well as moral reforms, including restricting the antitrust laws of monopoly groups and enacting laws to protect labor interests, the environment, food safety, and so on. That movement was conducive to stimulating the vitality of the country and safeguarding social stability, thus providing a powerful guarantee for the rise of the American economy.

From 1895 to 1914, during the rise of American maritime power, the United States' export revenue exceeded the cumulative number of import payments and reached USD 10 billion. During the same period, the United States' manufacturing industry doubled its size compared with the previous period, and the industrial exports of manufactured goods rose by nearly five times. The tonnage of the commercial transportation ships increased from 3.4 to 7 million tons, with an increase of 1.06 times over what it was before. From 1890 to 1914, the overseas investments of America increased by five times. While overseas markets and profit flows were expanding and growing, the expenditures of the US government for managing institutions and social welfare had also increased significantly.[2] In 1914, the US

---

[2] Shaibbe H. N., Watt H. G., and Faulkner H. U. (1983). *The Economic History of the United States in the Last Hundred Years* (Peng Songjian *et al.*, Trans.). Beijing, China: China Social Sciences Press, pp. 216–258.

national income reached USD 13.7 billion, which was 0.25 times higher than the United Kingdom's USD 11 billion, 1.28 times higher than the USD 6 billion of France, and 0.14 times higher than the USD 12 billion of Germany in the same period.[3] After WWI and WWII, the hegemonic countries in Europe, such as Britain and France, had generally declined greatly, and the United States became a global maritime power, holding a large share of the world's wealth and resource allocation. However, in the beginning of 1970s, the status of the United States in the traditional manufacturing industries, especially the four major industries of steel, textiles, automobiles, and electronics, faced strong challenges from Japan, Germany, and other emerging countries. This trend continued until the 1980s. The decline of the traditional manufacturing industry directly triggered a major discussion in the United States about the decline of US hegemony. It was not until the 1990s when the information revolution, which led to the phenomenon of the "Prosperity of the Clinton Government" in the United States, stopped this decline. Since the beginning of the 21st century, the bubble of the information economy in the United States has been shattered. The two wars against terrorism launched by the Bush administration greatly weakened the soft power of the United States. The outbreak of the financial crisis in 2008 was a more severe blow to the financial hegemony of the United States.

Karl Marx said that "For an industrial nation, when it reaches its historical peak generally, it will reach its peak of productivity. In fact, the industrial peak of a nation occurs when it does not give priority to its vested interests, but when it seeks its own benefits. Based on this fact, we can say the Americans are better than the British."[4] Today, the United States has undergone a change from a country that "fights for the interests of its own" to a country that "has vested interests as its mission." The "industrial peak" of America has been degenerated to the peak of the "arms industry." The historical peak of Britain had already become a thing of the past and the peak of the United States

[3] Zhang Yuefa, Liu Yangjie. (1999). *Nation State and World Economy: 1500–1900.* Beijing, China: Current Affairs Press, p. 365.
[4] *Selected Works of Marx and Engels* (Volume II). Beijing, China: People's Publishing House, 1972, p. 89.

may soon become a legend that can exist only in Hollywood block-busters. The most important thing for China at present is to sum up their experiences and learn from their lessons, in order to prepare well for China's future sustainable development.[5]

1.2 *The Evolutionary Change of the Global Economic Center*

In the era of the ancient agricultural society, Asia was the center of the world's economy. In terms of the population or total economic distribution, Asia occupies more than half of the world. In the 700 years since about 1000 AD, China has been the largest economic power in the world. Via the Silk Road, the ceramics and silk from China had swept the world. According to the statistics, by 1730, the output of China's finished products had even reached 1/3 of the world's total. China's current share of global manufacturing is approximately 12%. Before the 18th century, the Asian economy was always at the forefront of the world. The East had always been the focus of the global economy. From the 5th century BC onward, China's total economic output was ahead of the other countries in the world, and it was then the largest economy and the economic center of the world (Table 5.1).

With the discovery of the New World and the change in the world's navigating routes, the overseas forces of the Netherlands became fully developed. The Netherlands was the first European country to rule the world. In the 1760s, the United Kingdom initiated the Industrial Revolution and became the first industrial country in the world, which established the leading position of "the British Empire on which the sun never sets" in the world's economy, and made it the center of the world's economy. From the end of the 19th century to the beginning of the 20th century, the world's economic center began to gradually move from the United Kingdom to the United States. In 1894, the United States surpassed the United Kingdom in its industrial

---

[5] Zhang Wenmu. (November 6, 2012). Reading the "McIndre Paradox" and the Decline of British and American Hegemony from the Perspective of China. *Guanchazhe*. Retrieved from https://www.guancha.cn/zhang-wen-mu/2012_11_02_107430.shtml.

Table 5.1 World Economic Distribution in the Year 1–1000 AD (Unit: 1990 International Dollars)

	National GDP in 1 AD	National GDP in 1000 AD	Global Economic Share in 1 AD (%)	Global Economic Share in 1000 AD (%)	The Compound Annual Growth Rate in 1–1000 AD (%)
Europe	17,949	16,365	17.0	13.5	–0.01
The descendants of Western countries	448	748	0.4	0.6	0.05
Latin America	2,240	4,560	2.1	3.8	0.07
Asia	76,735	85,815	72.8	70.8	0.01
Africa	8,030	13,720	7.6	11.3	0.05
The Globe	105,402	121,208	100	100	0.01

Note: In Madison's book, the United States, Canada, Australia, and New Zealand are called "the descendants of Western countries."

Source: *Historical Statistics of the World Economy: 1–2006 AD* (Copyright Angus Maddison).

output and became the top economic power then. The scale of the United States' economy started its era with an unparalleled advantage. The US economy had experienced two periods of rapid growth. One was from the 1880s to the early 20th century after the completion of the Industrial Revolution, and the other was the so-called capitalist golden stage from the post-war period to the 1960s. Afterward, the "East Asian Miracle" initiated by Japan and the "Four Asian Tigers" have made East Asia the center of the global economy (Table 5.2).

The Atlantic era has been declining. In the future, the world economic center may gradually shift from the "Christian Civilization Circle" centered on "The US–Atlantic–Europe" to the "Plural Civilization Circle" centered on "China–Eurasian Hinterland–Western Europe." The process of human civilization seems to have returned to its starting point after a circle around the globe.[6]

---

[6] Bao Shenggang. (April 9, 2015). On the Shift of the World's Economic Centers from the Perspective of the AIIB. *Qiushi*. Retrieved from http://www.qstheory.cn/wp/2015-04/09/c_1114920571.htm.

Table 5.2   The Rise and Fall of the World's Economic Centers

Stage of Development	China	The Netherlands	The United Kingdom	The United States
Rising	4th–10th centuries	1575–1590	1789–1815	1897–1913/1920
Prosperity	10th–13th centuries	1590–1620	1815–1850	1913/1920–1945
Maturity	14th–15th centuries	1620–1650	1850–1873	1945–1967
Decline	15th–16th centuries	1650–1672	1873–1897	1967–(?)

Source: Adapted from Goldberg (2003).

Figure 5.1 shows the changing path of the global economic center since 1000 AD.

This map was drawn based on a study by the McKinsey Global Institute in the United States. It uses the estimates of the GDP of the countries throughout history by Angus Maddison, a British economist. With the increase in the GDP of the United States, the world's "economic center" began to shift westwards. However, at present, it seems to be moving back because developing countries, especially those in Asia, are developing rapidly. This is a return for a long-term historical trend. In 1000 AD, China and India accounted for 2/3 of the global economy. The global economic center was firmly set up in the East. After 820 years of keeping this position and with the advent of the British Industrial Revolution, the economic center began to shift to Europe and later to North America. However, over the past few decades, East Asia has experienced an astonishing rate of economic rise and an amazing process of urbanization. Together with the rise of India and other emerging economies, East Asia has quickly brought the world's economic center back to its original starting point.[7]

---

[7] American Media: The Shifting of the World's Economic Center Back to Its Original Starting Point in the East after a Thousand Years. (June 5, 2015). *Reference News*. Retrieved from http://www.cankaoxiaoxi.com/finance/20150605/807271.shtml.

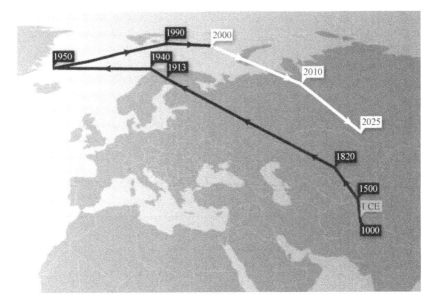

Figure 5.1   The Shifting Pattern of the World's Economic Center, 1000–2025

Figure 5.2 reflects China's position in the world's economy since 1960.

In the first 30 years of reform and opening-up, China's economy showed an obvious characteristic of giving priority to the heavy chemical industry, but China's overall status in the world's economy showed a downward trend. In 1978, when China opened up its doors to the road of reform and opening-up, the economy of the "Four Asian Tigers" and "Tiger Cub Economics" successively lifted, and the Indian economy began to develop rapidly after the 1990s. In 2001, after China joined the World Trade Organization (WTO), its economy was integrated into the globalized flood and entered into the fast lane of economic development. China's position in the world's economy has shown a continuous rise since then. In 2010, China became the second largest economy in the world. In 2014, although the growth rate of the Japanese economy was only a slight 0.2%, China and India both reached 7.4%, South Korea 3.2%, Indonesia 4.8%, and Malaysia 5.2%. The average growth rate of the Asian economies reached 5.5%, far exceeding the world's average of 2.6%. The growth

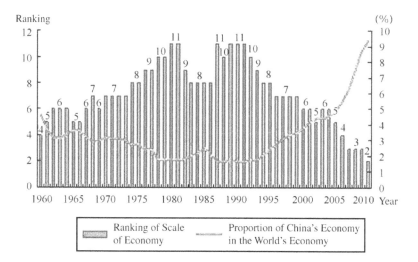

Figure 5.2   Change of China's Position in the World's Economy
Source: World Bank WDI data.

rate of the United States and the United Kingdom was 2.8%, Germany 1.6%, and France only 0.9%. According to the latest data from the International Monetary Fund (IMF), Asia's contribution to global economic growth is more than 50%, of which China's contribution rate is 29.7%, exceeding 22.4% of the United States and 16.8% of the whole euro area. The IMF predicted that the global economic growth rate would be 3.8% in 2015, while the forecasted growth rate of Asia was 5.5%. However, Asia will still remain the first driving force for world economic development. The era of the Asian countries as the center of the world's economy has arrived.

2. The Belt and Road Initiative to Improve Eurasian Development

The Belt and Road Initiative covers Central Asia, Southern Asia, Western Asia, Southeastern Asia, Central and Eastern Europe, and other countries and regions. The total population involved is around 4.4 billion and the total economic volume is USD 21 trillion, accounting for 63% and 29% of the world's total, respectively. From the perspective of its content, the Belt and Road Initiative contains extremely rich connotations, including both traditional free trade agreements and regional cooperation, as well as building economic corridors, economic development zones, interconnections, humanity and cultural exchanges, transnational transportation lines, financial cooperation, and so on. The construction of the Belt and Road Initiative is not only conducive to China's opening-up to the west but also to the European Union (EU)'s opening-up to the east. This is a truly and mutually beneficial and win–win arrangement. By participating in the construction of the Belt and Road Initiative, Europe can gain more business opportunities in Asian countries, which can also help the EU expand its allocation of resources and potential customers.

2.1 *New Economic Growth Drive Brought by the Belt and Road Initiative*

China's Belt and Road Initiative is an attempt to find a new driving force for economic growth. It is both a strategic initiative for China and for the countries along the Belt and Road; it is both a new way to promote China's economic development and to promote development of the world's economy, especially in the developing countries. As an important initiative, it is also a long-term one. It cannot be achieved in a year or two. Because, for the construction of the economic belt, whether it is on land or at sea, it requires large amount of investment. It needs to be based on long-term development plans and financing institutions. Therefore, after proposing this initiative, China has actively committed itself to the various activities in encouraging and advocating the Asian Infrastructure Investment Bank (AIIB), the Silk Road Fund, and emerging economies such as the Shanghai Cooperation Organization Development Bank to solve the financing problems. In addition, the proposed interconnections and interoperability either integrated with the Belt and Road Initiative or organic components themselves, which are all pragmatic practices. Most countries along the route of the Belt and Road Initiative are emerging economies and developing countries. They are generally in the rising period of their development. Therefore, the implementation of the Belt and Road Initiative is conducive to the economic development of countries along the route and thus may make them together one of the global economic powers. For China, expanding the space for foreign economic and trade cooperation will also benefit the steady growth of China's economy.

After the proposed concept of the Belt and Road Initiative, China has been connecting with its neighboring countries through infrastructures, such as railways. The high-speed rail networks with eight lines in China have been completed across the main routes, and a Pan-European railway line has been proposed. According to the plan of the Pan-European railway line, it will be possible to reach Istanbul within 16 hours from Chengdu, the capital city of Sichuan Province, and to arrive in Hamburg, Germany, within 18 hours from Chongqing. There will also be a railway line that crosses Pakistan and goes directly to the Strait of Hormuz. The three-dimensional routes of land, water, and airline determine a global leadership in trade. Compared with the current maritime transportation, the high-speed railway transportation will save people 15 times the amount of time in trade and economic exchanges, reduce transaction costs by more than 10 times and at the same time, reduce oil pollution by 100 times.

In addition to the opening of a number of intercontinental railways, including Madrid, Spain, and so on, China also reached a consensus with Russia on the construction of China–Russia high-speed railways. The idea of connecting high-speed railways between South China and Singapore is also underway. In addition, plans are also being made to build a railway linking Xinjiang directly to the Gwadar Port in the southwest of Pakistan, where Chinese enterprises exercise the management of the port. "All roads lead to Beijing," Beijing's diplomats commented as such on the Belt and Road Initiative. The rejuvenation of the ancient commercial routes clearly demonstrates the idea of building an economic circle centered on China. China hopes to rejuvenate the economic and cultural exchanges established along the ancient Silk Road and through the transportation network of the Belt and Road Initiative. The Silk Road Economic Belt is expected to connect Eastern China and Western Europe via Central

Asia and Eastern Europe, and the 21st-century Maritime Silk Road is a sea route connecting the east coast of China and Piraeus via the Red Sea and the Mediterranean Sea. China regards these plans of establishing a new trade route between the East and the West as one of the ways to accelerate the convergence and integration of the European market by linking the Mediterranean Sea and the European continent. The launch of the new project of the Belt and Road Initiative means that the Eurasian Economic Community is showing up. The increasing participation of Europe in Asian projects also adds new vitality to the European economy. The *Japanese Economic News* reported that China has proposed a new type of international relationship based on "cooperation" and "win–win" results. Through the strengthening of economic forces and cooperation with other countries, China has formed a loose economic circle known as the "community with a common destiny," in order to ensure its national security. France's *Le Monde* said that the Belt and Road Initiative, such as the AIIB, is conducive to the formation of a multipolar world order and allows more countries to actively participate in it. Rudolph, an expert at the Mercator China Research Center in Germany, pointed out that by opening up new trade routes, China is expected to stimulate its economic growth and to reduce dependence on certain countries and markets. The Belt and Road Initiative can strengthen China's position as a major trading country.[8]

2.2 *China–Europe Railways Connecting Eurasia*

With the implementation of the Belt and Road Initiative, China–Europe railways have also become one of the major plans in local governmental decisions for meeting the demands of the national plans, seizing a large share of the international market and boosting stable economic growth, which has gradually laid the transportation basis for the construction of the Silk Road Economic Belt Initiative. Since the first

---

[8] The Belt and Road Initiative Ignited the World's Enthusiasm, the Era of the Eurasian Economy Is Coming. (March 30, 2015). *China Internet Information Center.* Retrieved from http://news.china.com.cn/world/2015-03/30/content_35190730.htm.

train began to run in 2011, eight major railway lines between China and European countries have been built, including the Chongqing–Xinjiang–Europe, the Chengdu–Europe, the Zhengzhou–Xinjiang–Europe, the Suzhou–Manzhouli–Europe, the Wuhan–Xinjiang–Europe, the Xiangtan–Europe, the Yiwu–Xinjiang–Europe, and the Europe–Haerbin–Shenyang lines. In addition to the abovementioned eight lines, many trains, such as the Hefei–Xinjiang–Europe train (whose destination is currently in Central Asia), the Tianma train (Wuwei–Central Asia), and so on, are under way currently. Heilongjiang plans to open its international Haerbin–Russia–Europe route in June 2015, and the Urumqi Railway Container Center, which has an investment of RMB 1.38 billion from Xinjiang, is also under construction. According to the statistics of the Chinese Railway Corporation, in 2014, 308 China–Europe trains were launched and 26,070 twenty-foot equivalent units were sent to Europe, which was 228 lines more than that of the previous year and the ratio increased by 285%. It is estimated that by the end of 2015, the number of railway lines between China and the European countries would exceed 20. Currently, China and Europe have more than 70 million tons of land transportation and more than 200 million tons of sea transportation each year. However, most of the goods are exported from China to Europe, while European goods that are exported to China contain only a small amount of high-quality equipment, machinery, and first-class clothes. The Eurasian continent is a huge international market, which covers 60% of the world's population and about 30% of the world's GDP along the Belt and Road Initiative. Compared with other parts of the world, the Eurasian continent is the most potential market in the future. Through the Belt and Road Initiative, China's opening-up can be upgraded well in order to facilitate its trade and investments.

China and Central and Eastern European countries will cooperate on the construction of infrastructures such as high-speed railways, power stations, and highways. Chinese companies will also provide the energy equipment and electronic products industries needed by Central and Eastern European countries through financial investment and building factories. Since the outbreak of the debt crisis in the eurozone in 2011, Chinese companies have invested more than 10 billion Euros in Portugal. The construction of the Serbian E763 highway, the two highways in Macedonia, and the Stanari Thermal Power Plant in Bosnia and Herzegovina, which have been initiated by China cooperatively, have already started their program and are progressing smoothly. At the same time, the North–South Expressway project in Montenegro will also be launched very soon. At present, some Chinese companies are actively taking part in the investment and construction of nuclear power, thermal power, and highway projects in Central and Eastern European countries. According to the customs statistics, the volume of bilateral trade between China and the countries in Central and Eastern Europe increased from USD 52.1 billion in 2012 to USD 60.2 billion in 2014, with an increase of 15.6% in just two years. Among them, Chinese exports increased from USD 38.8 billion to USD 43.7 billion while imports increased from USD 13.4 billion to USD 16.5 billion, which increased by 12.6% and 24.6%, respectively. In 2003, China's volume of trade with Central and Eastern Europe was only USD 8.7 billion. According to part of the statistics, Chinese companies have currently invested more than USD 5 billion in Central and Eastern European countries. Experts have pointed out that Central and Eastern Europe is an important part of the Belt and Road Initiative and it has many common interests and opportunities for win–win cooperation with China in many areas.[9]

Chen Zhiwu, a tenured professor at Yale University, said that the gradual implementation of China's Belt and Road Initiative will continue to strengthen Asia's position. It was around 2010 that the proportion of Asian countries' GDP in the world began to exceed that of the Western developed countries. In the next 20 years, the overall economic volume of Asian countries will continue to rise throughout the world. At present, the influence and the power of discourse of Asian countries in international affairs have been lifted gradually. Statistics show that in 2010, Asia's contribution to the world's economic growth exceeded 50% and Asia's exports accounted for 31.6%

---

[9]Wang Junling. (June 5, 2015). The Chinese "Going-global" Enterprises Aim at Central and Eastern Europe. *People's Daily Online*. Retrieved from http://world.people.com. cn/n/2015/0605/c1002-27108892.html.

of the global exports, with an increase of approximately 5% over that of 2000. The Asian trade accounted for 52.6% of the total foreign trade of the Asian countries, which increased by 3.7% over that of 2000. It has already formed a multilayered and complementary regional cooperation pattern in Asia. According to the report of the Standard Chartered Bank, although the slowdown in the development of some major emerging economies is troublesome, a few reforms in the larger emerging economies including China, India, and Indonesia will trigger a new cycle of economic revitalization. The IMF forecasted that the Asian economic growth rates in 2014 and 2015 will be 5.4% and 5.5%, respectively. The Asian Development Bank predicted that the growth rates of Asian developing economies in 2014 and 2015 would be 6.3% and 6.4%, respectively. Calculated at the exchange rate, the Asian economy accounts for more than 27.5% of the global economy. By 2020, Asia will become the largest economic zone in the world, with an increasingly important status in the world economy. Since the beginning of the 21st century, the intraregional trade volume in Asia has increased from USD 800 billion to USD 3 trillion, and the volume of trade between Asia and the other parts of the world has increased from USD 1.5 trillion to USD 4.8 trillion, which fully demonstrates the attractive cohesion of Asian regional cooperation.

Since the reform and opening-up, China's economic and trade cooperation with the countries along the Maritime Silk Road has been increasing gradually. In 2012, China's total volume of trade with countries along the Maritime Silk Road was USD 690 billion, accounting for 17.9% of China's total volume of foreign trade. The nonfinancial direct investments by Chinese companies in 2012 were USD 5.7 billion, accounting for 7.4% of Chinese enterprises' foreign investments. In 2012, Chinese companies constructed projects that are equal to the value of USD 42.2 billion in the countries along the route, accounting for 37.9% of the total foreign contracted projects of China.[10] The abovementioned three sets of data are much higher than

---

[10] Ni Mingya. (December 19, 2013). Ministry of Commerce of the People's Republic of China: Construction of Free Trade Zone along the Silk Road will be accelerated. China Securities News-China Securities Network. *Sina Finance*. Retrieved from http://finance.sina.com.cn/china/20131219/013017678618.shtml.

those of the Silk Road Economic Belt. Therefore, although the construction of the Maritime Silk Road is not equivalent to the China-ASEAN "10 + 1" pattern of the free trade zone, it has been able to distribute the resources of all related parties and greatly increase the trading in goods, services, and investments in this area. Therefore, we can consider the Maritime Silk Road as an "upgraded version" of the comprehensive economic cooperation of China-ASEAN countries.[11]

With the clear and concrete construction of the Belt and Road Initiative, the outside world has a more comprehensive understanding of it. However, due to factors such as the different manner of thinking and differences in ideas and interests, Western countries have misunderstood the Belt and Road Initiative and have attempted to influence related countries and interfere with the smooth progress of the Initiative. One of the most severe and common misunderstandings is that the West regards the Belt and Road Initiative as the Chinese version of the "Marshall Plan" and believes that the Initiative reflects China's intentional purpose to exert its influence in the surrounding areas. They deliberately emphasize the formal similarities between the two plans that they all send their funds and technology to the countries and regions that need them urgently. In addition, due to the absence of the US participation, the Belt and Road Initiative has been misunderstood as a strong counterattack against the United States' pivot to the Asia-Pacific and its Trans-Pacific Partnership (TPP). They believe the China-led AIIB is a direct challenge to the US-led World Bank. Kathleen Collins, an associate professor of political science at the University of Minnesota, believes that the Belt and Road Initiative has led Central Asian countries to establish closer economic and trade relationships with China, thereby weakening the strength of the United States' New Silk Road Initiative that aimed to trade through energy channels in Afghanistan. At the hearing of the House of Representatives in February 2014, James Clapper, the National Intelligence Director of the United States, stated that China has shown strong aggression when it claims their theory of "Manifest

---

[11] Gu Yuanyang. (2015). Great Powers Meet in Asia and China and Other Issues — On the Construction of the 21st-century Maritime Silk Road. *Asia & Africa Review*, Issue 4, pp. 46–56.

Destiny." Influenced by those remarks, Dr. Patrick Mendis, from the School of International Policy, George Mason University, curiously compared the Belt and Road Initiative with the "Monroe Doctrine" proposed in the early days after the foundation of the United States. He believes that China is trying to restore the prosperity it enjoyed during the Han and Tang Dynasties and in the early Ming Dynasty, disseminate its culture in Asia, and promote the Chinese version of "Manifest Destiny." Behind this view is that China wants to divide the domestic sphere of its influence in Asia, disseminate its ideas to establish the "Asian order under Chinese leadership," and exclude the United States from Asia. Some Western media and scholars have also caused quite a big splash. They believe that China has taken advantage of the Belt and Road Initiative to accelerate the construction of a modern navy and continuously enhance its naval power, aiming at global maritime hegemony. James Holmes, an expert on naval affairs at the US Naval War College, believes that China is cutting the link between the United States and its allies through the Belt and Road Initiative, and is continuing to rule out the influence of the United States in Asia. According to Christopher Sharman, a scholar at the Pacific Command Center of the National Defense University of the United States, the Maritime Silk Road means the gradual escalation of China's oceanic naval forces. At the same time, it is inferred in the West that China will take a more aggressive attitude toward the South China Sea issue, encircle India's maritime strength in the Indian Ocean region, and try to bypass the Straits of Malacca to build Asian maritime traffic routes under China's leadership. Another small number of Western media and scholars believe that China is promoting "neocolonialism" by its Belt and Road Initiative. This view holds the idea that the main goal of China's construction of the Belt and Road Initiative is to obtain the oil and mineral resources in related countries. It is also inferred that Chinese companies are pursuing the maximization of profit while ignoring local environmental protection and public welfare, thus threatening the ecological security of and social stability in the related countries.[12]

---

[12] Huang Rihan, Cong Peiying. (May 13, 2015). Outside Misreading of and Rational Reflections on the Belt and Road Initiative. *Chinese Social Sciences Today.*

The goal of the Belt and Road Initiative is to achieve the mutual integration of the entire region and the ultimate goal of it is to reach the mutual understanding of people in the region. The increasingly urgent task for this initiative in the future is to make more international friends who can help China tell its stories well and air its voice clearly, especially scholars, young people, and common people with a good reputation in related countries. Only in this way can the Belt and Road Initiative be viewed positively by people throughout the world.

2.3 *The Belt and Road Initiative Helps Restore the Global Economy*

Since the founding of the People's Republic of China, we have traversed a difficult period of 66 years. Tribulation and glory have coexisted in the past. In the 30 years before the reform and opening-up, we went through some detours on the road in exploring the socialist system and had many problems. However, there is no doubt that the achievements we made also amazed the world. The well-known scholar, Jin Chongji, concludes these achievements as follows: China had achieved national independence, people's liberation, and national unity; It had established a comprehensive basic socialist system; and from the rubble left over from the old China, Modern China took much less time than the Western countries to build an independent and relatively complete industrial system and national economic system, which together laid a solid material and technological foundation for the modernization of China. On comparing the index statistics of 1978 with those of 1949, China's GDP increased by 7.78 times from RMB 46.6 billion to RMB 362.41 billion. Among these amounts, the total value of industrial output increased from RMB 14 billion to RMB 423 billion, an increase of 30.21 times; the total value of agricultural output increased from RMB 32.6 billion to RMB 139.7 billion, an increase of 4.29 times; the grain output increased from 113.18 million tons to 304.77 million tons, an increase of 2.69 times; the cotton output increased from 444,000 tons to 2.167 million tons, an increase of 4.88 times; the steel production increased from 160,000 tons to 31.78 million tons, an increase of 198.63

times; the coal production increased from 32 million tons to 618 million tons, an increase of 19.31 times; the power generation capacity increased from 4.3 billion kWh to 256.6 billion kWh, an increase of 59.67 times. During the 29-year period, the average annual growth rate of the GDP was 8.43%. Excluding the recovery period of the national economy from 1949 to 1952, the average annual growth rate is 7.78%.[13]

It has been more than 30 years since the implementation of the reform and opening-up in China during which China has made the strategic decision to open up its doors to the outside world, it has joined the WTO and has taken an active part in the wave of globalization. Since 1978, with more than 30 years already gone by, China has undergone many economic and political reforms under the leadership of the Chinese Communist Party, such as the land management system in rural areas, the purchase and sales system of agricultural products, the national macro-management system, the price system, the economic system, the financial system, the investment system, the internal and external trade system, the systems for the management of science and technology, education and culture, and so on. The reforms in various areas are in-depth and profound. There is also an enormous change in the livelihood of the people. With the profound and extensive economic restructuring, China's socialist construction has undergone historic changes. "From the countryside to the cities, and from the economic field to other fields, the process of comprehensive reforms is indomitable; from the initial coastal cities to the border cities along the rivers, from the eastern parts to the central and western regions, the doors to the outside world are open in a way that is unprecedented in Chinese history. The large-scale reforms and opening-up have greatly mobilized the enthusiasm of hundreds of millions of people and enabled China to successfully achieve a great shift from a highly centralized planned economic system to a vibrant socialist market economic system, and from a closed or semi-enclosed historical stage to the all-round pattern of opening-up. Today, a socialist China that faces modernization, the outside world, and the

---

[13]Jin Chongji. (2009). The First 30 Years of Modern New China. *Literature of the Chinese Communist Party*, Issue 5.

future stands firmly in the East of the world."[14] In 2014, China's GDP broke through RMB 60 trillion, reaching RMB 63,646.3 billion, with a year-on-year increase of 7.4%. The national economy remained stable under the new normal economic development, showing a good momentum of steady growth, structural optimization, quality enhancing, and improvement of the livelihood of the people. This mode of development has freed China completely from poverty, and China is now moving toward a more comprehensive and moderately prosperous society in all respects.

In 2001, the US GDP accounted for 33% of the total global amount. In 2014, this ratio dropped to approximately 20%. In 2014, China's GDP accounted for 13.4% of the total global amount. For hundreds of years, we Chinese people have always taken Britain and the United States as our examples for economic and social development. The purpose of the Great Leap Forward Movement in the early days after the founding of the People's Republic of China was to catch up with the development of Britain and of the United States in 15–20 years. However, before the reform and opening-up, China's attempt to surmount Britain or the United States in economic development was only a dream. After the reform and opening-up, China experienced more than 30 years of continuous high-speed, uninterrupted economic and social development. Its economy surpassed that of the United Kingdom in 2005, surpassed Japan in 2010, and became the second largest economy in the world. Since China joined the WTO in 2001 and until 2015, its total GDP had risen directly to 63.4% of that of the United States from the formerly 10%. The World Bank even believes that based on parity purchasing power, China's GDP actually exceeds that of the United States. If calculated in US dollars, China's GDP in 2011 increased by 23% within a year. By 2014, it would increase by 11%. At this rate, China will probably surpass the United States as the world's largest economy by the advent of 2025.

---

[14] Hu Jintao (October 27, 2007). *Hold High the Great Banner of Socialism with Chinese Characteristics and Strive for New Victories in Building a Moderately Prosperous Society in All Respects: Report to the Seventeenth National Congress of the Communist Party of China.* Retrieved from http://www.most.gov.cn/yw/200710/t20071026_56736.htm.

At present, China's import and export trade in the fields such as steel, automotive products, electronic products, Internet users, food, and foreign investments have caught up with or surpassed those of the United States. After 2012, China's economic growth entered a new normal state. On the one hand, the rate of the growth of China's GDP had stayed well under 10%, and by the first half year of 2015, it had dropped to 7%. Import and export trade has dropped from the original annual growth rate of more than 20% to a freezing point. On the other hand, China is making efforts to adjust its industrial structure and technological upgrading.

China's economy has increasingly exerted a huge influence on the global economy. Two things that happened in China and the United States in the second half year of 2015 showed this trend clearly. In July, the Chinese stock market plunged. The Chinese central bank issued a series of measures to rescue the market. Since August, the central parity rate of RMB against the USD had depreciated by approximately 4%, and the same depreciation of the RMB against the euro, yen, and pound sterling happened to varying degrees. The global stock market and foreign exchange market fluctuated substantially. On September 17, the Federal Reserve System ("Fed") announced that it had decided to keep the current federal funds rate and would not raise its interest rates temporarily due to the weakness of the global economy and the continued low inflation in the United States. The Fed is much concerned about the risks of emerging markets including China, but it is not surprised to see the slowing down of the Chinese economy. The World Bank report said that although the Fed has disseminated the information of increasing the interest rate to the financial markets and the public and has elaborated austerity measures, raising interest rates may still trigger issues of a volatile market, and raise the risks of large capital outflows from the emerging markets. Due to China's abundant foreign exchange reserves and fact that the capital accounts in China have not been fully opened to the outside world, the direct influence of the Fed's interest rate hike on China's real economy and financial market is still controllable. However, emerging economies with weak economic fundamentals and fragile financial system may be affected greatly by the Fed's interest rate hike and then indirectly affect China's economy through trade, investments, and financial channels.[15]

In such a situation at home and abroad, China's Belt and Road Initiative will undoubtedly provide a possible developmental path for the recovery of the global economy. The Belt and Road Initiative is a major plan proposed by China based on the new situation of continuous development and changes at home and abroad and the new security concept of diplomacy with neighboring countries. It is also an important decision for the Party Central Committee to profoundly understand China's position in the new period of time and deepen and expand its reform and opening-up. It will play an important role in shaping the new pattern of China's opening-up to the outside world and forming China's multilayered and all-round integration of land and sea, the eastern and western parts at the same time. Furthermore, it will promote regional economic development and accelerate the modernization of developing countries along the route. As one of China's major initiatives for deepening reforms and advancing neighborly diplomacy, the Belt and Road Initiative upholds the spirit of "peaceful cooperation, openness, inclusiveness, mutual learning, mutual benefit and win–win results."[16] It has given the ancient Silk Road new meanings and has promoted China's further opening-up to the outside world through the pattern of "one body system and two wings of plans." The Initiative also provides an open and inclusive cooperation platform for all countries along the route to communicate and cooperate closely with the economically prosperous China. It conforms to the requirements of the times and meets the demands for prosperity and stability shared by people of all the countries along the route. It is profoundly based on the historical past and the humanity exchanges among countries, connecting the "China Dream" with the

---

[15] Xue Bai. (September 18, 2015). The Fed Will Not Raise Interest Rates Temporarily Due to the Unclear Economic Situation. *People's Daily Online*. Retrieved from http://finance.people.com.cn/bank/n/2015/0918/c202331-27604896.html

[16] The Speech of Xi Jinping Delivered at the Opening Ceremony of the Sixth Ministerial Conference of the China–Arab States Cooperation Forum. (June 6, 2014). *Xinhuanet*. Retrieved from http://www.xinhuanet.com//politics/2014-06/05/c_1111002498.htm.

great "World Dream" of rejuvenation and shared development and prosperity. As of April 20, 2015, China has signed tax treaties with 53 countries along the route to avoid double taxation and tax discrimination, in order to encourage Chinese companies to go out and participate in the construction of the Belt and Road Initiative.[17]

The Belt and Road Initiative expands and deepens the exchanges and cooperation between China and the countries along the Asia–Europe route, promotes the diversification of foreign trade markets, builds a new pattern of opening-up to the world, emphasizes the equal importance of import and export trading, and the harmonious cooperation among agriculture, industrial, and service industries. It helps China to set up the coordinated all-round system of opening-up with the developed countries, developing countries, and transitional countries in its course of reform and opening-up. At the same time, the Belt and Road Initiative focuses on Central Asia and Western Asia. It will accelerate the "westward" pace of opening-up while maintaining the level of its eastward integration. It will turn the political and geographical advantages and economic structure complementarity of the central and western regions in their inland and border integrations to economic growth that is based on pragmatic cooperation and sustainable development. The inland hinterland of the past has become the open frontier; thus, the central and western regions will usher in many new opportunities to further increase their openness and achieve leaping growth in their foreign trading.[18] The Belt and Road Initiative is conducive to promoting the modernization of the developing countries along the route. The Initiative is a grand concept that benefits all participating countries. It has common interests with the countries along the route, taking into account the needs of each country's development and coordinating the two directions of development of the mainland and that of the ocean. It covers a wide

---

[17] Wei Zhimin. (2015). The Belt and Road Initiative: The Intrinsic Logic, Difficult Breakthroughs and Path Selection. *Academic Exchanges*, Issue 8, pp. 108–112.
[18] Zhong Sheng. (February 26, 2014). Openness and Tolerance, Common Development for a Win–Win Cooperation — Focusing on the Epochal Significance of the Belt and Road Initiative. *People's Daily Online*. Retrieved from http://opinion.people.com.cn/n/2014/0226/c1003-24463885.html.

range, has great inclusiveness, and exerts a radiating effect throughout the world. The developing countries in Eurasia are all at the critical stage of economic transformation and upgrading. There is an urgent need for them to further stimulate the potential for domestic demands, create new chances for economic growth, and enhance their endogenous power and capacity for risk resistance for economic development.[19] The great achievements China has made in its economy since the reform and opening-up have enabled China to assist the neighboring countries in terms of trade, transportation, capital, and cultural exchanges and help them benefit from China's reform and opening-up. The Belt and Road Initiative has also responded to the internal needs of those countries along the route and has provided new opportunities for promoting the free flow of production factors along the route, optimizing resource allocation, reducing the cost of trade and investment, and developing the remote and backward areas. In terms of traditional manufacturing, China can not only provide products with cheap prices and high quality for the countries along the route, but it can also provide the necessary technology and equipment for the development of their manufacturing industries.[20] In terms of the construction of infrastructures, China has a huge production capacity in raw materials such as steel, cement, and other building materials, which can effectively meet the needs of the construction of infrastructures of the countries along the route. China is at the world's advanced level in high-end projects such as manned space flights, lunar exploration, supercomputers, and high-speed railways. Exports of related technologies can not only stimulate economic growth in the region, but they can also provide the countries along the route with technical support. In terms of finance, the substantial foreign exchange reserves of China have enabled it to join forces with countries in the region to

---

[19] Zhong Sheng. (February 25, 2014). The Spirit of the Silk Road, and a New Story Unfold through the Old — Focusing on the Epochal Significance of the Belt and Road Initiative. *People's Daily Online*. Retrieved from http://opinion.people.com. cn/n/2014/0225/c1003-24452306.html.

[20] Wang Jingwen. (August 11, 2014). Xi Jinping's Concept of the Initiative: The Belt and Road Initiative Has Enough Room for Building Dreams. *China Economic Net*. Retrieved from http://www.ce.cn/xwzx/gnsz/szyw/201408/11/t20140811_3324310.shtml.

withstand international financial risks. The AIIB and the Silk Road Fund initiated and cooperated by China and other relevant countries can provide strong financial support in the construction of infrastructures such as railways, aviation equipment, ports, highways, water conservation, electricity, and telecommunications for countries along the route. In addition, a large scale of overseas investment is launched by China in the areas such as resource exploration, industrial cooperation, financial cooperation, and other fields, aiming at all-round interconnection, mutual sharing, and mutual benefit among China and the neighboring countries. China hopes to share its achievements in economic development with its neighbors, in order to create new opportunities for common development.[21]

The Belt and Road Initiative is a road of common development and shared prosperity for both China and the countries along the route, whose goal is to rely on the onshore and offshore economic cooperation corridors to achieve diverse, autonomous, balanced, and sustainable economic development among all of the countries along the route. By interconnecting, interoperating, and opening up to each other further, creating a dynamic market environment of fair competition, and tapping the great potential of regional markets, the Belt and Road Initiative aims to promote the free flow of production factors, increase the allocation efficiency of production factors, stimulate investment and consumption on the market in those regions, and create many employment opportunities. In a word, it definitely meets the fundamental interests of both China and the international community well.

3. China's Experience Influences the Whole World

Since the global financial crisis erupted in 2008, the world's economy has undergone a slow recovery. The US-led TPP and the Transatlantic Trade and Investment Partnership (TTIP) proposed by the European countries and the US aimed to promote the liberalization of trade and investment in the Asia-Pacific region and achieve the zero-tariff policy between the United States and Europe, whose volume of trade accounts

---

[21]Wei Zhimin. (2015). The Belt and Road Initiative: The Intrinsic Logic, Difficult Breakthroughs and Path Selection, *Academic Exchanges,* Issue 8, pp. 108–112.

for more than 1/3 of the world's total volume of trade. Together, they have built a new international trading system and strengthened its dominant position in the world trading system.[22] The Belt and Road Initiative is a major initiative decision made by China when taking into account the overall situation and conforming to the worldwide trend. It is an important measure for cultivating new advantages in its opening-up and actively adapting to new rules and changes in international trade. It will promote China's economy and integrate it with the world's economy to a much higher level. The Belt and Road Initiative expands and deepens the exchanges and cooperation between China and the countries along the Asia–Europe route, promotes the diversification of foreign trade markets, builds a new pattern of opening-up to the world, emphasizes the equal importance of import and export trading, and the harmonious cooperation among agriculture, industrial, and service industries. It helps China to set up a coordinated all-round system of opening-up with the developed countries, developing countries, and transitional countries in its course of reform and opening-up.[23]

Some scholars believe that in today's world, many countries have built their own "dreams" to set up their own goals and boost the motivation of their people. The Americans have their "American Dream," which represents the ideals of the capitalist world. The "China Dream" is undoubtedly one of the inviting and attractive dreams with its unique and specific connotations in the world. Just as we once used "the well-off society" and "the cosmopolitan world" to describe the staged goals of our modernization and depict the blueprint of the future communist society, the "China Dream" contains the profound historical heritage and cultural elements of China.[24]

---

[22] Shen Xianjie, Xiao Jincheng. (2014). The New Situation of International Regional Economic Cooperation and China's Belt and Road Cooperation Initiative. *Macroeconomics,* Issue 11, pp. 30–38.

[23] Zhong Sheng. (February 26, 2014). Openness and Tolerance, Common Development for a Win–Win Cooperation — Focusing on the Epochal Significance of the Belt and Road Initiative. *People's Daily Online.* Retrieved from http://opinion.people.com.cn/n/2014/0226/c1003-24463885.htm.

[24] Qu Qingshan. (July 14, 2014). To Grasp the Connotation and Significance of the China Dream from Five Perspectives. *People's Daily Online.* Retrieved from http://theory.people.com.cn/n/2014/0714/c49150-25276823.html.

China's proposal of the Belt and Road Initiative is undoubtedly one form of realizing the "China Dream," which will finally help to realize "the cosmopolitan world" of harmonious and peaceful development together with the dreams of the countries along the route. The developmental concepts of China and developed countries, including the United Kingdom and the United States, are being tested by the era and are bringing new experiences of growth to the world via different paths toward development.

3.1 *China Expands Bilateral Free Trade Areas*

On June 1, 2015, the China–South Korea Free Trade Agreement was officially signed. The agreement covers a total of 17 areas, such as trade in goods, services, investment, regulations, and so on, including the heated topics of the 21st century, such as the issues regarding e-commerce, competition policy, government procurement, environmental protection, and so on. With regard to the tariff concessions, it stated that since the China–South Korea Free Trade Agreement until at the most 20 years after it as a transitional period, China's zero-tariff products will reach 91% of the tax value and 85% of the import value, while South Korea's zero-tariff products will reach 92% of the tax value and 91% of the import value, respectively. In addition, a total of 310 items, including products from the North Korea's Kaesong Industrial Park, are eligible for labeling as Korean origin, and they will immediately benefit from the tariff concessions once the China–South Korea Free Trade Agreement is implemented. In terms of market liberalization, China and South Korea will provide reciprocal treatment to each other's financial companies when they enter into their domestic capital markets, which means that the relevant approval procedure will be simplified and the access standard for both financial markets will be lowered to a certain degree. The agreement also states that Korean construction companies in the Shanghai Free Trade Zone can undertake joint projects in Shanghai without restrictions on the proportion of foreign investments (which stipulates more than 50% of foreign investments) and China will ponder over allowing South Korean travel agencies to recruit tourists in China to visit South Korea or the third-party tourist destinations. In 2014, the bilateral

China–South Korea trade volume reached USD 290.5 billion, which made a record in history and was nearly 50 times what it was when they first established their diplomatic relations. It basically reached the goal once set up by China and South Korea in 2008 in which they would expect the volume of trade to reach USD 300 billion in 2015. According to China's estimation, once the China–South Korea Free Trade Agreement is implemented, the real GDP growth rate of the two countries will increase by 0.34% and 0.97% points, respectively, and China's exports to the world will increase by 1.81% and South Korea's by 2.3%. The China–South Korea Free Trade Agreement is the first free trade agreement set up in Northeast Asia. It will play an important and positive role in promoting economic cooperation among China, Japan, and South Korea, and further promoting regional economic integration in East Asia and the Asia-Pacific regions. As the respective second and 14th largest economies in the world, with the signing of the China–South Korea Free Trade Agreement between China and South Korea, China marks the birth of a super free trade zone covering 1.4 billion people and an economic volume of nearly USD 12 trillion. This will add new and powerful impetus to the joint development of China and South Korea, and effectively promote the process of economic integration and prosperity in the Asia-Pacific, which will in turn benefit countries around the world and the global economy as a whole.[25]

On June 17, 2015, China and Australia signed the *Free Trade Agreement between the Government of Australia and the Government of the People's Republic of China*. The China–Australia FTA negotiations began in April 2005 and lasted for 10 years. The negotiating talks were substantially finished in November 2014. This was the second bilateral free trade agreement signed by China in the same month after the China–South Korea FTA. The China–Australia Free Trade Agreement covers more than a dozen fields of goods, services, and investments and has achieved the goal of "comprehensive, high-quality, and balanced mutual interests." It is one of the most advanced trade

---

[25] Chen Hongna, Xu Hongqiang. (June 15, 2015). The China–South Korea Free Trade Agreement Will Have Multiple Win–Win Effects. *China Economic Times*. Retrieved from http://www.chinado.cn/?p=2573.

agreements with regard to the maximization of investment liberalization that has been established between China and other countries to date. Once the China–Australia Free Trade Agreement has been implemented, it will further promote the flow of funds, resources, and personnel between the two countries, and promote the sustainable and in-depth development of their complementary economic advantages, which will not only benefit the industrial sector and the consumers in both countries but it will also benefit the two peoples. The Australian government stated that under this agreement, more than 85% of Australian exports to China will enjoy zero tariffs once the agreement is implemented, which will rise to 93% 4 years after implementation and to 95% when the agreement is fully carried out. According to the agreement, tariffs on dairy products will be cut by 20% within 4–11 years, and the tariffs on beef products of about 12%–25% will all be canceled within at the most 9 years. In addition, tariffs on wines, up to 20%, will also be reduced to zero tariffs within 4 years. China's growing middle class has a growing demand for wine consumption, which will help Australia more on the highly competitive market of wine sales around the world. According to the forecast in 2013, after the implementation of the China–Australia FTA, the trade increase between the two countries could exceed USD 16 billion (about RMB 100 billion), accounting for approximately 10% of the volume of bilateral trade for a total amount of USD 136.46 billion in 2013.

At present, China has signed 14 free trade agreements with 22 other countries or regions. They are the agreements achieved between China and the ASEAN countries, New Zealand, Singapore, Pakistan, Chile, Peru, Costa Rica, Iceland, Switzerland, South Korea, and Australia; China has also signed the Mainland-Hong Kong and Mainland-Macao Closer Economic Partnership Arrangement, and Mainland–Taiwan Cross-Strait Economic Cooperation Framework Agreement.

3.2 *The Hollowing Out of the United States' Real Economy and the Containment Strategy*

The hegemony of the United States used to be built on the real economy. In the early part of the 20th century, the United States accumulated a colossal industrial foundation through low-end product processing, based on which the innovation and cutting-edge technologies began to burst locally in the United States. At that time, of all large mechanical equipment and elementary steel that are needed for manufacturing airplanes, tanks, and cannons in the world, the production capacity of the United States alone increased over 60%. Therefore, the United States rose rapidly after WWII and got rid of the influence of Europe completely, thus marching along the road to power and prosperity. The United States became a world leader of economy relying upon the three supports, that is, its strong foundation of manufacturing, a favorable trading position, and the US dollar's position as the world's dominant currency by having replaced gold. Since the 1960s and the 1970s, however, the United States' industries of automobile manufacturing, electrical appliances, steel, and textiles have had a strong impact from Western Europe and Japan. Faced with threats of industrial competition from other countries and regions, the US government has adopted unusual interruptive measures to cope with the threats: First, the US government subsidized its exporters by artificially reducing the USD exchange rate via the "Plaza Accord" in 1985 to improve the profit-making capability of the US manufacturing industry; second, the US government kept the growth rate of actual wages at a very low level for manufacturing workers by repressing the strength of labor unions. These measures stopped the decline of US manufacturers temporarily, but they failed to solve the root cause. In 1995, the implementation of the "strong dollar" policy interrupted the trend of revitalization of US manufacturing that started in 1985, and its manufacturing industry suffered a decline again, causing a trend of decline in its exports. The number of people involved in the manufacturing industry in the United States has been diminishing since the 1980s, and the reduction sped up at the end of the 1990s. From 1998 to 2010, this number dropped by 35%, and the number of people working in the manufacturing industry contributed a smaller portion in the private economy, shrinking from around 30% in the 1960s to 10% in 2010.[26]

---

[26] Tian Hui. (October 23, 2014). Enlightenment from Economic Transformation and Two Asset Bubbles of the USA Today. *China Economic Times*. Retrieved from http://www.drc.gov.cn/xslw/20141023/182-473-2884647.htm.

The American economy was highly "virtualized" during the process of "deindustrialization." The imbalance between the virtual economy that had undergone unprecedented expansion and the real economy that has greatly declined boosted the emergence of the two bubbles, and the bubble bursting in turn highlighted this fundamental defect in the economic transformation. Statistics show that the share taken by the real economy in the GDP of the United States declined to 33.99% in 2007 from 61.78% in 1950, and the contribution of manufacturing declined to 11.7% in 2007 from 27% in 1950; after WWII, the backbone position of the automobile, steel, and building industries was replaced by the financial service industry and the real estate service industry. A conservative estimation by the Bank for International Settlements showed that, at the end of 2006, the market value of stocks, securities, and bonds, foreign currencies, bulk commodity futures, and financial derivatives was around USD 400 trillion, about 36 times that of the real economy of the United States. There has been a tremendous change in the internal structure of the United States, but the serious "hollowing out" of the real economy indicates that such change will not last long. There have been two large-scale asset bubbles: the first one was the Internet bubble chiefly characteristic of the soaring stock prices of emerging network companies, and the second one was the real estate bubble created by various factors. There is a close connection between the two bubbles: The Fed's easy money policy for the sake of rescuing the Internet bubble nurtured profound soil for the real estate subprime mortgage bubble following that, which ultimately led to the global financial crisis.

The fact that the two asset bubbles burst made the Americans realize the issue that their economy was highly hollowing out. Therefore, the US government proposed the plan of "Rejuvenating the American Manufacturing Industry" after the crisis and began to lay focus on automobiles, housing, and green industries in a selective way by taking the advantage of government assistance. These measures all aimed to boost more sustainable development of the US economy, and they have achieved some positive effects and some progress has been made in the adjustment of the US economic structure, but on a whole, the progress is still some distance away from the expectations.

It is shown in the *Report on the Living Conditions of U.S. Households in 2014* published by the Fed on May 27, 2015 that nearly one half of American families could not afford a USD 400 contingency fund without selling something or borrowing. According to a British media, research conducted by the Urban Institute of the US showed that the number of American families that rely on usurious loans to pay their basic living expenses is increasing. "It depends on the measurement standard you are taking. About 1/3 to 1/2 of American families are already at a huge risk," remarked the researcher. "Nowadays, many American families resort to usurious loans not only in case of emergencies, but for most elementary daily expenditures." Many families that seek financial assistance are middle-class and upper-middle-class families. The investigation of the Fed shows that most American tenants want to have their own house, but many of them said that financial barriers had stopped them from buying houses. The most common reason for renting a house rather than buying one is that they cannot afford the down payment (taking up to 50%) or are unable to obtain a mortgage loan (taking up to 31%). Fourteen percent of the property owners under mortgage loans believed that the money they owed has exceeded the value of the house. A total of 47% of the interviewees said that they could not afford a USD 400 contingency fund without selling something or borrowing money, and 31% of the interviewees said that they had not received any medical service in any form in the past 12 months, because they could not afford it. Moreover, 20% of the interviewees said that what they owned in the past year could not cover what they had spent. Twenty-three percent of the adults are in educational debt of some sort. Of all the interviewees, 15% of the educational debts were owed by themselves, 6% were owed by their spouse or partner, and 6% were owed for their younger generations. A total of 39% of the nonretirees seldom or never think about their financial plan for their life after retirement at all, and 31% do not have retirement savings or pensions. Of the families with an annual before-tax income of USD 40,000 (RMB 250,000 approximately), 2/3 said they need to sell or borrow to pay a USD 400 contingency fund, or just cannot in any way afford it. On the last day of 2014, the total amount of debt of the US soared by USD 98 billion. The debts of American families for 2014 reached USD 11.83 trillion, a year-on-year increase of USD 306 billion. In 2012, the total trade deficit of the United States was USD 540.4 billion, and that amount was USD 559.9 billion for 2011. The United States' trade deficit for 2014 was USD 505.05 billion, and USD 476.39 billion for 2013.

Industrialization and the development of science and technology facilitate each other. Science and technology provide theoretical instructions for industry and raise its technological level; industry provides space and time for the application of science and technology, whose feasibility is attested to by practice, and industry also provides equipment for research in science and technology. The high-tech equipment and products all come from industry. Boasting 39 classes, 191 categories and 525 kinds, China is the only country that has all the entries that are included in the UN industrial categorization, having developed an industrial system with a complete set of categories. This foundation provides the possibility for China to become the no. 1 power of science and technology in the world. The results of a research study published in *The New England Journal of Medicine*, a top medical journal in the United States, on January 2, 2014 show that the United States is losing its position as a global leader in the area of biomedicine and the challenger is Asia with China as the most prominent one.

Today, the rise of emerging countries is the strongest driving force to push forward the reform of the global economic pattern and governance. While their active participation in shaping the international order and global economic governance and making the trend of the global economic strength shift from the West to the East becomes increasingly obvious, the position of developed countries is declining remarkably. The trend that the focus of global economic growth is shifting from developed countries to emerging economies and the relative power of developing countries is rising has not reversed. From 2004 to 2008, the period before the outbreak of the crisis, the contribution by developed countries to global economic growth was lower than that by the developing countries (44%:56%). After the crisis, from 2008 to 2012, this difference between the two sides had widened (13%:87%). Correspondingly, the ratio of the economic aggregate of developed countries to developing countries changed to around 2:1 from 4:1 in the 1980s. In emerging economies, China's performance is the most outstanding. Since 2008, China has become the strongest engine driving the global economic growth by transcending the United States and the EU. In 2012, China's GDP accounted for 11.5% of the world's total. However, the relative advantages in economic power, technologies, and rules of developed countries will not change tremendously in a short time; thus, it is a long-term process of twists and turns for the international power shift and global economic governance reform to happen. For the present, developed countries are not willing to honor their commitment to reform; instead, they adopted selfish measures to transfer their own economic risks and pressure and repress the rise of emerging countries by making use of their existing advantages and close cooperation with each other.[27] Of the major representations, one is that they try to weaken the competing edges of the emerging developing countries through formulating new global trade and investment rules that are exclusive and feature higher standards. They also implant various non-economic conditions out of their wishes, which is a mix of complicated intentions of geopolitics and geo-economics, bringing a complicated and significant impact on the shaping of new global economic rules and the progress of global economic governance.

Currently, the new global economic rules that are mainly being shaped by developed countries include the TPP and the TTIP, whose negotiations are pushed forward by the United States toward both the Asia-Pacific and Europe and the negotiations on the Plurilateral Services Agreement (PSA) or Trade in Service Agreement. The essence is for developed countries, the United States in particular, to weaken developing countries' advantages in manufacturing and the market and continue to be dominating in the world economy through formulating new global rules under a new global economic structure.

---

[27] Zou Zhiqiang. (2014). Enlightenment of the Reform of Global Economic Governance on Cooperation between China and Emerging Countries. *Forum of World Economics & Politics,* Issue 4, pp. 72–84, 127.

The TPP, the TTIP, and the PSA constitute the future strategy of the United States for the 21st century and also the fundamental strategy for the United States, Europe, and Japan, the so-called "powerful triangle" to stabilize the global trading order that has been dominated by them.[28]

3.3 *China Is Becoming One of the Decisive Forces for Today's Reform of Global Economic Development and Governance*

Since the financial crisis, China has been playing an excellent role in leading global economic cooperation and pushing forward the reform of global economic governance. There is more demand for economic cooperation among China and the other developing countries and developed countries. China needs to firmly represent the common interests of developing countries on the one hand, and on the other hand, China also has to make every effort to maintain the global trend of economic cooperation between developing countries and developed countries, and strive to consolidate the common understanding of all countries to jointly cope with new global economic challenges. Meanwhile, China should stick to the principle of equality, mutual benefit, and a win–win situation, play the critical role of pushing forward global economic growth and development, and enhance the proactivity and initiative as a global giant to undertake a commitment to driving forward the economic growth of developing countries through investments, trade, and monetary cooperation, as well as development assistance, to a greater extent. China aims to play a critical role rather than a dominant role, lead global economic cooperation and development with a new concept of economic cooperation, and push forward the balanced, sustainable, and inclusive growth that benefits all.[29]

---

[28] Gong Shengli. (2013). The 21st Century: Three Rules of the New Strategy of the United States. *International Finance,* Issue 5, pp. 30–33.

[29] Zou Zhiqiang. (2015). Post-2015 Developmental Agenda and the Formation of New Global Economic Rules: Connections and Challenges. *Journal of International Relations,* Issue 2, pp. 85–96.

It is fair to say that the launch of the reform and opening-up drive pushed China to undergo a fundamental change in its attitude toward the international system. It was pointed out in the report to the 12th National Congress of the Communist Party of China (CPC) in 1982 that it was China's firm strategic guidelines to implement opening-up and enlarge outward economic and technological exchanges under the principle of equality and mutual benefit. It was called for in the report to utilize the international market, earnestly expand foreign trade, and attract foreign funds for construction at the same time.

It was pointed out in the report to the 13th National Congress of the CPC in 1987 that, as needed by the international situation and the construction of China's modernization, China would adjust its diplomatic structure and the Party's foreign relations by focusing on the two themes of peace and development and develop a diplomatic policy featuring independence, objection to hegemony, and maintaining world peace. With the rapid development of the reform of new technology, the increasing intensified market competition, and ever-changing international politics, China was still faced with pressing and severe challenges. Therefore, China must have its presence on the global economic stage with a more courageous stance, choose the right import and export strategy and utilize the foreign investment strategy, and further expand economic and technological cooperation and trade exchanges with the other countries, including developed and developing countries, in order to create better conditions for China to accelerate its scientific and technological advancement and improve economic efficiency. The report to the 13th National Congress of the CPC explicitly pointed out that "the world is an open world," and such a consensus has set a strategic precondition for the continuous, steady, and furthered development of the reform and opening-up, and made important conceptual preparation for the coexistence and common prosperity between the world's economy and China's economy.

The report to the 14th National Congress of the CPC in 1992 pointed out from a strategic perspective that the world was undergoing a historical period of big changes by referring to the new trend in the international situation, but peace and development were still the two major themes of the world. With the ending of a two-pole structure and various forces being redivided and reorganized, the world was moving toward multiple poles. The formation of the new structure is a long-term and complicated process. Therefore, China must cooperate with other countries in building a new international order that features peace, stability, justness, and rationality.

The report to the 15th National Congress of the CPC in 1997 further elaborated China's expectations and vision for building an international system. It was pointed out in the report that the new international order had to be based on the Five Principles of Peaceful Coexistence, conform to the objective and principles of the Charter of the United Nations, and reflect the trend of the times, that is, peace and development. Meanwhile, it was acutely pointed out in the report that "the unjust and irrational old international economic order is still destroying the interests of developing countries," thus highlighting the necessity for and urgency of reforming the international economic order.

The report to the 16th National Congress of the CPC in 2002 made a proactive and positive comment on the international situation and the developmental trend of the international system at that time, believing that "the ongoing trend of multi-polarization of the world and the globalization of the economy has brought opportunities and favorable conditions for world peace and development." The report further elaborated China's determination and confidence in participating in the international system and pushing forward the reform and development of the international economic system, stating that China "is willing to make joint efforts with the international community to advance the multi-polarization of the world, push forward the harmonious coexistence of various forces, and maintain the stability of the international community and to actively push economic globalization in the direction of facilitating common prosperity, making each country, developing countries in particular, benefit from it."

The report to the 17th National Congress of the CPC in 2007 again affirmed the multipolarization of the world and the deeper development of economic globalization, believing that "the comparison of international strengths is developing in the direction that is helpful to maintaining world peace." However, it was undeniable that the imbalance of the world's economy was intensified and the gap between the North and the South was further widened. Therefore, China hoped that each country might be able to cooperate with each other on the economy, draw upon the advantages of each other, and push forward economic globalization to achieve balanced development, shared benefits, and win–win progress.[30] Despite the unexpected global financial crisis that later came to cause considerable trouble to the stable development of the world's economy, the crisis did not stop the trend of the world's multipolarization, economic globalization, and cooperation diversification.

Following the theme of "peace and development" for the times, the report to the 18th National Congress of the CPC pointed out that "Global cooperation is expanding at multiple levels and on all fronts. Emerging market economies and developing countries are gaining in overall strength, tipping the balance of international forces in favor of the maintenance of world peace. All this has created more favorable conditions for ensuring general stability in the international environment." Meanwhile, the report also objectively pointed out various negative factors that hindered the healthy development of international economic development. For example, it pointed out that "the global financial crisis is producing a far-reaching impact on the world. World economic growth is overshadowed by growing factors of instability and uncertainty, and imbalance in global development has widened. There are signs of increasing hegemony, power politics and neo-interventionism …"[31]

---

[30] Hu Jintao. Hold High the Great Banner of Socialism with Chinese Characteristics and Strive for New Victories in Building a Moderately Prosperous Society in All Respects: Report to the Seventeenth National Congress of the Communist Party of China. (October 15, 2007). Retrieved from Communist Part of China website http://www.most.gov.cn/yw/200710/t20071026_56736.htm.

[31] Hu Jintao. (2012). Firmly March along the Path of Socialism with Chinese Characteristics and Strive to Complete the Building of a Moderately Prosperous Society in All Respects: Report to the Eighteenth National Congress of the Communist Party of China. Retrieved from http://politics.people.com.cn/n/2012/1109/c1001-19529914.html.

According to the reports to the national congress of the CPC since the reform and opening-up, it is easy to see that China has been very concerned with the development of and changes in international systems, the international political and economic systems in particular. More importantly, the basic judgment of the international situation has directly determined the corresponding adjustment of China's foreign economic policies and China's decision regarding how to establish its international position and responsibilities in the international economic system. "China's achievements in development throughout the over 30 years of reform and opening-up has changed the comparison of forces in international systems and has also enriched and developed the understanding of the developmental regularities of human society."[32] China is a royal supporter to multilateral decision-making mechanisms, and it is more a force against hegemony and power politics, to prevent them from monopolizing the power of formulating international economic rules and the say in doing so. Additionally, China is a major defender of the benefit of developing countries, represented by China, in their participation in global multilateral cooperation mechanisms. This is also beneficial to the development and improvement of a just and equal international economic system. According to Barry Buzan, a famous expert on international relations, "A sign that marks a really successful kind of power is to what extent and for how long the country is able to maintain the security community that is established based on the needs of itself and the world; it is also decided by the extent to which the country is able to enhance shared values and a stable international order."[33] "China is an emerging giant; China is a rational and responsible member of the international community. China is expected to become a participant and cooperator in the existing international system and international order, a follower of the existing system of international law, and a party to the shaping of a more just and reason-

---

[32] Guo Jiping. (August 29, 2012). Guard Morality and Justness in International Relations through Development. *People's Daily.* Retrieved from https://wenku.baidu.com/view/bc374972f46527d3240ce0e6.html.

[33] Barry Buzan. (2006). China–Japan and China–US Relationships during China's Rise. *World Economics and Politics,* Issue 7. Retrieved from https://wenku.baidu.com/view/bc374972f46527d3240ce0e6.html.

able international order; China is a socialist country that holds high the banner of reform and opening-up."[34]

By advocating the incorporation of the important concept that "development is the ultimate driving force" into the global economic governance, China respects and allows individuals to independently and freely choose the right path for their own development while pursuing the common goal of economic growth. In fact, this emphasizes the understanding of the dialectical relationship between "development" and "governance." It first requires strength and ability if anyone wants to participate in global economic governance and contribute to the world's economy, which is also a basic material guarantee. China hopes that the global economic governance will closely catch up with the times in its main concerns and feel the pulse of the current era, and at the same time the governance model needs to be able to maintain the steady pace with the times in reforms and progress-making. In today's world, a large number of emerging market countries and developing countries have embarked on the fast lane of economic growth, billions of people are involved on their way toward accelerating modernization, multiple development centers have gradually taken shape in various regions of the world, and the checking and balancing among international forces prove to be continuously conducive to world peace and common development. Today is an era of big changes. The outdated idea of hegemony is gradually declining. No country or group of countries can dominate international affairs alone. Instead, the idea of hegemony is replaced with a new concept of peaceful coexistence and common development among all countries in the world. China advocates that global economic governance must actively combat trade protectionism and promote the liberalization of global trade and the integration of the world's economy. While participating in the global economic governance, China has sincerely and confidently exported to the world its important achievements and ideas of reform and innovation. The white paper entitled *China's Peaceful Development*, issued by the State

---

[34]Cai Tuo. (2010). Some Ideas on China's International Position Today. *Social Sciences in China,* Issue 5, pp. 121–137.

Council Information Office in 2011, pointed out that "China's contribution to world economic growth has reached more than 10% in recent years. The Asian financial crisis in 1997 caused a significant depreciation of currencies in neighboring countries and regions. In this circumstance, China has maintained a basically stable RMB exchange rate so that it has contributed to the stability and development of the regional economy. By the end of 2009, China had provided RMB 256.3 billion in assistance to 161 countries, more than 30 international and regional organizations, reduced or exempted 50 heavily indebted poor countries and the least developed countries on 380 debts. China has sent a total of 120,000 trainees, 2.01 million medical aid team members overseas, and nearly 10,000 foreign aid teachers to developing countries. China has actively promoted the expansion of exports to China from the least developed countries, and has promised to provide zero-tariff treatment to 95% of the products exported to China from all the least developed countries that have established diplomatic ties with China."[35] China emphasizes that the global economic governance must properly handle the complex relationship between "morality" and "interests," and strive to achieve a perfect balance between profits and righteousness. To this end, China not only upholds the principle of honesty and righteousness, promotes the development of the international economic system in a fair and just direction, but it also insists on developmental efficiency, deepens cooperation, and maintains the good momentum of a stable growth of global economic interests.[36]

In academic circles, the Chinese model is also known as the "Beijing Consensus." This concept implies a completely different approach compared to that of Western politics, economic institutions, and some universal values and attitudes toward balancing different powers. It has resulted from the continuous exploration of the developmental path with Chinese characteristics that has been

---

[35] The State Council Information Office of the People's Republic of China. (September 2011). *China's Peace and Development*. Retrieved from http://www.china.com.cn/aboutchina/zhuanti/xwbd/2011-05/27/content_22659107.htm.
[36] Chen Youjun. (2014). Global Economic Governance and China: Integration of Reform, Innovation, and Ideas. *Asia-Pacific Economic Review*, Issue 1, pp. 89–96.

followed in the past 30 years of successful practices in China's rapid economic growth and political stability. The state and the government play important roles in promoting development. Our ruling party has the great capacity of political mobilization and cohesive power. It is the mainstay of our country and the society. The ruling party can concentrate its energies on the establishment of enterprises and building our country so that it can prevent the internal frictions and chaos in some developing countries when they blindly copy the Western multiparty democracy. China pursues an independent foreign policy of peace in the international community, advocates multilateralism, and opposes the unilateralism of hegemony. All countries are treated equally by China regardless of their sizes. These concepts and actions were warmly welcomed and praised by the developing countries, overshadowing the "Washington Consensus."

China's success is conditioned by and closely bound to the global economy. Foreign trade and attracting foreign direct investments (FDIs) have been important driving forces for China's rapid economic development over the past 30 years. The proportion of China's foreign trade in its GDP has soared from 30% in 1990 to 65% in 2007. Although it declined afterward, it remained at 50% from 2010 to 2011. China's dependence on foreign trade (the ratio of exports in GDP) increased from 16% in 1990 to 36% in 2007, and it remained at 26% in 2011 and 46% in 2013.[37] Even in terms of the degree of China's opening-up, the proportion of China's imports in its GDP rose from 5% in 1978 to 30% in 2005 and remained at 24% in 2011. This ratio is almost twice that of the United States and three times that of Japan in the same period.[38] In terms of attracting FDIs, from 1979 to 2008, China's total FDI reached USD 852.613 billion.[39] Thus, China became the developing country that had attracted the largest amount of FDIs in the world at that time. Its FDI reached the

---

[37] Calculated according to statistics of relevant years based on the *China Statistical Yearbook* compiled by the National Bureau of Statistics.
[38] C. Fred Bergstein, Bagtes Gill, Nicholas R. Lardy, and Derek Mitchell. (2006). *China: The Balance Sheet*. New York: Public Affairs, p. 84.
[39] Wang Zhengyi. (2010). *An Introduction to International Political Economics*. Beijing, China: Peking University Press. p. 495.

highest, USD 124 billion in 2011. In 2014, foreign investments in China reached USD 128 billion, making China the world's largest country in foreign capital inflow.[40] Driven by foreign trade and FDIs, the ratio of industry in GDP reached 46.4% from 1995 to 2010, and China became a worldwide factory for manufacturing.[41] From 1998 to 2013, the average annual growth rate of imports of the foreign-invested enterprises was 17.41% and of exports was 18.90%; thus, we can see that the average annual value of exports was 1.49% points higher than that of imports. According to the arithmetic mean percentage, the average proportion of imports by foreign-invested enterprises accounted for 53.74% of the total amount of imports in China, and exports accounted for 52.54% of China's total amount of exports. The average ratio of imports to exports was 53.08%. In China's ongoing trade surplus, the proportion of foreign-invested enterprises is 45.87% on average, and it reached a percentage as high as 84.12% in 2011.[42]

In September 2013, the Chinese government issued an official paper on the Post-2015 Development Agenda, advocating that poverty eradication and the promotion of development should be regarded as the priorities so that it can make sure not to deviate from the theme of development among a large amount of contents of the agenda. The paper states that China should uphold the principle of the diversification of developmental models so that each country can independently choose the developmental model and developmental path suited to its own national conditions. The paper adheres to the principle of "common but differentiated responsibilities" in the international affairs and sets up a lot of priorities in the key fields, such as eliminating poverty and hunger issues, promoting social progress and

---

[40] Global Foreign Direct Investment Declined in 2014 (January 30, 2015). *People's Daily Online*. Retrieved from http://world.people.com.cn/n/2015/0131/c1002-26483320.html.

[41] Wang Zhengyi. (2013). The Rise of China: The End or the Continuation of the World Development System? *Journal of International Security Studies,* Issue 3, pp. 3–20.

[42] Yearly statistics from the *China Economic Statistical Yearbook*. Retrieved from https://www.docin.com/p-1206482772.html.

improving people's livelihood, promoting the inclusive economic growth, strengthening the construction of an ecological civilization, promoting sustainable development, and strengthening the global partnerships.[43] In September 2014, Wang Yi, Chinese Minister of Foreign Affairs, again emphasized the consistent statements of the Chinese government at the UN Climate Summit. China's proposals are precisely from the perspective of the developing countries and based on the goal of promoting common global development, which strive to balance multiple goals and their internal contradictions and have taken into account the interests of all the parties involved.

3.4 *The China Dream Influences the World*

Since the 18th National Congress of the CPC, General Secretary Xi Jinping has put forward the "China Dream." This concept has quickly triggered heated discussions among people from all walks of life at home and abroad. Joseph Gregory Mahoney, an American scholar, commented that "the China Dream reminds us of the American Dream easily, but the American Dream has always been built on policies and practices characterized by exploitation and hegemony. Thus, it cannot be sustainable whether with regard to politics, economics, or the environment. The world today does need some paradigm shifts, or, more further, it requires a kind of fissile update on political and economic reforms, and China may prove to be the best candidate in promoting and leading the trend of these changes." The British scholar Martin Jacques, in his book *When China Rules the World* published in 2010, believes that the rapid growth of China's economy has had a profound impact on and has been well received by the international community. However, its influence is far more than this. The rise of China marks the end of the global dominance by the Western countries. At the same time, the rise of China far not only exceeds the scope of the economy, but also includes its culture and politics, and the

---

[43] The Chinese Official Document for the Post-2015 Development Agenda. (August 3, 2015). *Xinhuanet.* Retrieved from http://www.xinhuanet.com//world/2015-08/03/c_128086615.htm.

impact of the rise of China is far greater than that of the United States. The Australian scholar Peter Halcher believes that the influence of the Chinese developmental model is increasing day by day. China's development has achieved such splendid achievements; thus it is not the Chinese system but the Western system that has now been challenged. For the Western developmental model, the Chinese model has proved to be a powerful alternative and a challenge to it. To a certain extent, the Chinese developmental model dwarfs some arrogant ideas of Western countries and their democracy and freedom.[44]

The East has a tradition of "war-dislike, aggression-free and free religious beliefs." The Western missionary Matteo Ricci once pointed out that "It is a kingdom that can be said to be vast in its territory, has innumerable populations, and diverse and extremely rich in products. Even though the people there have the forces which are well-equipped and can easily conquer the armies of its neighboring countries, they never even thought of the idea of getting into a war of aggression, whether it is the king or the common people. They are totally satisfied with what they have and they do not desire to conquer others. In this respect, they are completely different from the Europeans ..."[45] The splendid culture of our Chinese nation for more than 5,000 years contains valuable ideological resources and noble moral values. It contains important revelations for people today to solve the contemporary problems, such as the ideal of "Great Harmony" and "An All-round Well-to-do Society," the concept of ruling the country by "guaranteeing the safety of the people because they are the foundation of the country," the spirit of a "gentleman's striving for continuous self-improvement," the important idea of "harmony with diversity," and the broad mind of "being loyal and honest" and "harmonious with all things," and so on. All of them imperceptibly affect the way people think and behave in China.

---

[44] Li Jianguo. (2014). Where Did the International Influence of Socialism with Chinese Characteristics Come from? *Beijing Daily,* Issue 10. Retrieved from http://www.bjqx.org.cn/qxweb/.

[45] Stavrianos. (1999). *The Global History: The World after 1500* (Wu Xiangying and Liang Chimin, Trans.). Shanghai, China: Shanghai Academy of Social Sciences Press, pp. 12–13.

Since the beginning of the reform and opening-up, China has always insisted that peace and development are the basic themes of the times. China has repeatedly demonstrated to the world that it did not seek hegemony in the past and it does not and will not seek hegemony now or in the future. China chooses the basic road of peaceful development and win–win cooperation to achieve national modernization and national rejuvenation. It is not engaged in power diplomacy and always holds high the banner of peace, development, and cooperation, providing opportunities for the development of the whole world. China's insistence on walking the road of peaceful development and building a harmonious world breaks the traditional model of the rise of great powers in history. The most powerful country was always hegemonic in the past. The Former Indian Prime Minister Singh said that China's reform has promoted India's development. In the past few decades, the reform and opening-up in economy have not only benefited China but also deeply benefited India. King Abdullah II of Jordan pointed out that "China's pattern of development has set a model for many Middle Eastern countries. As a country with an important international status, China's voice is respected here." The World Bank also believes that the Chinese model has an exemplary effect on other developing countries.

After more than 30 years of sustained and rapid growth, the Chinese economy has undergone profound changes. Judging from the quantitative indicators, China's GDP totaled RMB 51.9 trillion in 2012, which was approximately 24 times higher than that at the initial period of reform and opening-up and has an average annual growth rate of approximately 9.8% at comparable prices and nearly USD 8 trillion according to the current exchange rate. It is the second largest economy in the world, accounting for about 10% of the world's total GDP, with the per capita GDP of RMB 38,000, which was about 17 times higher than that during the initial period of reform and opening-up, and with an average annual growth rate of 8.7% calculated at comparable prices. Calculated at the current exchange rate, it reached USD 5,800, exceeding the average of USD 3,400 in the middle-income countries of the contemporary world. According to the purchasing power assessment method, the World Bank estimates that it had reached 6,710 international dollars in 2009, surpassing the average of 6,340 international dollars in contemporary middle-income countries and reaching the upper middle-income level in the world. China is the world's fastest-growing economy to date, surpassing Japan that had once made the "Japanese Miracle" in the past. The average GDP of China doubled in less than 6 years. Since 1978, the growth of the GDP has far exceeded the expectations. In 2014, China's GDP reached USD 10.4 trillion and the World Bank predicts that China will become the world's largest economy by 2020.

In the process of moving from a developing country to achieving its modernization, China has shown remarkable changes in many aspects. First of all, the proportion of the employment of agricultural laborers has reflected the level of agricultural modernization. According to the current level of employment of agricultural laborers, the proportion of employment has dropped by about 2% points each year. The proportion of the employment of Chinese agricultural workers will have dropped from 36% of the total employment in 2011 to around 18% by 2020. Although there is still a gap between the proportion and the average level of 10% in 70 other high-income countries, it is very close to the critical point of the high-income level and will probably reach that level in the future. Second, compared with the high level of some modern international industrialized countries, at the present stage, China has entered the late stage of industrialization from the perspective of the realization of its goals of industrialization. For instance, the eastern developed provinces and cities such as Shanghai, Beijing, Tianjin, Jiangsu, and Guangdong have basically achieved their industrialization, and Zhejiang, Fujian, Shandong, and Liaoning will achieve industrialization soon. According to the current development, it is possible to achieve all-round industrialization in the country by 2020. Third, from the perspective of urbanization, China has now entered an accelerated period of urbanization driven by modernization and industrialization, and by 2020, it is entirely possible that the rate of urbanization will reach about 70%, the average level of the high-income countries, from the current 51.3%. Finally, from the perspective of the development of modern information services, under the circumstances of an advanced level of informatization along with economic development, the modern service industries based on information technology will achieve rapid development in the process of the integration of agricultural modernization, new-type industrialization, and accelerated urbanization.[46]

It has taken China only several decades to walk the course of development that took developed countries hundreds of years to go through, and it has achieved a historic leap from poverty to an overall well-to-do society. The Chinese nation has taken great strides to catch up with the times and welcome the great rejuvenation of the Chinese nation. Taking economic development as an example, from 1979 to 2012, China's GDP grew at an average annual rate of 9.8%, which was much higher than the 2.8% average annual growth rate of the world's economy in the same period. China's total economic output ranks second in the world, which accounts for nearly 12% of the total share of the world's economy from the former less than 2% in 1979. China has become today's "world factory" and is approaching the "center of the world stage" from its once destitute situation of shortages of material and products in the past. Faced with the international financial crisis, China has taken the lead in stabilizing the economy and becoming an important engine for helping the world's economy out of recession. In recent years, China's contribution to world economic growth has exceeded 20%, and it is now reaching as high as 30%. Regarding the great changes in China, some foreign politicians and scholars have called it "the most important event of the present era." They believe that China's achievements are "unmatched and unprecedented." The former U.S. Secretary of State Henry Kissinger commented on this with the words "unbelievable" and "beyond imagination," with strong emotional feelings.[47]

It is worth noting that in 2010, China surpassed the United States to become the world's largest manufacturing country. In 2010, the world's manufacturing output was worth USD 10 trillion. Among the world's output then, China's manufacturing output was 19.8%, which

---

[46] Liu Wei. (2013). Efforts to Build an Upgraded Version of China's Economy. *Qiushi*, Issue 9, pp. 22–25.

[47] Liu Qibao. (2014). Understanding the Road of Socialism with Chinese Characteristics. *Qiushi*, Issue 20, pp. 3–8.

was slightly higher than that of the United States, which was 19.4%. However, according to the exchange rate at the beginning of 2011 based on the statistics of the UN, the value of China's manufacturing output was USD 2.05 trillion whereas that of the United States was USD 1.78 trillion. So, China's manufacturing output was not only 0.4% higher than that of the United States, but was as high as 15.2%. However, it does not matter how much higher than the United States is China in the percentages. What matters is that from 1895 to 2009, the United States sat on the "throne" of the world's manufacturing industry for 114 consecutive years, but China has been able to so rapidly surpass America in its manufacturing industry output. This is undoubtedly a great "historical leap" for China and it has ushered in a new era of human economic development.

From the historical perspective of world economic development, although in different historical periods, the 70 high-income countries in the contemporary world generally experienced a period of about 12 years' development before they entered into the high-income stage. At present, China has reached the upper middle-income level. Can we take 10 years to achieve the leap to the high-income stage, which means, to build a well-off society by 2020? Based on the economic quantitative indicators, as long as China can maintain an average annual growth rate of 7.2%, its total GDP will double by 2020 compared with that of 2010, nearly RMB 90 trillion (at constant prices), which is USD 14 trillion according to the exchange rate and is roughly equivalent to the GDP of the United States at the beginning of the 21st century. As long as the natural population growth rate is controlled at the current level (below 5‰), the per capita GDP can be doubled correspondingly, approaching RMB 70,000 (at constant prices), which is USD 12,000, reaching the standard starting point of the high-income countries today.

At present, the Chinese economy has entered a new normal state and is shifting from high-speed growth to a steady growth, which has aroused widespread concern in the world. Judging from the relationship between China and the world, China is changing from the current export-oriented economy to the world's largest open economy. According to the current USD exchange rate, China's contribution to the growth of the world's GDP reached 19.2% from 2000 to 2013, which was higher than the United States' contribution rate (15.5%). According to the purchasing power parity international dollar calculation, from 2000 to 2013, China's contribution to the growth of the world's GDP reached 23.0%, which is also higher than that of the United States (12.0%). In 2000, the US GDP reached USD 10 trillion whereas at that time, China's GDP was only USD 1 trillion. In 2014, China's GDP climbed to USD 10 trillion and the US GDP was USD 16.8 trillion. From 2000 to 2012, the rate of the contribution to the growth of China's importation and exportation of goods and services to the world reached 12.8%, which was higher than the United States' rate of contribution (8.1%), and it made China the world's largest engine for trade growth. In 2000, China's import and export trade volume in goods was only USD 474.3 billion, whereas in 2013, it had reached a new stage of USD 4 trillion. China is already the largest trading partner of 140 countries or regions, and the second or the third largest trading partner of dozens of countries or regions in the world. It is also notable in trade in services. In 2014, Chinese citizens made more than 100 million trips overseas, and their total expenditure exceeded RMB 1 trillion. According to the data of the World Intellectual Property Organization, from 2000 to 2012, the proportion of China's invention patent applications in the world increased from 3.77% to 27.80%, and its contribution rate to the global total growth rate reached 61.95%, which was higher than that of the United States (25.46%), which has also made it possible for China to become the largest engine of invention patent growth. In 2014, the number of applications for invention patents in China was 928,000; in 2015, the number exceeded 1 million, reaching 1.102 million. China has surpassed the total patent applications of the United States, Germany, and Japan, ranking first in the world for five consecutive years. The number of Patent Cooperation Treaty international patent applications was 26,000, ranking third in the world. In addition, China is still the largest sales market of high-tech products and the fastest-growing market of high-tech applications. China is not only the world's largest engine of economic growth, trade growth, and invention patent growth, but it will also contribute much more to the world and bring more and greater room for developmental opportunities to all countries in the world. Since the beginning of the 21st century, China's relations with the world have undergone historical and fundamental changes. China's interests are more closely linked with the interests of other countries in the world, and it is the world's largest trading partner, economic entity, and technological innovation market. It is also the largest stakeholder in international relations and is greatly concerned about the world's common interests. China's development can make an increasingly significant contribution to human development. This includes four major aspects as follows: First, its contribution to the promotion of world economic growth as the world's largest economic engine; second, promoting global economic integration, trade and investment liberalization, and service facilitation in order to contribute to promoting the growth of world trade; third, promoting a global green energy revolution, green industrial revolution, green transportation revolution, green building revolution, and so on, in order to contribute to the promotion of global energy conservation and emission reduction; fourth, promoting global fair development and actively providing developmental assistance and experience for the underdeveloped countries, in order to promote the rise of the countries in the Southern Hemisphere, further narrow the developmental gap between the North and the South, and make positive contributions to all mankind for an equal, fair, and inclusive development.[48]

In such a developmental environment at home and abroad, many scholars believe that the proposal of the Belt and Road Initiative has made a declaration of cooperation and mutual benefit to the world: the China Dream of great rejuvenation of the Chinese nation is connected with the dreams of all the people in the world. It will set up four bridges of peace, growth, reform, and civilization high above for the whole world, and will definitely provide new opportunities for global cooperation and common development.

---

[48] Hu An'gang. (March 26, 2015). The Economic New Normal Helps China Leap a Big Step. *China Internet Information Center*. Retrieved from https://news.china.com/domesticgd/10000159/20150326/19431277.html.

Bibliography

1. Hu Angang, Yang Fan. (2000). *Strategy of a Giant Country: China's Interest and Mission.* Shenyang, China: Liaoning People's Publishing House.
2. Hu Angang, Zheng Yunfeng, and Gao Yuning. (2015). Evaluation of the Comprehensive National Strength of China and the United States (1990–2013). *Journal of Tsinghua University* (Philosophy and Social Sciences), Issue 1.
3. Asian Development Bank Institute. (2012). *The Construction of Asia's Infrastructures.* Beijing, China: Social Sciences Academic Press.
4. Luis Cabral. (2002). *Introduction to Industrial Organization.* Beijing, China: Posts & Telecom Press.
5. Contemporary China Series Editorial Department. (1990). *China's Railway Cause Today,* Volumes I, II. Beijing, China: China Social Sciences Press.
6. Rui Chuanming. (2009). *Guidance to Studies on the Silk Road.* Shanghai, China: Fudan University Press.
7. Guan Chudu. (2000). *Location Theory of Transportation and Its Application.* Beijing, China: China Communications Press.
8. Chongyang Institute of Economics, University of China. (2014). *The Eurasian Era: The Blue Book of Studies on the Silk Road Economic Belt*

(2014–2015) (2 Volumes). Beijing, China: China Economic Publishing House.

9. International Monetary Fund (Ed.) (2014). *Global Financial Stability Report: Shift from the Flow-driven Market to the Market Driven by Economic Growth.* (He Tao *et al.*, Trans.) Beijing, China: China Financial Publishing House.

10. Goldberg. (2003). *World Economy Hegemony 1500–1990.* Hong Kong, China: The Commercial Press, p. 78.

11. Liu Guoguang. (2006). *Research on Ten Five-Year Plans in China.* Beijing, China: People's Publishing House.

12. Wang Haibo. (2010). *An Industrial Economic History of Modern China.* Taiyuan, China: Shanxi Economic Publishing House.

13. Xu Haiyan. (2014). *An Approach to Building the Green Silk Road Economic Belt — Agricultural Modernization, the Aral Sea Governance and New Energy Development in Central Asia.* Shanghai, China: Fudan University Press.

14. Hanban's Statistics, 2015. Retrieved from http://www.moe.gov.cn/jyb_xxgk/xxgk_jyta/jyta_gjhb/

15. Albert Otto Hirschman. (1991). *Economic Developmental Strategies* (Cao Zhenghai *et al.* Trans.). Beijing, China: Economic Science Press.

16. International Bank for Reconstruction and Development, the World Bank. (2013). *The World Bank Report — The Changing Wealth of Nations· Measuring Sustainable Development in the Millennium.* Beijing, China: Xinhua Publishing House.

17. International Monetary Fund. (2014). *Global Financial Stability Report: A Difficult Journal Transiting to Stability* (Wang Huirong, *et al.* Trans.). Beijing, China: China Financial Publishing House.

18. Martin Jacques. (2010). *When China Rules the World: The Rise of the Middle Kingdom and the End of the Western World.* Beijing, China: CITIC Press.

19. Wu Jianhong. (2002). *The WTO and China's Railways.* Chengdu, China: Southwest Jiaotong University Press.

20. Zhang Jie (ed.). (2015). *2015: Evaluation of the Belt and Road Initiative and Peripheral Strategy According to the Situation of China's Peripheral Security.* Beijing, China: Social Sciences Academic Press.

21. Zou Lei. (2015). *Political Economics of China's Belt and Road Initiative.* Shanghai, China: Shanghai People's Publishing House.

22. Wu Li. (2010). *A History of the Economy of the People's Republic of China.* Beijing, China: China Times Economic Publishing House.

23. Ma Lili, Ren Baoping. (2014). *Report on Silk Road Economic Belt Development 2014.* Beijing, China: China Economic Publishing House.

24. Huang Maoxing. (2015). *Echoes of History and Reality: The Revival of the 21st-Century Maritime Silk Road.* Beijing, China: Economic Science Press.

25. David Miller, *National Responsibility and Global Justice.* Chongqing, China: Chongqing Publishing House, 2014.

26. Lu Ming *et al.* (2008). *Economic Developmental Path of China as a Giant Country.* Beijing, China: Encyclopedia of China Publishing House.

27. David M. Newbery. (2002). *Privatization, Restructuring, and Regulation of Network Utilities.* Beijing, China: Posts & Telecom Press.

28. Ragnar Nurkse. (1966). *Problems of Capital Formation in Underdeveloped Countries.* Hong Kong: The Commercial Press.

29. Bill Porter. (2013). *The Silk Road: Tracing the Most Glorious Chapter of China's Civilization.* Chengdu, China: Sichuan Literature and Art Publishing House.

30. W. W. Rostow. (1962). *The Stages of Economic Growth.* Hong Kong, China: The Commercial Press.

31. Huang Shiling. (1988). *Studies on Traffic and Transportation.* Beijing, China: China Communications Press.

32. Xie Shiqing. (2014). *China and the World Bank: Advancing Capability Development.* Beijing, China: Economic Science Press.

33. State Planning Commission. (2005). *Yearbook of China: Transportation & Communications.* Beijing, China: China Transportation & Communications Year Book Press.

34. Stavrianos. (2005). *A Global History.* Beijing, China: Peking University Press.

35. Immanuel Wallerstein. (1998). *The Modern World-System.* Beijing, China: Higher Education Press.

36. Lu Wei. (2002). *Industrial Reorganization and Competition.* Beijing, China: China Development Press.

37. Liu Xiahui *et al.* (2008). *Economic Growth and Structural Transformation in the Years of Reform.* Shanghai, China: Truth & Wisdom Press.

38. Ma Xiaohe *et al.* (2009). *Change in China's Industrial Structure and Industrial Policy Evolvement.* Beijing, China: China Jihua Press.

39. Jiang Xiaojuan (2007). *The Openness and Growth of China's Economy (1980–2005).* Beijing, China: People's Publishing House.

40. Jiang Xiyuan. (2003). *Strategy of a Giant Country and a Future China.* Beijing, China: China Social Sciences Press.

41. Ouyang Yao. (2011). *Comprehensive Advantages of a Giant Country.* Shanghai, China: Truth & Wisdom Press.
42. Sun Li & Wu Hongwei (Eds.) (2014). *The Yellow Book of Central Asia — Annual Report on the Development of Central Asia (2014): Featuring the Silk Road Economic Belt.* Beijing, China: Social Sciences Academic Press.
43. Liu Yingsheng. (2014). *The Silk Road.* Nanjing, China: Jiangsu People's Publishing.
44. Wang Yiwei. (2015). *The Belt and Road Initiative: Opportunities and Challenges.* Beijing, China: People's Publishing House.
45. Liu Yuhong. (2014). *Traffic Infrastructure and Regional Economic Growth in the New Silk Road Economic Belt.* Beijing, China: China Social Sciences Press.
46. Ji Yunfei. (ed.). (2014). *Yearbook: Studies on China's Maritime Silk Road (2013).* Hangzhou, China: Zhejiang University Press.
47. Yang Yunlong. (2008). *Changes in China's Economic Structure and Industrialization.* Beijing, China: Peking University Press.
48. Shi Yuntao. (2007). *Changes in the Silk Road from the 3rd Century to the 6th Century.* Beijing, China: Culture & Art Publishing House.
49. Dong Zhiwen. (2014). *The China Maritime Studies Series: Studies on China's Maritime Silk Road.* Beijing, China: China Economic Publishing House & Guangzhou, China: Guangdong Economic Publishing House.
50. Huang Zhiyong, Kuang Zhong, Tan Chunzhi. (2013). *Onto the Path of the Community with a Common Destiny: Preparing for the Establishment of the Asian Infrastructure Investment Bank First Made Breakthroughs in the China-ASEAN Region.* Nanning, China: Guangxi People's Publishing House.
51. Li Zhongmin. (1990). *A Study on the Silk Road Economic Belt Development.* Beijing, China: Economic Science Press, 2014.
52. А.Н. чисбаев. (1990). *Development, Theories and Research Methods on Economic Zones.* Beijing, China: Haichao Press.

Index